ACADEMIC DICTIONARY OF AGRICULTURAL SCIENCE

Editor
Ajay Kumar Ghosh

ISHA

ISHA BOOKS
Delhi-110033

Academic Dictionary of Agricultural Science

ISBN : 9788182051812

Published in 2005 in India by
Isha Books
D-43, Prithviraj Road,
Adarsh Nagar, Delhi - 110033
e-mail : ishabooks@hotmail.com

Laser Typesetting at : Global Printers, New Delhi
Printed at : Ajit Printers

ACADEMIC DICTIONARY OF AGRICULTURAL SCIENCE

A

Acaulis : Having no stem

Accent plant : This could be a focal point plant. A plant to catch attention. Could also be called an anchor plant.

Acceptor control : The regulation of the rate of respiration by the availability of ADP as a phosphate acceptor.

Acceptor junction site : The junction between the 3' end of an intron and the 5' end of an exon.

Accessory bud : A lateral bud occurring at the base of a terminal bud or at the side of an axillary bud.

Accidental host : Humans are not part of the life cycle, they accidentally entered into that organisms life cycle and got the disease. Examples : ringworm, rabies.

Acclimate : To adapt to new environmental conditions.

Acclimatization : The adaptation of a living organism (plant, animal or micro-organism) to a changed environment that subjects it to physiological stress. Acclimatization should not be confused with adaptation.

Accrete : Grown together

Acequia : An irrigation ditch or canal.

Acetretin : A Retinoids which is a synthetic derivatives of vitamin A.

Acetyl co-enzyme A (acetyl coA) : A compound formed in the mitochondria when an acetyl group (CH_3CO-) - derived from breakdown of fats, proteins, or carbohydrates - combines with the thiol group (-SH) of co-enzyme A.

Acheve : A one seeded fruit which does not split open to release it's seed, ie. the "seeds" on a strawberry.

Acicular : Needlelike spine; pointed; bristle

Acid deposition / acid rain : Abnormally acidic (low pH) precipitation (or dry deposition) resulting from emissions of sulfur and nitrogen compounds that transform during chemical processes in the atmosphere. Acid deposition can affect the chemistry of soils and acidify lakes, adversely affecting forests and fish. It does not adversely affect cropland.

Acid detergent fiber : ADF The amount of residue (primarily cellulose, lignin and variable amounts of silica) left after boiling a feed sample in an acid detergent solution. The ADF value is used to predict the energy content (TDN, NE) of forages.

Acid soil : Soil that is lower than 7.0 ph (higher would be alkaline). Acidity is measured by the amount of calcium in the soil, as is alkaline soil.

Acquired : Developed in response to the environment, not inherited, such as a character trait (acquired characteristic) resulting from environmental effect(s). cf acclimatization.

Acreage limitation : With respect to commodity policy, acreage limitation might refer to planting constraints under an acreage reduction program, set-aside, or paid land diversion. In relation to water policy, it is the maximum number of acres that may be irrigated with less than full-cost water from Bureau of Reclamation projects. Generally, the acreage limitation for individuals or legal entities representing 25 people or fewer is 960 acres; however, amounts vary depending on a landowner's legal status. Also referred to as ownership limitation, ownership entitlement, or non- full-cost entitlement.

Acre-foot : The volume of water that would cover one acre of land (43,560 square feet) to a depth of one foot, equivalent to 325,851 gallons of water. An acre-foot is the basic measure of agricultural water use. On average, irrigators apply almost 2 feet of water on each acre through the crop growing season; the amount ranges from 4 feet in the Southwest to a half foot in some eastern states. Irrigation accounts for about 85 maf (million acre-feet) of water use annually.

Acridine dyes : A class of positively charged polycyclic molecules that intercalate into DNA and induce frameshift mutations.

Ad libitum (ad lib) : Feed offered free-choice, allowing animals to eat as much as they desire.

Ad valorem duty : A tariff expressed as a fixed percentage of the value of the imported commodity or product.

Adaptation : Adjustment of a population to changes in environment over generations, associated (at least in part) with genetic changes resulting from selection imposed by the changed environment. Not acclimatization.

Adaptive radiation : The evolution of new species or sub-species to fill unoccupied ecological niches.

Adenocarcinoma : A form of cancer that occurs in the prostate gland.

Adenosine : The (ribo)nucleoside resulting from the combination of the base adenine (A) and the sugar D-ribose. The corresponding deoxyribonucleoside is called deoxyadenosine.

Adenovirus : One of a group of DNA-containing viruses found in rodents, fowl, cattle, monkeys, and man. In man they are responsible for respiratory-tract infections, but they have been exploited as a vector in gene therapy, especially for genes targeted at the lungs.

Adrenal gland : A gland located close to the kidneys that produces several hormones including cortisol.

Adrenaline : Also known as epinephrine. A hormone that stimulates the heart and increases blood pressure.

Adrenergic : Drugs that mimic the action of the sympathetic nervous system.

Adventitious plant : A young plant that develops in an asexual manner on the leaves or stems of the mother plant.

Adverse event : Any undesirable occurrence, either injury or death, following the use of an immunobiological product.

Aflatoxin : A highly carcinogenic toxin produced by a fungus, which occurs when crops are stored under warm, humid conditions. Most commonly associated with corn, peanuts and soybeans. Shipments of grain containing high levels of aflatoxin are generally rejected.

AFLP : Amplified Fragment Length Polymorphism.

Africanized honey bee : "Killer bees." A threat to people involved in outdoor activities throughout the state including hiking, hunting, fishing, and farming.

Agarose : The main functional constituent of agar.

Agarose gel electrophoresis : A matrix composed of a highly purified form of agar that is used to separate larger DNA and RNA molecules ranging 20,000 nucleotides.

Age specific data base : The minimum amount of information that is planned to be collected on all patients of a certain age; for example pediatric or geriatric databases.

Agglutination : An abnormal clumping of red blood cells. Often seen in patients with immune-mediated anemia.

Agrobacterium tumefaciens-mediated transformation : The process of DNA transfer from Agrobacterium tumefaciens to plants, that occurs naturally during crown gall disease, and can be used as a method of transformation.

AIDS defining diseases : If a person is HIV+ and is diagnoses with one of several disease conditions, by definition the person has AIDS. Included among the AIDS defining diseases are several zoonotic diseases (toxoplasmosis, cryptosporidiosis).

AIF : Animal Industry Foundation

Air layering : A method of propagating single-stem plants, such as Ficus elastica decora, which have lost their lower leaves and become leggy. An incision is made to a portion of outer stem layer, damp sphagnum moss is wrapped in a bag around it until roots develop. Then it is cut and replanted with its shorter stem size.

Alar : Trade name for daminozide, a plant regulator and therefore classed as a pesticide, that makes apples redder, firmer, and less likely to drop off trees before harvest. It was also used to a lesser extent on peanuts, tart cherries, concord grapes, and other fruits.

Alata : Winged

Albumin : A small protein in blood that acts like a "sponge" to keep fluid within the blood vessels. If albumin is low, fluid leaks out of the blood vessels and causes edema.

Alkaline Phosphatase (AP) : Also known as serum alkaline phosphatase (SAP). An enzyme found in many tissues but most often elevated in serum in response to cholestasis, bone remodeling or glucocorticoid excess.

Alkaline soil : Soil that has a pH level of about 7.0 or more. Sometimes referred to as "sweet" soil.

Alkalinity : Having a pH greater than 7.

Allele frequency : The relative number of copies of an allele in a population, expressed as a proportion of the total number of copies of all alleles at a given locus in a population.

Alleles : Alternate forms of genes. Because genes occur in pairs in body cells, one gene of a pair may have one effect and another gene of that same pair (allele) may have a different effect on the same trait.

Allelic exclusion : A phenomenon whereby only one functional allele of an antibody gene can be assembled in a given B lymphocyte.

Allo : Combining form denoting differential characteristics or forms; differentiation from normal

Allodynia : Pain from a stimulus that would normally be non-painful.

Allogamy : Cross fertilization in plants.

Allogenic : Differing at one or more loci, although belonging to the same species. Thus an organ transplant from one human donor to another is allogeneic, whereas a transplant from a baboon to a human would be xenogeneic.

Allotype : A classification of antibody molecules according to the antigenicity of the constant regions; a variation that is determined by a single allele.

Allowable Sale Quantity (ASQ) : A forestry term defined in law as the maximum amount of timber that can be sold every year, forever, from a national forest; in forest planning, the annual timber sale target for a national forest.

Allozygote : A individual that is heterozygous for two different mutant alleles.

Alopecia : Loss of hair.

Alpine : Plants from high mountain regions. Anything that is from above the tree line. They are able to overwinter beneath deep snow protected from extreme low temperature by their moisture.

Alpine house : A special greenhouse created to meet the requirements of alpines. It is usually kept cool in the summer by shading the glass. In the winter it is unheated unless it needs to provide protection from very severe cold.

Alternate host : A secondary host that becomes infected and is necessary for alternating generations of a disease-causing organism.

Alternative agriculture : A systematic approach to farming intended to reduce agricultural pollution, enhance sustainability, and improve efficiency and profitability.

Alternative fuels : Substitutes for traditional liquid, oil- derived motor vehicle fuels like gasoline and diesel. Includes methanol, ethanol, compressed natural gas, and others.

Ambient temperature : Air temperature, i.e., the temperature of the air around the pile and not affected by the heat of the pile.

Amendment : Usually referring to some form of organic material being added to the soil for the purpose of improvement.

Amino acid : A compound containing both amino ($-NH_2$) and carboxyl (-COOH) groups. In particular, any of 20 basic building blocks of proteins having the formula NH_2-CR-COOH, where R is different for each specific amino acid.

Aminoacyl tRNA synthetase : An enzyme that catalyses the attachment of an amino acid to its specific tRNA molecule.

Amiodarone : A class III antiarrhythmic drug.

Amitosis : A cell division (including nuclear division through constriction of the nucleus) that occurs without chromosome differentiation as in mitosis. The mechanism whereby the genetic integrity is maintained during amitosis is uncertain.

Amitraz : Mitaban (Pharmacia). A treatment for demodectic mange. Mechanism of action is unknown, probably a monamine oxidase inhibitor.

Amlodipine : A long-acting calcium channel blocker that is the drug of choice for management of hypertension in cats.

Amniotic fluid : Liquid contents of the amniotic sac of higher vertebrates, containing foetal, but not maternal cells.

Amniotic vesicle : Another name for the embryonic vesicle.

Amorph : A mutation that abolishes gene function.

Amphotericin b : Systemic antifungal drug.

Ampicillin (beta-lactamase) : An antibiotic derived from penicillin that prevents bacterial growth by interfering with cell wall synthesis.

Ampicillin : A penicillin-type antibiotic that prevents bacterial growth by interfering with synthesis of the cell wall. Commonly used as a selectable marker in the creation of transgenic plants.

Amplexicaul : Clasping the stem

AMTA : Agricultural Market Transition Act

Anabolic pathway : A pathway by which a metabolite is synthesized; a biosynthetic pathway.

Anabolism : One of the two subcategories of metabolism, referring to the building up of complex organic molecules from simpler precursors.

Anaerobe : An organism that can grow in the absence of oxygen.

Anaerobic respiration : Respiration in which foodstuffs are partially oxidized, with the release of chemical energy, in a process not involving atmospheric oxygen. A notable example is in alcoholic fermentation, where sugar is metabolized into ethanol.

Anagen : The phase of the hair cycle during with the hair is synthesized.

Analgesia : Refers to the absence of pain in the presence of stimuli that would be expected to be painful. In clinical practice we use the term analgesia to mean a reduction in pain.

Anaphylaxis : A severe hypersensitivity reaction often resulting in bronchoconstriction and hypotension.

Anastomose : When one vein unites with another, the connection forming a reticulation

Anchor gene : A gene that has been positioned on both the physical map and the linkage map of a chromosome, and thereby allows their mutual alignment.

Androgenesis : Male parthenogenesis, i.e. the development of a haploid embryo from a male nucleus. The maternal nucleus is eliminated or inactivated subsequent to fertilization of the ovum, and the haploid individual (referred to as androgenetic) contains in its cells the genome of the male gamete only.

Anemia : Anemia is a decrease in PCV or hemoglobin resulting in decreased oxygen carrying capacity of the blood.

Anisocytosis : Varied sizes of red blood cells. May be an indicator of regenerative anemia.

Anneal : The pairing of complementary DNA or RNA sequences, via hydrogen bonding, to form a double-stranded polynucleotide. Most often used to describe the binding of a short primer or probe.

Annual : Any plant which completes its entire life cycles and dies within one year or less.

Antagonism : An interaction between two organisms (e.g. moulds or bacteria) in which the growth of one is inhibited by the other.

Antagonist : A compound that inhibits the effect of an agonist in such a way that the combined biological effect of the two becomes smaller than the sum of their individual effects.

Anterior chamber : Space between the cornea and iris and filled with aqueous.

Anthocyanin : A water-soluble blue, purple or red flavonoid pigments found in vacuoles of cells of certain plants.

Anthropomorphism : Projecting human needs or wants on to an animal.

Antiauxin : A chemical that interferes with the auxin response, sometimes by the prevention of auxin transport. Some antiauxins may promote morphogenesis in vitro (e.g. 2,3,5-tri-iodobenzoate (TIBA) and 2,4,5-trichlorophenoxyacetate (2,4,5-T)) and are therefore used to stimulate the growth of some cultures.

Antibiosis : The prevention of growth or development of an organism by a substance or another organism.

Antibiotics : Drugs that kill bacteria, but not viruses.

Antibody (Ab) : An immunological protein produced by the lymphocytes in response to contact with an antigen. Each antibody recognizes just one antigenic determinant of one antigen and acts by specifically binding to it, thus rendering it harmless. Those from the IgG antibody class are found in the bloodstream and used in immunoassay.

Antibody binding site : The part of an antibody that binds to the antigenic determinant.

Antibody class : The class to which an antibody belongs, depending on the type of heavy chain present. In mammals, there are five classes of antibodies: IgA, IgD, IgE, IgG, and IgM.

Antibody structure : Describes the molecular architecture of an antibody, which consists of two identical "light" chains and two identical "heavy" chains and has two antigen-binding sites. Each chain consists of a constant region which is the same between antibodies of the same class and sub-class, and a variable region that is antibody-specific.

Antibody-mediated immune response : The synthesis of antibodies by B cells in response to an encounter of the cells of the immune system with a foreign antigen.

Anticonvulsant : Drugs administered to reduce seizures.

Anticous : The fore-part, i.e. that most remote or turned away from the axis

Antidiuretic Hormone (ADH) : A hormone produced by the hypothalmus and stored in the pituitary gland. ADH regulates the ability of the collecting ducts of the kidneys to reabsorb water. In the absence of ADH the animal voids large amount of urine.

Antiemetics : Drugs administered to reduce vomiting.

Antifungal : A drug used in the treatment of a disease caused by a fungus.

Antioxidant : Compounds that slow the rate of oxidation reactions.

Antiparallel orientation : The normal arrangement of the two strands of a double-stranded DNA molecule, and of other nucleic-acid duplexes (DNA-RNA, RNA-RNA), in which the two strands are oriented in opposite directions so that the 5'-phosphate end of one strand is aligned with the 3'-hydroxyl end of the complementary strand.

Antipyretics : Drugs that suppress a fever in an attempt to bring the temperature to normal.

Antisense : DNA One of the two strands of double-stranded DNA, usually that which is complementary (hence "anti") to the mRNA, i.e. the non-transcribed strand. However, there is not universal agreement on this convention, and the preferred designations are coding strand for the strand whose sequence matches that of the mRNA, and non-coding strand or template strand for the complementary strand (i.e. the transcription template).

Antisense gene : A gene that produces an mRNA complementary to the transcript of a normal gene (usually constructed by inverting the coding region relative to the promoter).

Antisense rNA : A complementary RNA sequence that binds to a naturally occurring (sense) mRNA molecule, thus blocking its translation.

Antixenosis : The modification of the behaviour of an organism by a substance or another organism. Particularly used in the context of a plant's apparent resistance against insect feeding, when the insects are presented with a choice of plant genotypes.

Antrorse : Turned backwards, directed upwards

Anus : The muscular tissue at the end of the rectum that keeps stool in the rectum until the animal defecates.

Apicule : A short and sharp, but not stiff, point

Apoenzyme : Inactive enzyme that has to be associated with a co-enzyme in order to function. The apoenzyme/co-enzyme complex is called a holoenzyme.

Apomixis : The production of an embryo in the absence of meiosis. Apomictic higher plants produce asexual seeds, derived only from maternal tissue.

Appressed : Lying flat for the whole length of the organ

Aptamer : A polynucleotide molecule that binds to a specific molecule, often a protein.

Aqueous : The clear liquid produced by the cells of the ciliary body which fills the anterior chamber (between the cornea and iris) and the posterior chamber (between the iris and lens).

Arabidopsis : A genus of flowering plants in the Cruciferae. A. thaliana is used in research as a model plant because it has a small fully sequenced genome, can be cultured and transformed easily, and has a rapid generation time.

Arbitrage : The simultaneous buying and selling of the same commodity or foreign exchange in two or more markets to take advantage of price differentials.

Arbitrarily Primed Polymerase Chain Reaction (AP-PCR) : An application of the polymerase chain reaction to generate DNA fingerprints. The technique uses arbitrary primers to amplify anonymous stretches of DNA.

Arbitrary primer : An oligonucleotide primer whose sequence is chosen at random, rather than one whose sequence matches that of a known locus. These primers therefore amplify DNA fragments which have not been pre-selected.

Arteries : Blood vessels that carry blood from the heart to the organs and tissues. Arteries contain more oxygen and nutrients than veins and are under higher pressure.

Arthropod : Invertebrate animals (insects, arachnids and crustaceans) that have a jointed body and limbs and usually a hard shell or exoskeleton that is molted periodically.

Artificial inembryonation : Non-surgical transfer of embryo(s) to a recipient female. As in vitro embryo technology develops, artificial inembryonation may replace artificial insemination.

Artificial insemination : Deposition of bull semen in the reproductive tract of the cow as means of impregnation.

Artificial seed : Encapsulated or coated somatic embryos that are planted and treated like seed.

Artificial selection : The practice of choosing individuals from a population for reproduction, usually because these individuals possess one or more desirable traits.

As-applied map : Is a map containing site-specific information about the location and rate of application for fertilizer or chemical input. Usually created with a GPS equipped applicator and data logger.

Ascites : Abnormal accumulation of fluid in the peritoneal cavity, occurring naturally as a complication of cirrhosis of the liver, among other conditions. In the context of monoclonal antibody production, hybridoma cells are injected into mice to induce their proliferation in the resulting ascites. This method has been largely superseded by in vitro culture of hybridomas.

Ascospore : One of the spores contained in the ascus of certain fungi.

Asexual propagation : The duplication of a plant from a cell, tissue or organ of the plant.

Asexual reproduction : Nonsexual means of reproduction which can include grafting and budding.

Ash : The inorganic mineral elements of animals and plants, determined by burning off the organic matter and weighing the residue (ash).

A-site : Aminoacyl Site.

Assortative mating : Mating in which the partners are chosen on the basis of phenotypic similarity.

Asymmetric hybrid : A hybrid formed, usually via protoplast fusion, between two donors, where the chromosome complement of one of the donors is incomplete. This chromosome loss can be induced by irradiation or chemical treatment, or can occur naturally.

Asynapsis : The failure or partial failure in the pairing of homologous chromosomes during the first meiotic prophase.

Asystole : Cardiac arrest.

Atomic clock : The world's most accurate clock. Each GPS satellite has an atomic clock on-board, which is used by GPS receivers to calculate position.

Atopy : Allergic inhalant dermatitis or atopic dermatitis. Allergens are true antigens which are usually inhaled or penetrate the skin as complete allergens or haptens. Allergens may also be ingested or injected.

Atresia : Regressing or shrinking in size.

Atria : The heart has 4 chambers; the two chambers that make up the top of the heart are the atria.

Atrium : A structure that provides lots of above light for plants. Commercial buildings often have their foyer as an atrium. Many homes have built in atriums.

Atropine : A parasympatholytic drug which competitivly blocks acetylcholine at muscarinic receptors and increases sinus node automaticity and atrial-ventricular conduction resulting in an increase in heart rate.

Attack rate : The proportion of a defined population affected during an outbreak.

Attenuated vaccine : A virulent organism that has been modified to produce a less virulent form, but nevertheless retains the ability to elicit antibodies against the virulent form.

Attenuation : A mechanism for controlling gene expression in prokaryotes that involves premature termination of transcription.

Attenuator : A nucleotide sequence in the 5' region of a prokaryotic gene (or in its RNA) that causes premature termination of transcription, possibly by forming a secondary structure.

Auscultation : To listen with a stethoscope. The heart and lung sounds are heard by auscultation.

Authentic protein : A recombinant protein that has all the properties - including any post-translational modifications - of its naturally occurring counterpart.

Autocatalysis : Catalysis in which one of the products of the reaction is a catalyst for the reaction.

Autologous cells : Cells taken from an individual, cultured (or stored), and, possibly, genetically manipulated before being transferred back into the original donor.

Autolysis : The process of self destruction of a cell, cell organelle, or tissue, through the action of lysosomic enzymes.

Autonomous : A term applied to any biological unit that can function on its own, i.e. without the help of another unit, such as a transposable element that encodes an enzyme for its own transposition.

Autonomous operation : Vehicle guidance without the need for human intervention. A tractor may be driven by a series of on-boards sensors and GPS for precision driving without damage to crops.

Autonomous(ly) Replicating Segment (or Sequence) (ARS) : Any eukaryotic DNA sequence that initiates and supports chromosomal replication; they have been isolated in yeast cells.

Autopolyploid : A polyploid whose constituent genomes are derived from the same or nearly the same progenitor. In an autotetraploid, each chromosome is present in four copies, so meiotic configurations may include many (or exclusively) quadrivalents (four paired chromosomes), and the inheritance of alleles will be quadruplex. Quadrivalents do not always segregate normaly at meiosis, resulting in lowered fertility, so some established autotetraploid species that reproduce sexually have restricted quadrivalent formation.

Autoradiograph : A technique for visualizing the presence, location and intensity of radioactivity in histological preparations, paper chromatograms or electrophoretic gel separations, obtained by overlaying the surface with X-ray film and allowing the radiation to form an image on the film.

Autosome : Any of the chromosomes except the sex chromosomes.

Autotroph : Organism capable of self-nourishment utilizing carbon dioxide or carbonates as the sole source of carbon and obtaining energy from radiant energy or from the oxidation of inorganic elements, or compounds such as iron, sulphur, hydrogen, ammonium and nitrites.

Average Daily Gain (ADG) : Measurement of daily body weight change in animal on a feed test. Most tests for bulls are 140 or 160 days long.

Avidin : A glycoprotein present in egg white, which has a strong affinity to biotin. Can lead to biotin deficiency if given in large quantities. Used as a biological reagent in the same way as streptavidin.

Avidity : A measure of the binding strength of an antibody to its antigen.

Avirulence gene (Avr gene) : Many plants contain R genes, which confer simply-inherited resistance to a specific pathogen race. The plants are able to recognize the presence of the pathogen by an interaction between their R gene and the matching pathogen's avirulence gene. Successful recognition triggers a cascade of further genes, often leading to a hypersensitive response.

Axenic culture : Free of external contaminants and internal symbionts; generally not possible with surface sterilization alone, sometimes used incorrectly to indicate aseptic culture.

Axillary bud proliferation : Propagation of plant tissue in vitro to promote axillary growth, to generate large numbers of plantlets in culture.

Axis : 1) Upper angle formed between thc stem or branch and any other branch, leaf or other organ arising from them 2) The main line of growth in a plant or organ, e.g., the stem, from which the other parts such as the leaves and flowers grow

Azathioprine : An immunosuppressive drug used in cancer chemotherapy and in treatment of immune mediated diseases.

Azoospermia : The complete absence of sperm in an ejaculate.

B

Backbulb : refers to the propagation of an orchid. It is the old, dormant pseudobulb, it may be leafless, but will still produce a new plant.

Backcross : Crossing an individual with one of its parents or with the genetically equivalent organism. The offspring of such a cross are referred to as the backcross generation or backcross progeny.

Backfill : Replacing dirt from the original hole after planting.

Backup : A computer backup is a duplicate set of data that can be used to retrieve files in the event of data loss. Backups are often stored using CD-R, DVD, or USB external hard drives.

Backyard wildlife habitat : A dreamy situation where native plant materials are providing food and shelter for protection and reproduction for birds, insects, and mammals in ones own backyard.

BACT : Best available control technology

Bacteremia : Bacteria in the blood.

Bacteria : Microorganisms that break down organic materials in the first stages of composting. It is bacteria that generate the heat associated with hot composting. The three types of bacteria are psychrophilic, mesophyllic, and thermophilic.

Bacterial artificial chromosome : A plasmid vector that can be used to clone large inserts of DNA (up to 500 kb).

Bacteriocin : A protein produced by bacteria of one strain and active against those of a closely related strain.

Bacteriophage (phage or phage particle) : A virus that infects bacteria. Altered forms are used as cloning vectors.

Bacteriostat : A substance that inhibits or slows down growth and reproduction of bacteria.

Balance of payments : An accounting statement measuring the value of goods, services and capital exchanged between a country and all foreign countries. A nation is said to have either: 1) a balance of payments deficit if it sends abroad less in goods, services, and capital than it receives from foreigners; or 2) a balance of payments surplus if it sends abroad more in goods, services, and capital than it receives.

Balance of trade : The difference in value between a country's merchandise imports and exports in a specified period. A country's balance of trade is only one factor -- though an important one -- in its balance of payments.

Balanced lethal system : A system for maintaining a recessive lethal allele at each of two loci on the same pair of chromosomes. In a closed population with no crossing-over between the loci, only the double heterozygotes for the lethal mutations survive.

Balanced polymorphism : Two or more phenotypes maintained in the same breeding population.

Balanced ration : A 24-hour feed allowance that provides an animal with appropriate amounts and proportions of all nutrients required for a given level of performance.

Band fertilize : To apply fertilizer in a narrow line along a row of plants or in a circle around individual plants.

Banks for Cooperatives (BC) : Lending institutions within the Farm Credit System that provide credit to agricultural cooperatives and rural utility cooperatives nationwide. Currently, there are two BCs with national charters -- the St. Paul Bank for Cooperatives and CoBank Agricultural Bank (Denver).

Barbate : Bearded; barbed

Bare root : Plants that have been dug out of the ground when dormant. The soil is shaken free, washed and stored until shipment. Roses and daylilies commonly come this way, as well as smaller shrubs and bushes, sold in their dormancy.

Bargaining association : A farmer cooperative intended primarily to influence farm prices or other terms of trade between the members and the buyers of the commodities they produce.

Barnase : A bacterial ribonuclease, which, when transformed into plants and expressed in the anthers, generates a male sterile phenotype. Thus it is a technology applicable to F1 hybrid seed production, which relies on the ability to genetically sterilize genotypes to ensure that all seed borne on the plant are the result of outcrossing. The sterility phenotype is suppressed by the barstar protein, which can therefore be used to reverse the sterility where this is necessary.

BASAL : At the base of an organ or part such as the stem or pseudobulb

Basal fluid loss : The basal fluid loss is the typical loss of fluids by both insensible and sensible routes. For a normal adult dog or cat, the net basal loss is about 20-30 ml/lb/day.

Base : One of the components of nucleosides, nucleotides and nucleic acids. Four different bases are found in naturally occurring DNA - the purines A (adenine) and G (guanine); and the pyrimidines C (cytosine) and T (thymine, the common name for 5-methyluracil). In RNA, T is replaced by U (uracil).

Base analogue : A non-natural purine or pyrimidine base that differs slightly in structure from the normal bases, but can be incorporated into nucleic acids. They are often mutagenic.

Base Pair (BP) : The two separate strands of a nucleic acid double helix are held together by specific hydrogen bonding between a purine and a pyrimidine, one from each strand. The base A pairs with T in DNA (with U in RNA); while G pairs with C in both DNA and RNA. The length of a nucleic acid molecule is often given in terms of the number of base pairs it contains.

Base period price : The average price for an item in a specified time period used as a base for an index -- such as 1910-14, 1957-59, 1967, 1977, or 1982. Time series of data are often deflated to a base period price. Such deflated time series are referred to as constant dollar values.

Base property : For the Bureau of Land Management: land or water resources, owned or controlled by a holder of a grazing permit or lease, that are suitable to support livestock for a part of the year. For the Forest Service: lands and improvements owned and used by a permittee for a farm or ranch and designated by the permittee to qualify for a grazing permit. One must own or control base property to be eligible for permits or leases to graze private livestock on federal lands.

Basing point : A geographical site used to establish fixed rates and/or prices for federal milk marketing orders. Generally, rates or prices increase according to the distance from the basing point.

Basipetal : Developing, in sequence, from the apex towards the base.

Basis : The difference between the current spot price (or cash price) of a commodity and the price of the nearest futures contract for the same or a related commodity. Basis is usually computed in relation to the futures contract next to expire and may reflect different time periods, product forms, qualities, or locations.

Basis risk : The possibility of unexpected variation in basis and a resulting loss of expected revenue when a futures contract is liquidated and the commodity sold on the cash market.

Basophil : A type of leukocyte produced by stem cells in the red bone marrow.

BAT : Best available technology

Batch furrow system : A management system where pigs are raised in batches from piglets to market hogs and as they mature the raising area they left is cleaned, disinfected, and left vacant until the next batch of pigs is purchased.

Batch process : An entire cubic-yard pile is built at the same time, and finishes decomposing at the same time. This is the opposite of the "add as you go"method. Because the entire pile is built at one time, factors such as moisture, C:N ratio, variety of textures and sizes, etc. can be more closely controlled for fast decomposition.

Bedding plant : Usually an annual plant temporarily in a garden display. Some interstates have "smiley faces" that are done in a bedding plant display. Sometimes called carpet bedding.

Beef (cattle) Price index (BPI) : An index of the weighted average annual price for beef cattle, excluding calves, for an 11 western state area as compared with a specific base period equal to 100. This index is used in calculating federal grazing fees.

Beef carcass data service : A program whereby producers, for a fee, can receive carcass evaluation data on their cattle by using a special "carcass data" eartag for their slaughter animals.

Beef Improvement Federation (BIF) : A federation of organizations, businesses and individuals interested or involved in performance evaluation of beef cattle. The purposes of BIF are to bring about uniformity of procedures, development of programs, cooperation among interested entities, education of its members and the ultimate consumers of performance evaluation methods, and to build confidence of the beef industry in the principles and potentials of performance testing.

Bench-scale process : A small- or laboratory-scale process; commonly used in connection with fermentation.

Beneficial insect : These are insects that will improve and work in our gardens. By improving the soil, going after harmful insects, and will pollinate plants. Ladybeetles, earthworms, and bees are well known.

Benign : Not malignant. Sometimes taken to mean noncancerous although some cancers are called benign if they do not spread to other parts of the body.

Benign Prostate Hypertrophy (BPH) : A condition in which the prostate gland enlarges under the influence of sex hormones. BPH can lead to infection of the prostate gland.

Best Management Practices (BMP) : A conservation practice or combination of practices designed to maintain agricultural productivity while reducing point- and nonpoint- source water pollution. State water quality agencies (or their designees) determine BMPs to fit local conditions and to make the most efficient use of natural resources and purchased inputs.

Beta-DNA : The normal form of DNA found in biological systems, which exists as a right-handed helix.

Beta-Glucuronidase (GUS) : An enzyme produced by certain bacteria, which catalyses the cleavage of a whole range of beta-glucuronides. Because this activity is largely absent in plants, the encoding bacterial gene has been widely used as a reporter gene in plant transgenesis.

Beta-lactamase : An enzyme that detoxifies penicillin group antibiotics, such as ampicillin. The â-lactamase gene is commonly used as a marker for successful transformation, where only transformed cells are able to tolerate the presence of ampicillin.

Bicolour : A flower with petals which bear two distinctly different colors.

Biennial : A plant that will require two growing seasons to complete its life cycle. In the first year leaves. In the second year has blooms and seeds.

Bigeneric : A hybrid that is created by crossing two different genera.

Bilateral : Involving both sides.

Bile : A yellow fluid produced by the liver and stored in the gall bladder that helps in the digestion of fats.

Bile acids : Substances produces by the liver and secreted in the bile that aid digestion.

Binomial nomenclature : A system in which the scientific name of a plant consists of two parts indicating the genus and species.

Bio-accumulation : A problem that can arise when a stable chemical such as a heavy metal or DDT is introduced into a natural environment. Where there are no agents present able to biodegrade it, its concentration can increase as it passes up the food chain and higher organisms may suffer toxic effects. This phenomenon may be employed beneficially for the removal of toxic metals from wastewater, and for bioremediation.

Bioavailability : The proportion of a nutrient or administered drug etc. that can be taken up by an organism in a biologically effective form. For example, some soils high in phosphorus have a low level of P availability because the pH of the soil renders much of the P insoluble.

Biocatalysis : The use of enzymes to improve the efficiency of chemical reactions.

Biochemical Oxygen Demand (BOD) : A measure of the amount of oxygen consumed in 5 days due to natural, biological processes that break down organic matter, such as those that take place when manure or sawdust is put in water. High levels of oxygen-demanding wastes in waters deplete dissolved oxygen (DO), thereby endangering aquatic life. Sometimes referred to as "biological oxygen demand. Chemical oxygen demand (COD) is a measure of the oxygen consumed when organic matter is broken down chemically rather than naturally. COD can be determined much more quickly than BOD and more accurately reflects the amount of organic matter in a water sample.

Biocontrol : Pest control by biological means. Any process using deliberately introduced living organisms to restrain the growth and development of other organisms, such as the introduction of predatory insects to control an insect pest.

Biodesulphurization : The removal of organic and inorganic sulphur from coal by bacterial and soil micro-organisms. Certain bacteria can oxidize insoluble sulphur compounds into soluble sulphates, which can be washed away with the bacteria.

Biodiversity (or biological diversity) : In general, the variety and variation among plants, animals, and microorganisms, and among their ecosystems. It has 3 levels: ecosystem diversity, species diversity, and genetic (within species) diversity. The concept of maintaining biodiversity holds that civilization should preserve the greatest possible number of existing species so that a highly diverse genetic pool, which can be tapped for useful and beneficial characteristics, will be available into the future. Genetic diversity provides resources for genetic resistance to pests and diseases. In agriculture, biodiversity is a production system characterized by the presence of multiple plant and/or animal species, as contrasted with the genetic specialization of monoculture.

Bio-energetics : The study of the flow and the transformation of energy that occur in living organisms.

Biofilms : A layer of micro-organisms growing on a surface, in a bed of polymeric material which they themselves have made. Biofilms tend to form wherever a surface on which bacteria can grow is exposed to some suitable medium and a supply of bacteria.

Biofuel : A gaseous, liquid or solid fuel derived from a biological source, e. g. ethanol, rapeseed oil or fish liver oil.

Biogas : A mixture of methane and carbon dioxide resulting from the anaerobic decomposition of waste such as domestic, industrial and agricultural sewage.

Bio-informatics : The use and organization of information of biological interest. In particular, concerned with organizing bio-molecular databases (particularly DNA sequences), utilizing computers for analysing this information, and integrating information from disparate biological sources.

Bioleaching : The recovery of metals from their ores, using the action of micro-organisms, rather than chemical or physical treatment. For example, Thiobacillus ferroxidans has been used to extract gold from refractory ores.

Biolistics : A technique to generate transgenic cells, in which DNA-coated small metal particles (tungsten or gold) are propelled by various means fast enough to puncture target cells. Provided that the cell is not irretrievably damaged, the DNA is frequently taken up by the cell. The technique has been successfully used to transform animal, plant and fungal cells, and even mitochondria inside cells.

Biological containment : Restricting the movement of organisms from the laboratory. Can take two forms: making the organism unable to survive in the outside environment, or making the outside environment inhospitable to the organism. For micro-organisms, the favoured approach is to engineer organisms to require a supply of a specific nutrient that is usually available only in the laboratory. For higher organisms (plants and animals), it is more possible to ensure that the outside environment is unsuited to growth, spread and reproduction.

Biological control : The practice of using beneficial natural organisms to attack and control harmful plant and animal pests and weeds is called biological control, or biocontrol. This can include introducing predators, parasites, and disease organisms, or releasing sterilized individuals. Biocontrol methods may be an alternative or complement to chemical pest control methods.

Biological diversity : Richness and abundance of species, and variety of natural communities. Both the number of species and the number of individuals within each species are important in considering the extent of biological diversity in an area. Also referred to as biodiversity.

Biological Oxygen Demand (BOD) : The dissolved oxygen required for the respiration of a population of aerobic organisms present in water. Expressed in terms of the oxygen consumed in water at a temperature of 20°C per unit time. The BOD is used as an indication of the degree to which the sample of water is polluted, particularly by inorganic nutrients for plants.

Biopharming : The use of genetically transformed crop plants and livestock animals to produce valuable compounds, especially pharmaceuticals.

Biopiracy : The patenting of genetic stocks, and the subsequent privatization of genetic resources collections. The term implies a lack of consent on the part of the originator.

Biopolymer : Any large polymer produced by a living organism. Includes some materials suitable for use as plastics.

Bioprocess : Any process that uses complete living cells or their components to effect desired physical or chemical changes.

Biosilk : A biomimetic fibre produced by the expression of the relevant orb-weaving spider genes in yeast or bacteria, followed by the spinning of the expressed protein into a fibre.

Biosorbents : Micro-organisms which, either by themselves or in conjunction with a substrate are able to extract and/or concentrate a desired molecule by means of its selective retention.

Biosphere : The part of the earth and its atmosphere that is inhabited by living organisms.

Biosynthesis : Synthesis of compounds by living cells, which is the essential feature of anabolism.

Biotic stress : Living organisms which can harm plants, such as viruses, fungi, and bacteria, and harmful insects.

Biotoxin : A naturally produced compound which shows pronounced biological activity, toxic to some or many organisms.

Biotransformation : The conversion of one chemical or material into another using a biological catalyst: a near synonym is biocatalysis, and hence the catalyst used is called a biocatalyst. Usually the catalyst is an enzyme, or a fixed whole, dead micro-organism that contains an enzyme or several enzymes.

Bi-parietal diameter : The diameter of the skull as determined using ultrasound. This diameter can be used to determine age of the fetus.

Birth Weight (BW) : The weight of a calf taken within 24 hours after birth. Heavy birth weights tend to be correlated with calving problems, but the conformation of the calf and the cow are contributing factors.

Black spot : A disease on the foliage of roses. It is caused by moisture. To avoid, plant disease - resistant roses. Clean up after pruning. One can use fungicide during damp weather - captan, copper, or lime sulfur are most effective when you follow the instructions carefully. One can also use baking soda (sodium bicarbonate) at a rate of one teaspoon to one gallon. Use in the morning to prevent sun scald. One can also try neem oil.

Bladder : The sac-like structure, which holds urine until the urine can be passed.

Blastula : In animals, an early embryo form that follows the morula stage; typically, a single-layered sheet (blastoderm) or ball of cells (blastocyst).

Bleeding : 1) Collection of blood from immunized animals. 2) Used to describe the occasional purplish-black colouration of media due to phenolic products given off by (usually fresh) transfers.

Blend price : Primarily used in the federal milk marketing order program. Represents the weighted average price of milk, per hundred pounds, paid to each farmer based on how Grade A (fluid grade) milk is allocated to different usage classes (e. g., fluid, manufacturing) by processors.

Blending : In grain marketing, the combining of two different qualities of grain in order to change the total value of both lots. For example, it is common to blend grains of differing moisture or different foreign material content to achieve the requirements of a contract order.

Blue box : Direct payments, under the definition of 'production-limiting' measures as defined in Article 6 of the Uruguay Round Agreement on Agriculture, that are not subject to the commitment to reduce domestic support. To qualify for the exemption, payments must be based on fixed areas or yields, on a fixed number of livestock, or on 85% or less of the base level of production.

Blue eye : A post vaccination adverse event that had been reported by veterinarians vaccinating dogs with the modified-live canine adenovirus-1 vaccine (CAV-1).

Blunt end : The end of a double-stranded DNA molecule in which neither strand extends beyond the other.

Board foot : A measure for lumber, equal to a 1-inch thick board that is 1 foot long and 1 foot wide in nominal dimensions (a 2x4, for example, is less than 2 inches thick and 4 inches wide, but a 1-foot long 2x4 is still counted as 2/3 of a board foot); typically reported in thousands of board feet (mbf). Also used to estimate the volume of lumber that can be produced from logs and standing trees.

Body condition score : A score based on a scale of 1 to 5 that ranks the fatness of the animal. One is the thinest and five is the fatest.

Body Condition Score (BCS) : A score based on a scale from 1 to 5 that asseses the amount of body fat on an animal. One is emaciated, three is ideal, and five is obese.

Bog plant : Plants that preferred damp and most sail as their habitat.

Bole : The area of a tree trunk that is from the ground to the first major branch.

Boll weevil : An insect pest of cotton that is the subject of an Animal and Plant Health Inspection Service eradication program cooperatively funded and managed by cotton producers.

Bolt : The tendency of cool-season plants to grow rapidly and produce seeds when exposed to warm temperatures.

Bolus : The rapid administration of a fluid or drug over a short time period.

Bony orbit : The bony fossa within the skull separating the eyes from the cranial cavity.

Botanical pesticide : A pesticide whose active ingredient is a plant-produced chemical such as nicotine or strychnine. Also called a plant-derived pesticide. Being 'natural' pesticides, as distinct from synthetic ones, they are typically acceptable to organic farmers.

Bottle garden : A small terrarium created in a bottle. A miniature eco-system.

Bottom heat : An arrangement used in propagation. Usually electric heating cables will run through the base of the propagation medium. Great for seed germination and cuttings.

Bound water : Cellular water not released into the intercellular space upon freezing and thawing.

Bracteate : Bearing bracts

Bradycardia : An abnormally slow heart rate.

Bramble : Any shrub with thorns in the rose family; usually refers to blackberries and raspberries.

Branch crown : Plant tissue that is the junction of the roots and stem that forms on the side of a strawberry plant. These only form foliage.

Breastfeeding promotion : Relates to activities required to be carried out by state and local agencies using federal funds provided for nutrition education and administrative services under the WIC program.

Breech : Area around the tail and back of hind legs.

Breeding value : Value of an animal as a parent. The working definition is twice the difference between a very large number of progeny and the population average when individuals are mated at random within the population and all progeny are managed alike. The difference is doubled because only a sample half (one gene of each pair) is transmitted from a parent to each progeny. Breeding value exists for each trait and is dependent on the population in which the animal is evaluated. For a given trait, an individual can be an above average producer in one herd and a below average producer in another herd.

Bretylium : A drug which diminishes the release of norepinephrine from nerve endings with chronic oral dosing. It is used in treatment of ventricular fibrillation and ventricular tachycardia.

Brewer's yeast : Strains of the yeast Saccharomyces cerevisiae that are used for the production of beer.

Bridge : A filter paper or other substrate used as a wick and support structure for a plant tissue in culture when a liquid medium is used.

Broad-host-range plasmid : A plasmid that can replicate in a number of different bacterial species.

Broad-sense heritability : The proportion of the total phenotypic variation which results from genetic variation or interaction between the genotype and the environment.

Broiler : A young chicken, usually 6 to 8 weeks old and 3 to 5 pounds, raised primarily for its meat.

Broken mouth : A term describing a sheep who has lost one or more of its permanent incisors.

Broom snakeweed : Perennial. Same family as the sunflower. Shrub-like plant that competes with range vegetation and is poisonous to livestock.

Brown rot : A fungus that is very common disease on fruit. Buy disease resistant varieties. Remove all infected parts of the plant.

Browning : Discolouration of freshly cut surfaces of plant tissue due to phenolic oxidation. In plant tissue culture, it may indicate a nutritional or pathogenic problem, generally leading to necrosis.

Bt crops : Bt crops are genetically modified to carry genetic material from the soil bacterium Bacillus thuringiensis. Crops containing the Bt genes are able to produceBt-toxin, thereby providing protection against insects during the growth-stage of the plant..

Buffer : A substance used in livestock rations to help resist changes in the acidity of the digestive tract. Examples : sodium bicarbonate, bentonite.

Buffer strips : Small areas of erosion-resistant vegetation planted on fields, usually along the contour or along the boundaries, to slow the flow of runoff and reduce erosion.

Bulb : A storage organ, usually formed below ground level, used for propagation. A true bulb consists of fleshy scales surrounding the central bud. We often think of spring and fall bulbs.

Bulbil : A small bulb that forms along the stems of certain plants, such as tiger lilies and bladder ferns.

Bulblet : A small bulb that develops around a parent bulb and can be removed to propagate additional plants.

Bulbourethral glands : An accessory sex gland of the male.

Bulbous : Bulb-like

Bulbus glandis : The rounded base of the penis.

Bulgur : Wheat that has been parboiled, dried, and partially debranned for later use in cracked or whole grain form.

Bulk carrier : Refers to two types of cargo ships: the dry- bulk carrier and the liquid-bulk carrier, better known as a tanker. Bulk cargo is a shipment such as oil, grain, or ore, that is not packaged, baled, bottled, or otherwise packed and is loaded without counting or marking.

Bulk commodities : Generally, high volume, low value unprocessed agricultural commodities, which are treated as though they are homogeneous (fungible) in nature prior to processing. Grains, oilseeds, and cotton are considered bulk commodities. Contrasting categories are high value commodities, semiprocessed and processed commodities, and consumer ready commodities.

Bulk tank : A refrigerated milk storage tank for each dairy herd.

Bullous retinal detachment : The retina has detached from all points of contact except for around the periphery and at the optic disk.

Buoyant density : The intrinsic density which a molecule, virus or sub-cellular particle has when suspended in an aqueous solution of a salt, such as CsCl, or a sugar, such as sucrose. DNA from different species has different characteristic buoyant densities, determined largely by the relative proportion of the base-pairs G+C, to A+T.

Buphthalmos : Enlarged eye caused by glaucoma.

Butterfly catheter : A style of catheter that has a rigid needle attached to a plastic finger grip that looks like "wings" and then attached to a short piece of flexible tubing.

Button : The small heads of broccoli or cabbage that form as a result of seedlings being exposed to freezing temperatures.

By-pass flow : Water required by a regulating or permitting entity to be retained in-stream to protect fish habitat and other water-based functions and values. For example, the Forest Service requires some operators to allow a certain amount of water to bypass their dams to preserve endangered fish habitat.

C

Cage : An enclosure used to support a plant.

Calcinosis cutis : Hard crusts or white plaques in the skin of some patients with hyperadrenocorticism.

Calcitic limestone : A common material used for "liming" soil that has an acid level that is too high. this type is most commonly used and contains calcium carbonate.

Calcitriol : The active form of 1, 25 dihydroxycholecalciferol (vitamin D). Can be exogenously administered to patients with chronic renal failure to suppress PTH secretion by the parathyroid glands with reversal of some of the clinical manifestations and possibly a resultant slowing of the rate of progression of renal dysfunction.

Calcium channel blocker : These drugs inhibit the movement of calcium ion across cell membranes. Calcium channel blockers are used in the treatment of certain heart conditions. In CPR, they may be used after resusitation to protect the heart from the effects of calcium administered during CPR.

Calculi : Stones in the kidney, urinary bladder or occasionally gall bladder.

Calf crop : The number or percentage of calves produced within a herd in a given year relative to the number of cows and heifers exposed to breeding.

Calf hutch : Individual housing unit for young calves, assists in blocking transmission of disease.

Calf starter : Grain based mixes fed to young calves.

Callus : A protective tissue, consisting of parenchyma cells, that develops over a cut or damaged plant surface. 2. Mass of undifferentiated, thin-walled parenchyma cells induced by hormone treatment. 3. Actively dividing non-organized masses of undifferentiated and differentiated cells often developing from injury (wounding) or in tissue culture in the presence of growth regulators.

Callus culture : A technique of plant tissue culture, usually on solidified medium and initiated by inoculation of small explants. Used as the basis for organogenic (shoot or root forming) cultures, cell cultures or proliferation of embryoids. Callus cultures can be indefinitely maintained through regular sub-culturing.

Calorie (kcal) : A measure of energy; usually expressed as kilocalorie (kcal) or megacalorie (Mcal). 1 cal = the amount of energy required to increase the temperature of 1 g of water 1 degree C.

Cambial zone : Region in stems and roots consisting of the cambium and its recent derivatives.

Cambium : A one or two cells thick layer of plant meristematic tissue, between the xylem and phloem tissues, which gives rise to secondary tissues, thus resulting in an increase in the diameter of the stem or root. The two most important cambia are the vascular (fascicular) cambium and the cork cambium.

Camelids : Camelids are a large family including Old World camelids : camels and the bactrians, which are two-humped camels, and the New World camelids, llamas and alpacs.

Candidate gene : A gene whose deduced function (on the basis of DNA sequence) suggests that it may be involved in the genetic control of an aspect of phenotype.

Candidate-gene strategy : An experimental approach in which knowledge of the biochemistry and/or physiology of a trait is used to identify candidate genes.

Candle : The new shoot growth on needled evergreens before the needles expand.

Cap site : The site on a DNA template where transcription begins. It corresponds to the nucleotide at the 5' end of the RNA transcript which accepts the G cap.

Capacitation : The final stage, inside the female genital tract, in the maturation process of a spermatozoon, as it penetrates the ovum.

Capillary action : A force that causes liquids to rise or fall when inside very small tubular spaces.

Capillary electrophoresis : A form of electrophoresis used widely in current large-scale DNA sequencing facilities, where the sample is passed through a long, very-narrow-bore tube containing a re-usable matrix.

Caprine : Goat.

Capsid : The protein coat of a virus. The capsid often determines the shape of the virus.

Carbohydrates : Major energy providing substrates including starches, sugars, cellulose and hemicellulose. All carbohydrates contain carbon, hydrogen and oxygen, and are usually divided into two fractions - structural (fibre) and non-structural (sugars and starches).

Carbon dioxide, CO_2 : A colorless, odorless gas found in the air. It is absorbed by plants and exhaled by animals.

Carbonic anhydrase : An enzyme located in the eye and in the kidney tubules that is important in reabsorbing bicarbonate (kidney) and in the active secretion of aqueous in the eye.

Carbuncle : Multiple cutaneous abscesses that are connected by sinuses.

Carcass evaluation : Techniques of measuring components of quality and quantity in carcasses.

Carcass quality grade : An estimate of palatability based primarily on marbling and maturity and generally to a lesser extent on color, texture and firmness of lean. Days on feed and fat thickness (of 0.25 inches or more) are comparable to quality grade in estimating eating quality.

Carcass quantity : Amount of salable meat (muscle) the carcass will yield. Cutability is an estimate of this.

Card reader : A device that reads removable memory cards such as Secure Digital, Smart Media, CF, and Memory Sticks. Usually connects to PC using an USB port.

Cardiac pump theory : In CPR, when the chest is compressed the heart underneath the chest wall is directly compressed as well, squeezing blood out into the major blood vessels so it can return to the heart and then go to the brain. CPR in animals weighing less than 7 kg is probably using the cardiac pump theory.

Cardiomyopathy : A disease of the heart muscle. Weak heart muscle cannot pump blood normally.

Cardiopulmonary Resuscitation (CPR) : A life saving procedure that includes the external compression of the chest wall to stimulate blood flow and breathing (by mouth to mouth or other methods) to provide oxygen.

Cardiovascular : The organ system that includes the heart and blood vessels.

Carnivores : Macroorganisms that feed on other animals. Includes ant, beetle, centipede, enchytraed, fly, mite, mole, scorpion, slug, snail, spider, springtail.

Carotene : A reddish-orange plastid pigment involved in photosynthesis. A carotenoid and precursor of vitamin A.

Carotenoid : A group of chemically similar red to yellow pigments responsible for the characteristic colour of many plant organs or fruits, such as tomatoes, carrots, etc.

Oxygen-containing carotenoids are called xanthophylls. Carotenoids serve as light-harvesting molecules in photosynthetic assemblies and also play a role in protecting prokaryotes from the deleterious effects of light.

Carrying capacity : The maximum stocking rate for livestock possible without damaging vegetation or related resources. Carrying capacity may vary from year to year on the same area, due to fluctuating forage production. Used by the government in decisions about how much livestock will be allowed on an allotment on public lands.

Carryover : The supply of a farm commodity not yet used at the end of a marketing year and carried over into the next year. An excessively large carryover is typically described as a surplus condition that causes prices to fall. When the carryover falls below normal, there may be concerns of a shortage contributing to price escalation.

Cartel : An alliance or arrangement among industrial or commercial enterprises or nations aimed at limiting competition or exercising monopoly power in a market.

Cash grain farm : A farm where corn, grain sorghum, small grains, soybeans, or field peas and beans account for at least 50% of the value of farm products sold.

Cash in lieu of commodities : Refers to cash provided to food programme operators (e.g., elderly nutrition programmes, child care food programmes, and some school food programmes) in lieu of mandated commodity assistance. Recipients may use the cash to buy whatever foods they need to operate their meal service programmes.

Cash market : The market for the cash commodity (as contrasted to a futures contract), taking the form of : 1) an organized, self-regulated central market (e.g., a commodity exchange); 2) a decentralized over-the-counter market; or 3) a local organization, such as a grain elevator or meat processor, which provides a market for a small region.

Cash price : The price in the marketplace for actual cash or spot commodities to be delivered via customary market channels.

Castings : Manure, i.e., excretion, of earthworms. Earthworm castings are high in nutrients for plants and microorganisms.

Castration : Another term for neutering a male animal by removal of the testes.

CAT : Catastrophic crop insurance

Catabolic pathway : A pathway by which an organic molecule is degraded in order to release energy for growth and other cellular processes.

Catabolism : The breakdown of large molecules in living organisms, with the accompanying release of energy.

Catabolite activator Protein (CAP) : A protein which combines with cyclic AMP. The cAMP-CAP complex binds to the promoter regions of E. coli and stimulates transcription of the relevant operon.

Catabolite repression : Glucose-mediated reduction in the rates of transcription of genes that encode enzymes involved in catabolic pathways (e.g. the lac operon).

Catalytic antibody (abzyme) : An antibody selected for its ability to catalyze a chemical reaction by binding to and stabilizing the transition state intermediate.

Catalytic RNA (ribozyme) : A natural or synthetic RNA molecule that cuts an RNA substrate.

Catalytic site : The part of the surface of an enzyme molecule (usually only a small portion of the total) necessary for the catalytic process.

Caudal : Refers to the rear or in a direction toward the rear of the animal. For example the abdomen is more caudal than the chest. The opposite term is cranial meaning closer to the head of the animal.

Caudicle : Slender stalk-like appendage that attaches the VISCIDIUM (a sticky gland) to the POLLINIA (pollen packets).

Caulescent : Having no visible stem, or a very short one

Cauliflower Mosaic Virus (CaMV) : A DNA virus affecting cauliflower and many other dicot species. Its importance is due to the promoter of its 35S ribosomal DNA, which is constitutively active in most plant tissues, and has therefore been widely used as a promoter for the expression of transgenes.

Caulogenesis : Stem organogenesis; induction of shoot development from callus.

CD molecules : Abbreviation for: cluster of differentiation molecules. Any group of surface antigens associated with a specific sub-population of T cells.

CDC : Centers for Disease Control and Prevention

CDNA : DNA synthesized from an RNA template using reverse transcriptase.

CDNA clone : A double-stranded cDNA molecule propagated in a vector, and used as a probe in RFLP analyses, as template for the production of EST sequences, and for gene expression studies.

CDNA library : A library composed of complementary copies of cellular mRNAs.

CD-R : A recordable compact disc. Most CD-R discs hold up to 650 MB. Can be used for moving large amount of data or as a data backup.

CED : County Executive Director

Cell : The fundamental level of structural organization in complex organisms. Eukaryotic cells contain a nucleus (with chromosomes) and cytoplasm with the protein synthesis machinery, bounded by a membrane. Prokaryotic cells have no nucleus.

Cell culture : The in vitro growth of cells isolated from multicellular organisms.

Cell cycle : The sequence of stages that a cell passes through between one division and the next. The cell cycle oscillates between mitosis (M) and the interphase, which is divided into the G1 phase (involving a high rate of biosynthesis and growth), the S phase (in which the DNA content is doubled as a consequence of chromosome replication), and the G2 phase (preparatory for cell division).

Cell generation time : The interval between the beginning of consecutive divisions of a cell, equivalent to the time that it takes for a population of single-celled organisms to double its cell number.

Cell line : 1) A cell lineage that can be maintained in vitro. Significant genetic changes can occur during lengthy periods in culture, so that the genotype of long-term cell lines may not be the same as that of the starter cell. 2) A cell lineage that can be recognized in vivo.

Cell Mediated Immunity (CMI) : Immunity mediated via lymphocytes and macrophages.

Cell number : The number of cells per unit volume of a culture.

Cell pack : A group of gardeners traveling together in a confined space for snipping and stealing plant material in a botanical garden.

Cell plate : The precursor of the cell wall, formed at the beginning of cell division. The cell plate develops in the region of the equatorial plate and arises from membranes in the cytoplasm.

Cell sap : Water and dissolved substances, sugar, amino acids, waste substances, etc., in the plant cell vacuole.

Cell selection : The process of selecting cells exhibiting specific traits within a group of genetically different cells. Selected cells are often sub-cultured onto fresh medium for continued selection and exposed to an increased level of the selection agent to eliminate false positives.

Centers of origin : Usually the location in the world where the oldest cultivation of a particular crop has been identified.

Centimorgan (cM) : Unit of map distance. For small recombination fractions, cM and % recombination frequency are equivalent.

Central dogma : The basic concept that, in nature, genetic information generally flows from DNA to RNA to protein. However, information contained in the RNA molecules of retroviruses can also flow back to DNA.

Central mother cell : A subsurface cell located in a plant apical meristem and characterized by a large vacuole.

Central test : A location where animals are assembled from several herds to evaluate differences in certain performance traits under uniform management conditions.

Central venous catheter : A long catheter with its tip placed in a large diameter vein such as jugular catheter, or a long, lateral saphenous catheter.

Central Venous Pressure (CVP) : Central venous pressure measures the ability of the right heart to accommodate the fluid load presented to it. Normal animals have a central venous pressure of less than 5 cm of water. Assuming there are no clots in the IV catheter, central venous pressures repeatedly above 10 cm of water are indicative of impending onset of edema and fluid overload. Measurement of central venous pressure requires a central catheter (jugular catheter) be in place. CVP readings can be influenced by catheter position and patency.

Centriole : An organelle in many animal cells that appears to be involved in the formation of the spindle during mitosis. During cell division, the two centrioles move to opposite sides of the nucleus to form the ends of the spindle.

Centromere : The eukaryotic chromosome structure, which appears as a constriction in karyotype analysis, to which the spindle fibres attach during mitotic and meiotic division. Composed of highly repetitive DNA.

Centrosome : A specialized region of a living cell, situated next to the nucleus, where microtubules are assembled and broken down during cell division. The centrosome of most animal cells contains a pair of centrioles.

Ceruminolytic agents : Agents that loosen and dissolve ear wax. Includes dioctyl sodium sulfosuccinate, squalene, propylene glycol, carbamide peroxide, and others.

Cervicitis : Inflammation of the cervix.

Cervix : Part of the female reproductive tract located between the vagina and uterus.

Cestodes : Tape worms.

Chaff : Husks or other seed coverings and other plant parts separated from seed during harvest or processing.

Channelization : Engineering watercourses by straightening, widening, or deepening them so water will move faster. While improving drainage, this process can interfere with waste assimilation capacity, disturb fish and wildlife habitats, and aggravate flooding.

Chaperone : A family of proteins that ensure the correct assembly and conformation of other polypeptides in vivo as they emerge from the ribosome, but are not themselves components of the functional assembled structures. The prokaryotic equivalents are known as chaperonins.

Characterization : Description of the essential properties of an organism or system.

Check-off programme : Usually, a reference to the generic research and commodity promotion programmes for farm products that are financed by assessments applied to sales of those products by producers, importers, or others in the industry.

Chemical defibrillator : In the absence of an electrical defibrillator machine, certain drugs may be used in an attempt to reverse the cardiac arrhythmia of atrial fibrillation.

Chemical mutagen : A chemical capable of inducing mutations in living organisms.

Chemically-defined medium : When all of the chemical components of a culture medium are fully known and defined.

Chemostat : A continuous and open culture in which growth rate and cell density are maintained constant by a fixed rate of input of a growth-limiting nutrient.

Chemosterilant : A chemical that controls pests by preventing reproduction, thereby causing the population to collapse. This contrasts with chemicals that directly kill pests.

Chemotaxis : The movement of a cell, or the whole or part of an organism, towards or away from an increasing concentration of a particular substance.

Chemotherapy : A treatment for cancers that involves administering chemicals toxic to malignant cells.

Chimeraplasty : A method designed to create defined alterations in DNA sequence at a target locus, with potential both for gene therapy and for investigating gene function. A synthetic nucleic acid that contains DNA interspersed with small amounts of RNA is introduced into the target cell, where it pairs with its target gene sequence and then triggers the cell's DNA repair machinery, resulting in the replacement of the native sequence by the synthetic one.

Chimeric gene : An engineered gene, where a coding sequence is fused to promoter and/or other sequences derived from a different gene. Most genes used in transformation are chimeric.

Chimeric selectable marker gene : A gene that is constructed from parts of two or more different genes and allows the host cell to survive under conditions where it would otherwise die.

Chlorinated hydrocarbons : Also known as organochlorines, these synthetic organic compounds contain chlorine. They tend to be persistent in the environment and to biomagnify in the food chain. Chlorinated hydrocarbons that are pesticides include DDT, aldrin, dieldrin, heptachlor, chlordane, lindane, endrin, mirex, hexachloride, and toxaphene. Most chlorinated hydrocarbon pesticide uses have been canceled because of their persistence, propensity to bioaccumulate, and toxicity to nontarget species.

Chlorosis : The appearance of yellow colour in plants, due to the failure of development or the breakdown of chlorophyll. This is generally a symptom of either nutritional disturbance or of pathogen infection.

Chorioditis : Inflammation of the choroid.

Chorioretinitis : Inflammation affecting the choroid and retina causing choroidal, +/- retinal, blood vessels to become leaky and either transudative fluid or exudative fluid and cells to leak into the space between the choroid and retina, elevating the retina.

Choroid : The posterior uvea lying between the sclera and retina, and joining the ciliary body anteriorly. The choroid provides nutrition to the outer layers of the retina and contains the tapetum.

Chromatid : Each of the two strands of chromatin comprising a duplicated chromosome. The term is applied only while the two chromatids are joined at the centromere. As soon as the centromere divides, setting the two chromatids adrift (during anaphase of mitosis; and during anaphase II of meiosis), they are called chromosomes.

Chromatin : Substance of which eukaryotic chromosomes are composed. It consists of a complex of DNA, histone and non-histone chromosomal proteins (mainly histones), and a small amount of RNA.

Chromatin fibre : The standard structural conformation of chromatin in strands of 30 nm average diameter.

Chromatography : A method for separating the components of mixtures of molecules by partitioning them between two phases, one stationary and the other mobile. Appropriate selection of partitioning mechanism can produce separation of very closely-related molecules.

Chromocentre : Body produced by fusion of the heterochromatic regions of the chromosomes in the polytene tissues (e.g. the salivary glands) of certain Diptera.

Chromoplast : Plastid containing pigments other than chlorophyll.

Chromosomal : An abnormal change in chromosome structure or number, including deficiency, duplication, inversion, translocation, aneuploidy, polyploidy, or any other change from the normal pattern.. Although it can be a mechanism for enhancing genetic diversity, most alterations are fatal or debilitating, especially in animals.

Chromosomal integration site : A chromosomal location where foreign DNA can be integrated, often without impairing any essential function in the host organism.

Chromosomal polymorphism : The occurrence of one to several chromosomes in two or more alteRNAtive structural forms within a population; the structurally changed chromosomes are the result of chromosome mutations (i.e. any structural change involving the gain, loss or re-location of chromosome segments).

Chromosome : In eukaryotic cells, chromosomes are the nuclear bodies containing most of the genes largely responsible for the differentiation and activity of the cell. Chromosomes are most easily studied in their contracted state, which occurs around the metaphase of mitosis or meiosis; they contain most of the cell's DNA in the form of chromatin. Each eukaryotic species has a characteristic number of chromosomes. Bacterial and viral cells contain only one chromosome, which consists of a single or double strand of DNA or, in some viruses, RNA, without histones.

Chromosome banding : Differential staining of chromosomes in such a way that light and dark areas occur along the length of the chromosomes in repeatable patterns. Identical banding pattern implies chromosome homology.

Chromosome jumping : A technique that allows two segments of duplex DNA that are separated by thousands of base pairs (about 200 kb) to be cloned together. After sub-cloning, each segment can be used as a probe to identify cloned DNA sequences that, at the chromosome level, are roughly 200 kb apart.

Chromosome landing : An alteRNAtive to chromosome walking for positional cloning. Clones of genomic DNA are fragmented so as to include both the target gene and a closely linked marker and are screened to select ('land on') those clones that contain the target gene.

Chronic : Exposure to the poison occurs over a period of weeks, months, or years; onset of signs may be sudden and dramatic, or can be insidious like a slow loss in body condition or reduced productivity.

Chronic Interstital Nephritis (CIN) : Chronic interstitial nephritis (CIN) is similar to the term end stage renal disease (ESRD) in that it is a non specific histologic finding on renal biopsy and may be the end result of renal disease of any etiology.

Chronic renal Disease (CRD) : Irreversible renal disease caused by damage to a large part of both kidneys. Two thirds of both kidneys must be damaged before the animal loses the ability to concentrate and dilute urine and 75% of both kidneys must be destroyed before azotemia is observed.

Chronic toxicity : The capacity of a substance to cause long-term or delayed adverse health effects. For example, a cancer resulting from exposure to a carcinogen may not appear for years or decades.

Chronological records : Records that are organized by arranging all the data in the record in the order in which it was collected.

Chrysotherapy : Gold salt therapy used in treatment of immune mediated disorders. Solganol®-Schering Co.

Chymosin : An enzyme that clots milk, used in the manufacture of cheese.

Cis-acting protein : A protein with the particular property of acting only on the molecule of DNA from which it was expressed.

Class switching : The process during which a plasma cell stops producing antibodies of one class and begins producing antibodies of another class.

Classified pricing : The pricing system of federal milk marketing orders, under which milk processors pay into a pool for fluid grade (Grade A) milk; its value is based on how the milk ultimately is used. Milk used for fluid (Class I) consumption receives a higher price than milk for processed (Class II, Class III, Class IIIa) dairy products.

Clay aggerate : A product that is manufactured exclusively in high tech kilns in Germany and used as a soil replacement on hydroponics. It once was very popular in the late '70's : '80's. Now making a comeback.

Clay soils : Soils with clay particles and small air pores. Water retention is high creating poor drainage conditions.

Clean wool : Wool after it has been "scoured" to remove the above materials.

Clear media : Includes the aqueous, lens and vitreous.

Clearcut harvest : A harvest and regeneration technique removing all the trees on an area. Clearcutting is commonly used with shade-intolerant species such as Douglas fir or lodgepole pine, which require full sunlight to reproduce and grow well. Clearcutting produces an even-aged stand of trees.

Clemastine : Tavist an over the counter antihistamine.

Climbers : Those gardeners who are willing to hike for distances to see an alpine specimen.

Clinandrium : A cavity, at the apex of a column in orchids, in which the anthers rest.

Cline : Variation in one or more phenotypic characters or allele frequencies across a geographical gradient.

Closed continuous culture : A culture system, in which the inflow of fresh medium is balanced by the outflow of corresponding volumes of spent medium. Cells are separated mechanically from outflowing medium and added back to the culture.

Coarse grains : Corn, sorghum, barley, rye, oats and millet.

Coast guard beacon : Coast Guard Beacon is a differential correction source for GPS. The Coast Guard built the system for maritime navigation. The signal is ground-based and generally available throughout the United States, but may be limited in some areas. The signal is free, but requires a special GPS antenna.

Coat protein (capsid) : The coating of a protein that enclosed the nucleic acid core of a virus.

CoBank : National Bank for Cooperatives

Coccus : A spherical bacterium.

Co-cloning : The unintentional cloning of DNA fragments, along with the desired one, that can occur when the source of DNA being cloned is not sufficiently purified.

Coding sequence : That portion of a gene which directly specifies the amino acid sequence of its product. Non-coding sequences of genes include introns and control regions, such as promoters, operators, and terminators.

Coding strand : The strand of a DNA double helix that contains the same base sequence (after substituting U for T) found in the mRNA molecule resulting from transcription of that segment of DNA. Sometimes called the sense strand. The mRNA molecule is transcribed from the other strand, known as the template or antisense strand.

Codling moth : Small moth that is problem in fruits and vegetables.

Co-dominance : Where both alleles are expressed in the heterozygous state, so that the phenotype reflects a contribution from both alleles. For example, roan coat colour in cattle results from a mixture of red hairs and white hairs, caused by heterozygosity for the red allele and the white allele.

Codon : One of the groups of three consecutive nucleotides in mRNA, which represent the unit of genetic coding by specifying a particular amino acid during the synthesis of polypeptides in a cell. Each codon is recognized by a tRNA carrying a specific amino acid, which is incorporated into a polypeptide chain during protein synthesis. In DNA, any informative triplet of bases, including both coding and control sequences.

Codon optimization : An experimental strategy in which codons within a cloned gene - ones not generally used by the host cell translation system - are changed by in vitro mutagenesis to the preferred codons, without changing the amino acids of the synthesized protein.

Co-fermentation : The simultaneous growth of two micro-organisms in one bioreactor.

Cognitive-evaluative dimension of pain : This relates to prior experience, level of anxiety, and conditioned responses that arise from the cerebral cortex and their influence on response to pain.

Coincidence : The ratio of the observed to the expected frequency of double cross-overs, where the expected frequency is calculated by assuming that the two cross-over events occur independently of one another.

Co-integrate : A chimeric DNA molecule formed by the incorporation at a single site of two different DNA molecules.

Co-integrate vector system : A two plasmid system for plant transgenesis. One plasmid is engineered to carry a T-DNA segment incorporating the gene(s) to be introduced. After introduction into Agrobacterium tumefaciens, the plasmid undergoes homologous recombination with a resident disarmed Ti plasmid to form a single plasmid carrying the genetic information for transferring the genetically engineered T-DNA region to plant cells.

Colchicine an alkaloid, obtained from the autumn crocus : Colchicum autumnale, which inhibits spindle formation. When applied during mitosis, chromosomes are unable to separate during anaphase. This property is used to achieve a doubling of the chromosome number. A further use is to halt mitosis at metaphase, the stage at which karyotypes are best viewed.

Cold compost : A method by which organic material just rots on its own. It may take months or years to naturally decompose. There may be a significant amount of weed seeds. And, there may be the danger of some disease organisms still in the compost.

Cold Hemagglutination Disease (CHD) : A form of autoimmune hemolytic anemia in which there is formation of cold acting anti-erythrocyte antibodies (IgM)resulting in agglutination of red cells in areas exposed to cold surface temperatures such as the extremities, ear margins and nose.

Cold nursery : A nursery where piglets older than four weeks old are kept and the ambient temperature is around 65F.

Cole crops : These are members of the cabbage family (ie. broccoli, cabbage, cauliflower, kale, collards, kohlorabi)

Coleoptile : Protective sheath covering the shoot apex of the embryo in the grasses.

Collateral relatives : Relatives of an individual that are not its ancestors or descendants. Brothers and sisters are an example of collateral relatives.

Collenchyma : A tissue of living cells, found particularly in midribs and leaf petioles. Characterized by cell walls unevenly thickened with cellulose and hemicellulose, but never lignified; it functions as a mechanical support in young, short-lived or non-woody organs.

Colloid : Microscopic particles suspended in a solution. The particles in a colloidal solution are large in molecular weight and can pull fluid into the intravascular space. Because the particles are large they stay in the vascular space longer than crystalloids and therefore exert their effect for a longer time.

Colloidal solutions : Colloidal solutions are solutions that contain large particles. These large particles are either proteins or complex sugars, such as dextrans or hetastarches. Colloidal solutions because they are physically large molecules, will stay in the bloodstream and hold water in the bloodstream by their oncotic effect.

Colloids : Colloidal solutions contain large particles, particles in excess of 50, 000 molecular weight units. These particles may be proteins or complex sugars.

Colon : Part of the large intestine.

Colony : 1) An group of genetically identical cells or individuals derived from a single progenitor. 2) A group of interdependent cells or organisms.

Colony hybridization : A technique that uses a nucleic acid probe to identify a recombinant bacterial colony carrying a particular inserted DNA.

Colostrum : The accumulated secretions of the mammary gland over the last few weeks of pregnancy. It is rich in IgG (65-90%) with variable levels of IgA and IgM. Form of passively acquired immunity (short-lived).

Column : The male and female reproductive organs of the orchid. The column (technically called a "gynostemium") is formed by the fusion of male portion of the flower (stamens) and female portion (pistils). This is one major characteristic that defines orchids and differentiates them from all other flowering plants.

Common name : The name by which plants are known by non-botanists. Plants that have a short history of cultivation may not have a common name. these names vary from country to country, even from region to region.

Companion planting : Different plants that are planted together for the benefit of each other. Whether it be color or roots deeper to bring up the nutrients for the secondary plant. Ground covers are great companion plants.

Comparative advantage : Refers to the economic theory that in international trade it is more advantageous for a country to devote its resources not to all lines of production in which it may have superiority (least cost production), but to those in which its relative superiority is greatest. Two countries may find trade mutually profitable even if one of the countries could produce all goods at lower cost than the other.

Comparative mapping : The comparison of map locations of genes and markers between species. In comparisons between closely related species, this will usually uncover a high degree of conservation of synteny and co-linearity. In these cases, the likely location of many genes can be predicted from model system data. Comparisons across wider phylogenetic distances reveal increasing loss of synteny.

Comparative positional candidate gene : Relates to an indirect means of assigning function to a QTL. Where a QTL has been linked to a marker in one species, and that same marker is linked to a known gene in a model system, inferences may be drawn as to the nature of the QTL.

Competency : An ephemeral state, induced by treatment with cold cations, during which bacterial cells are capable of uptaking foreign DNA.

Competent : 1) Bacterial cells able to take up foreign DNA molecules and thereby become genetically transformed. Can be genetically determined, or induced by physical treatment. 2) A competent cell is capable of developing into a fully functional embryo.

Complement proteins : Proteins that bind to antibody-antigen complexes and help degrade the complexes by proteolysis.

Complementary homopolymeric tailing : The process of adding complementary nucleotide extensions to DNA molecules, (e.g. deoxyguanosine) to the 3' end of one DNA molecule and deoxycytidine to the 5' end of another DNA molecule) to facilitate the ligation of the two DNA molecules.

Complementary nucleotides : Members of the pairs adenine-thymine, adenine-uracil, and guaninecytosine that have the ability to hydrogen bond to one another.

Complementation test : A genetic method to test whether or not independent mutations are allelic. In a cross between the two mutant individuals, the genotype will be m1m2 if the mutations are allelic and m1 +/+ m2 if non-allelic. The phenotype of the former will be mutant, but that of the latter will be wild type (normal).

Complete Blood Count (CBC) : A blood test in which the number of red and white blood cells and platelets are counted.

Complete digest : The treatment of a DNA preparation with a restriction endonuclease for sufficient time for all of the potential target sites within that DNA to have been cleaved.

Composting : The controlled biological decomposition of organic material, such as sewage sludge, animal manures, or crop residues, in the presence of air to form a humus-like material. Controlled methods of composting include mechanical mixing and aerating, ventilating the materials by dropping them through a vertical series of aerated chambers, or placing the compost in piles out in the open air and mixing it or turning it periodically.

Compound : To mix components following a "recipe" or protocol.

Compound chromosome : A chromosome formed by the fusion of two separate chromosomes, as in attached-X chromosomes or attached-X-Y chromosomes.

Compounding : To create a medication by combining parts or to change the formulation of a drug, for example from tablet to liquid.

Computerized Tomography scan (CT) : Many x-ray pictures are taken during a CT scan. A computer is used to put the x-ray pictures together to obtain a 3-dimensional view of a structure.

Concentrate : A classification of feedstuffs high in energy and low in fibre; usually further divided into energy and protein concentrates. Often used interchangeably with supplement. Examples : corn, barley, soybeans.

Congenital : A defect that is present at birth. The defect may either be inherited or be caused by something during gestation.

Conifer : An evergreen, generally green, sometimes cone shaped. Generally in a northern region.

Conjugation : 1)Union of gametes or unicellular organisms during fertilization. 2) The unidirectional transfer of plasmid DNA from one bacterium cell to another, involving cell-to-cell contact. The plasmid usually encodes the majority of the functions necessary for its own transfer. 3) Attachment of sugar and other polar molecules to less polar compounds, thus making them more water soluble.

Conjugative functions : Plasmid-based genes and their products that facilitate the transfer of a plasmid from one bacterium to another via conjugation.

Conjunctiva : The thin, moist, mucus membrane that lines the inside of the eyelids (palpebral conjunctiva) and curves around at the fornix to cover the eyeball up to the cornea (bulbar conjunctiva) ventrally it also covers both sides of the nictitans.

Conjunctive use : Water management methods. Usually used to describe the practice of storing surface water in a groundwater basin in wet years and withdrawing it from the basin in dry years. Often used in discussing water supplies and water conservation.

Conjunctivitis : Inflammation of the pink tissues (conjunctiva) surrounding the eye.

Consanguinity : Related by descent from a common ancestor.

Consensus sequence : The part of a gene or signal sequence that is shared over a wide range of members of a gene family, both within a given species, or in comparisons between species.

Conservatory : A building build partially or entirely of glass attached to the house and where a large number of plants are grown. Not to be confused with a greenhouse.

Conserved sequence : An identical or highly similar sequence of nucleotides or amino acids which occurs as part, or all of a number of different genes or proteins, in either the same or different species. This conservation can signify which part of the full sequence is responsible for the functionality.

Constitutive : The expression of a gene without any requirement for induction.

Constitutive gene : A gene that is continually expressed in all cells of an organism.

Constitutive promoter : An unregulated promoter that allows for continual transcription of its associated gene.

Constitutive synthesis : Continual synthesis of a gene product by an organism.

Construct : An engineered chimeric DNA designed to be transferred into a cell or tissue. Typically, the construct comprises the gene or genes of interest, a marker gene and appropriate control sequences as a single package. A repeatedly-used construct may be called a cassette.

Consumer Price Index (CPI-U) : The Bureau of Labor Statistics' general measure of retail prices (for goods and services) paid by urban wage earners and clerical workers. Includes prices of about 400 items, including food, clothing, housing, medical care, and transportation. The CPI-U is commonly used to deflate time series data and is the most widely accepted measure of inflation.

Consumer subsidy Equivalent (CSE) : A measure of the value of monetary transfers to consumers resulting from agricultural policies in a given year. If negative, it measures the implicit tax imposed on consumers by agricultural policies. The main component of the CSE is market transfers due to market price support to producers. The CSE can be measured in money terms, in money terms per unit of production, or in percentage terms.

Consumptive water use : Water removed from available supplies without return to a water resources system, e.g., water used in manufacturing, agriculture, and food preparation. Crop consumptive water use is the amount of water transpired during plant growth plus what evaporated from the soil surface and foliage in the crop area.

Containment : Measures and protocols applied to limit contact of genetically modified organisms or pathogens with the external environment.

Contaminant : 1) An undesired chemical present in a compound or mixture of compounds. 2) Any micro-organism accidentally introduced into a culture or culture medium. The contaminant may compete with the desired cells and consequently inhibit their growth, or totally replace them.

Contemporary group : A group of cattle that are of the same breed and sex and have been raised in the same management group (in the same location on the same feed and pasture).

Contig : A set of overlapping cloned DNA fragments that can be assembled to represent a defined region of the chromosome or genome from which they were obtained. Contig definition is a necessary step for assembling whole genome sequences.

Contiguous (Contig) map : The alignment of sequence data from large, adjacent regions of the genome to produce a continuous nucleotide sequence across a chromosomal region.

Continuous culture : A suspension culture continuously supplied with nutrients by the inflow of fresh medium. The culture volume is normally constant.

Continuous fermentation : A process in which cells or micro-organisms are maintained in culture in the exponential growth phase by the continuous addition of fresh medium that is exactly balanced by the removal of cell suspension from the bioreactor.

Continuous variation : Variation where individuals cannot be classified as belonging to one of a set of discrete classes.

Characters showing continuous variation are referred to as quantitative.

Contour farming : Field operations (such as plowing, planting, cultivating, and harvesting) at right angles to the natural slope to reduce soil erosion, protect soil fertility, and limit water runoff. Contour strip farming is a kind of contour farming in which row crops are planted in strips, between alternating strips of close-growing, erosion-resistant forage crops.

Contrast : A dye given by mouth or in the vein that will make some organs more visible on an x-ray (radiograph).

Controlled breeding : Also called a timed breeding technique. Modification of the physiology of the ovaries in such a way that one can predict exactly when that female is going to be ready and breed her only once.

Controlled environment : A closed environment in which parameters, such as light, temperature, relative humidity and sometimes the partial gas pressure, are fully controlled.

Controlling element : In eukaryotes, transposons which affect the activity of known genes. This can occur as a result of the integration within, or close to a gene, thereby disrupting its activity; or following its excision from such a site, thereby restoring activity.

Conventional agriculture : Generally used to contrast common or traditional agricultural practices featuring heavy reliance on chemical and energy inputs typical of large-scale, mechanized farms to alternative agriculture or sustainable agriculture practices. Mold-board plowing to cover stubble, routine pesticide spraying, and use of synthetic fertilizers are examples of conventional practices that contrast to alternative practices such as no-till, integrated pest management, and use of animal and green manures.

Conventional tillage : Tillage operations considered standard for a specific location and crop and that tend to bury the crop residues; usually considered as a base for determining the cost effectiveness of erosion control practices.

Conversion : The development of a somatic embryo into a plant.

Converted wetland : Under the swampbuster programme, these are wetlands that were drained or altered to improve agricultural production after December 23, 1985, the date swampbuster was enacted. On lands with this designation, no drainage maintenance and no additional drainage are allowed.

Conveyance loss : Water loss in pipes, channels, conduits, ditches by leakage or evaporation.

Cool-season crop : A crop that grows best during the cool temperatures of spring and fall.

Cool-season grass : Turfgrasses that actively grow during the cooler spring and fall weather. These include Kentucky bluegrass, the fescues, ryegrasses and bentgrass.

Coordinate repression : Correlated regulation of a structural gene within an operon by a molecule that interacts with the operator.

Corm : A short, thickened, underground, upright stem in which food is stored.

Cormel : A small corm that forms around the parent corm. It can be removed and planted to propagate a new plant.

Corn belt : That area of the United States where corn is a principal cash crop, including Iowa, Indiana, most of Illinois, and parts of Kansas, Missouri, Nebraska, South Dakota, Minnesota, Ohio and Wisconsin.

Corn rootworm : The larva stage of the corn rootworm beetle which historically has laid its eggs on corn/maize plants. When they hatch, the larva must feed on the roots of the corn/maize plant in order to live. Some strains of Bacillus thuringiensis (B.t.) have proven to be effective against the corn rootworm, when sprayed onto them or genetically engineered into the corn/maize plant.

Corneal degeneration : After certain corneal or scleral injuries, lipid or cholesterol can be deposited in the cornea.

Corneal reflex : Used to assess corneal sensation.

Corneal sequestrum : A focal area of collagen degeneration in the cornea with brown to black discoloration.

Corneoscleral transposition : A surgical technique used to patch conjunctiva over a corneal ulcer.

Cornification : The angular appearance of epithelial cells during estrus under the influence of estrogen.

Corolla : Inner of two series of floral leaves; petals

Coronary band : The tissue right around the top of the hoof, similar to a fingernail cuticle.

Coronavirus : A single stranded RNA virus.

Corpora nigra : Structures present mainly on the upper pupil margin in horses, upper and lower margins in the lamb. Quite obvious and elaborate on llamas and alpacas. Their function is not really known.

Corpus : A part of the apical meristem below the tunica. In the corpus, cells divide in all directions, and increase in volume.

Cos ends : The 12-base, single-strand, complementary extensions of bacteriophage lambda DNA.

Co-segregation : The joint inheritance of two characters, usually the result of genetic linkage.

Cosmid : A synthetic plasmid which incorporates the cos ends, and one or more selectable markers such as an antibiotic resistance gene. Cosmids were designed as vectors able to incorporate DNA fragments up to 40-50 kb in size.

Co-suppression : A natural gene silencing phenomenon, which probably evolved as part of plants' defence against viral attack, but which has become important in the context of plant transgenesis. Operates by inhibiting the expression of transgenes with homology to native DNA through the interaction of native and transgenic mRNA.

Cover : Vegetation or other natural shelter serving to conceal wildlife from predators.

Cover crop : A close-growing crop, planted primarily as a rotation between regularly planted crops, or between trees and vines in orchards and vineyards, to protect soil from erosion and improve it between periods of regular crops, or.

COX inhibitor : Drugs that block cyclooxygenase and that are intended to relieve pain and inflammation.

Creep area : An area where new born piglets crawl to, to keep warm and avoid being accidentally crushed by their mother.

Creeper : any plant that will make long shoots and grow along the ground such as creeping fig, ivy, or Virginia creeper.

Creutzfeldt-Jacob Disease (CJD) : A sporadic and rare, but fatal human disease that usually strikes people over 65. It occurs worldwide at an estimated annual rate of one case per million population. About 10-15% of CJD cases are inherited. A small number of cases occurred as the result of various medical treatments or procedures which inadvertently transferred the CJD agent. In March 1996, the British government announced a possible link between bovine spongiform encephalopathy (BSE) and CJD. The announcement was prompted by the discovery of several atypical cases of CJD in Great Britain.

Cria : The term describing a llama from the age of birth to weanling (4-6 months).

Crimp : The "wave" in the staple of wool.

Critical control point : An operation (practice, procedure, process, or location) at or by which preventive or control measures can be exercised that will eliminate, prevent, or minimize one or more hazards. Critical control points are fundamental to Hazard Analysis and Critical Control Point (HACCP) systems, which are now being adopted by the food industry to prevent health hazards in the food supply.

Crocking : Any material used in the bottom of containers to provide drainage (i.e. shells, rocks, broken pottery, Styrofoam.)

Crop insurance : A multiperil crop insurance programme available for a fee (premium) to the producers of most crops as protection against significant yield losses from natural hazards. The present Federal Crop Insurance Programme is a comprehensive, subsidized, all-risk programme that provides different degrees of protection for different premium amounts.

Crop residue : That portion of a plant, such as a corn stalk, left in the field after harvest. Crop residues are measured for farmers who use conservation tillage to implement their conservation plans to meet conservation compliance requirements. These farmers are required to maintain a minimum level of crop residue to be in compliance.

Crop rotation : The growing of different crops, in recurring succession, on the same land in contrast to monoculture cropping. Rotation usually is done to replenish soil fertility and to reduce pest populations in order to increase the potential for high levels of production in future years.

Crop year : The year in which a crop is harvested, as opposed to a marketing year, which refers to the 12-month period following harvest.

Cross-pollination : Fertilization of a plant from a plant with a different genetic makeup.

Crotch : The angle measured from the trunk of a tree to the upper surface of a branch.

Crown : The base of the stem of cereals and forage species from which tillers or branches arise. In woody plants, the root-stem junction. In forestry, the top portion of the tree.

Crown gall : A tumorous growth at the base of certain plants characteristic of infection by Agrobacterium tumefaciens. The gall is induced by the transformation of the plant cell by portions of the Ti plasmid.

Crutching : Removing the wool from around the breech area.

Cry proteins : A class of crystalline proteins produced by strains of Bacillus thuringiensis, and engineered into crop plants to give resistance against insect pests. These proteins are toxic to certain categories of insects (e.g. corn borers, corn rootworms, mosquitoes, black flies, armyworms, tobacco hornworms, some types of beetles, etc.), but are harmless to mammals and most beneficial insects.

Cryobiological preservation : The preservation of germplasm resources in a dormant state by storage at ultra-low temperatures, often in liquid nitrogen. Currently applied to storage of plant seeds and pollen, micro-organisms, animal sperm, and tissue culture cell lines.

Cryogenic : At very low temperature.

Cryoprotectant : Compound preventing cell damage during successive freezing and thawing processes. Cryoprotectants are agents with high water solubility and low toxicity. Two types commonly used: permeating (glycerol and DMSO) and non-permeating (sugars, dextran, ethylene glycol, polyvinylpyrrolidone and hydroxyethyl starch).

Cryptorchid : A condition seen in intact male animals where a testicle failed to descend into the scrotum.

Cryptorchidism : A condition in which one or both testes are not located in the scrotum.

CTP : Abbreviation for 1) cytidine 5'-triphosphate, which is required for RNA synthesis since it is a direct precursor molecule; 2) Chloroplast transit peptide.

CU : Consumers' Union

Culinary : Used in cooking.

Culinary herb : A plant grown for its strong flavor which is used to cook with in dishes and salads. the parts of the plant used are the leaves, flowers, or bulbs.

Cull : To select inferior animals from the herd for potential sale.

Cull cow : Cow removed from a herd due to poor profitability. Generally due to poor production, reproduction, or mastitis.

Culling : The process of eliminating less productive or less desirable cattle from a herd.

Cultigen : A cultivated plant species with no known wild progenitor.

Cultivar (CV) : An inteRNAtionally accepted term denoting a variety of a cultivated plant. Must be distinguishable from other varieties by stated characteristics and must retain their distinguishing characters when reproduced under specific conditions.

Cultivate : Breaking the topsoil so water and air can penetrate, and, to prevent weeds.

Cultivation : The technique of weeding and hoeing for the purpose of increasing the air in the to layers of the soil and to break up the soil so water will penetrate.

Cultivator : A machine used to till the upper portion of the soil, primarily used to destroy weeds or form a moisture retaining mulch.

Cultural control : The use of good gardening techniques to control pest populations.

Culture : A population of plant or animal cells or micro-organisms grown under controlled conditions.

Cush : The laying down position of the female camelid during mating.

Cushing's disease : A disease of the adrenal gland that produces too much of the hormone cortisol. Too much cortisol causes signs including drinking, eating and urinating increased amounts and loss of hair on the body. Also called hyperadrenocorticism.

Custom feeders : Producers who provide the service of feeding animals (e.g., cattle, hogs) they do not own, in return for a fee paid by someone else (such as a packer) who does own the animals. Custom feeding potentially provides packers with more control over supplies and prices of animals. Custom feeding is a form of vertical integration.

Cut back : Trimming or cutting moderately, making sure some of the last season's growth is left, to clean the plant up and the encourage new growth.

Cutaneous Lupus Erythematosus (CLE) : Discoid lupus. A form of systemic lupus erythematosus which only onvolves the skin.

Cutting : A detached plant part that, with appropriate treatment, can regenerate into a complete plant.

Cybrid : A hybrid, originating from the fusion of a cytoplast (the cytoplasm without nucleus) with a whole cell derived from a different species.

Cycad : An ancient group of plants that were very abundant in the "age of dinosaurs" (the Jurasic and Cretaceous periods). There are less than 200 species that survive today and are growing in the warmer regions of the world. Often thought of as long-lived flowerless plants. Most are palm or fern-like.

Cycle : Events that happen in the female such as ovulation, hormone production, receptivity, etc. In camelids the cycle does not follow regular time periods as it does in horses or cattle.

Cyclocryotherapy : A freezing probe is applied to sclera to destroy the underlying ciliary body in treatment of glaucoma.

Cyclodextrin : Cyclic oligomer of glucose.

Cycloheximide : A molecule that inhibits protein synthesis in eukaryotes, but not in prokaryotes. It blocks peptide bond formation by binding to the large ribosomal subunits.

Cyclophosphamide : Trade name is Cytoxan®-Mead Johnson. A chemotherapy drug also used in the treatment of immune mediated diseases.

Cycloplegic : A drug that paralyses the ciliary muscle and helps reduce pain.

Cystocercus : The larval stage of a tapeworm encysted in muscle.

Cytidine : The (ribo)nucleoside resulting from the combination of the base cytosine (C) and the sugar D-ribose. The corresponding deoxyribonucleoside is called deoxycytidine.

Cytochrome : A class of pigments in plant and animal cells, usually in the mitochondria. They function as electron carriers in respiration.

Cytokine : A generic name for a diverse group of soluble proteins and peptides which act as humoral regulators at extremely small concentrations and which, either under normal or pathological conditions, modulate the functional activities of individual cells and tissues.

Cytokines/Interleukins : Regulatory proteins secreted primarily by lymphocytes to facilitate interaction between other lymphocytes and macrophages e.g. IL-2, IL-12, CSF, TNF.

Cytokinesis : Cytoplasmic division and other changes exclusive of nuclear division that are a part of mitosis or meiosis.

Cytokinins : Organic compounds acting like hormones in plants. Stimulates or alters cellular RNA resulting in a modification to plant development. Generally acts by affecting cellular division and differentiation into roots and shoots. This inhibits aging in the plant.

Cytoplasmic genes : Genes located on DNA outside the nucleus, i.e. on plastids.

Cytoplasmic inheritance : Hereditary transmission dependent on cytoplasmic genes.

Cytoplasmic male sterility : Genetic defect due to faulty functioning of mitochondria in pollen development, preventing the formation of viable pollen. Commonly found or inducible in many plant species and exploited for some F1 hybrid seed programmes.

Cytoplasmic organelles : Discrete sub-cellular structures located in the cytoplasm of cells - mitochondria, plastids and lysosomes.

Cytotype : A maternally inherited cellular condition in Drosophila that regulates the activity of transposable P elements.

D

Data logger : Used to store electronic data sent by a measurement device. A yield monitor is an example of a data logging device.

dATP : Abbreviation for deoxyadenosine 5'-triphosphate. dATP is required for DNA synthesis since it is a direct precursor molecule.

Datum : A set of parameters and control points used to accurately define the three-dimensional shape of the earth. The datum defines part of a geographic coordinate system that is the basis for a planar coordinate system.

Day length : This merely is the number of hours from sunrise to sunset. Sometimes used interchangeably with photo period.

Day neutral : A plant whose blooming period is not affected by the length of day.

Day-neutral plant : A plant that will flower under any day length.

Days in milk : The number of days a cow has been milking in her current lactation, same as days since fresh.

Days open : The number of days between calving (parturition) and conception. Should be less than 120 days.

Days to maturity : The number of days between planting the seed and first harvest.

DC : District Conservationist

dCTP : Abbreviation for deoxycytidine 5'-triphosphate. dCTP is required for DNA synthesis since it is a direct precursor molecule.

ddNTP : Abbreviation for di-deoxynucleotide.

DDT : The abbreviated name of a chlorinated hydrocarbon insecticide, dichloro-diphenyl-trichloromethane. It is persistent in the environment and biomagnifies in birds of prey.

Dead weight : the vessel's total carrying capacity, i. e. , cargo plus fuel and water and constant (crew, machinery, spare parts, etc.) Dead weight cargo capacity is what remains after deducting fuel and water, etc. , as above, for total dead weight.

Dead-end host : It can not be transmitted from human to human. Example : brucellosis.

Deadhead : To remove spent blossoms of herbaceous plants.

Deadheading : Pinch here, snip there, removing spent flowers that have already bloomed. This is done for the benefit of the plant to prevent disease, prevent seed development and will encourage more vigorous blooming and a bushier plant.

Death phase : The final growth phase of cell culture, during which nutrients have been depleted and cell number decreases.

Debride : To clean out dead or dying tissue from a wound.

Debt-asset ratio : A financial ratio that measures the percentage of a farm operator's assets that are financed by debt. For example, a ratio of 0. 4 means that for every $100 of assets the operator has $40 of debt. The ratio indicates to a lender the degree of security of a loan. Higher values indicate greater risk. Although a safe or acceptable level varies greatly by enterprise, a debt-asset ratio in excess of 0. 4 may indicate financial stress. A ratio of 0 means that the operator owes no debt; a ratio greater than 1 means that the borrower's debts exceed the value of assets, indicating the insolvency of the farm business.

Deceleration phase : The phase of declining growth rate, following the linear phase and preceding the stationary phase in most batch-suspension cultures.

Deciduous : These are plants that loose their leaves at the end of the growing season. Maple trees are a good example.

Deciduous teeth : Non-permanent teeth(baby teeth)that will be shed and replaced with permanent adult teeth.

De-differentiation : The process, in response to wounding and in tissue cultures, by which plant cells can become unspecialized and start to proliferate by cell division to form a mass of undifferentiated cells (or callus) which, in response to appropriate stimuli, may later differentiate again to form either the same cell type or a different one.

Deep mycoses : Diseases incluing Histoplasmosis, Blastomycosis, Coccidioidomycosis and Cryptococcosis.

Defecation : To pass feces, stool or manure.

Defective virus : A virus that, by itself, is unable to reproduce when infecting its host cell, but that can grow in the presence of another virus. This other virus provides the necessary molecular machinery that the first virus lacks.

Deferred pricing : A cash forward contract that provides for determining price by formula at a later date. This also may be called 'booking the basis,' when the formula sets price relative to a futures price.

Deficiency : Lack of adequate supply of nutritional, enzymatic, or environmental requirements, so that development, growth or physiological functions are affected.

Deficiency payments : Direct government payments made to farmers who participated in an annual commodity program for wheat, feed grains, rice, or cotton, prior to 1996. The crop-specific deficiency payment rate was based on the difference between the legislatively set target price and the lower national average market price during a specified time. The total payment was equal to the payment rate, multiplied by a farm's eligible payment acreage and the program payment yield established for the particular farm. In the latter years of the program, farmers could receive up to one-half of their projected deficiency payments at program signup.

Defined : 1) Fixed conditions of medium, environment and protocol for growth. 2) Precisely known and stated elements of a tissue culture medium.

Degradable Intake protein (DIP) : Portion of intake protein that is degraded (broken down) by rumen microbes to ammonia and amino acids. DIP is used for microbial synthesis.

Dehalogenation : The removal of halogen atoms (fluorine, chlorine, bromine, iodine) from molecules, for example during biodegradation.

Dehiscence : The spontaneous and often violent opening of a fruit, seed pod or anther to release and disperse the seeds or pollen.

Dehydration : An inadequate amount of fluid in the body. The minimum amout of dehydration that can be detected is about 5% loss of total body weight as fluid loss.

Dehydrogenase : An enzyme that catalyses the removal of hydrogen atoms in biological reactions.

Dehydrogenation : A chemical reaction in which hydrogen is removed from a compound.

De-ionized water : Water from which most salts have been removed - with varying degrees of efficiency - by ion exchange.

DEIP : Dairy Export Incentive Program

Delivery : In settlement of a futures contract, the tender and receipt of the actual commodity, the cash value of the commodity, or of a delivery instrument covering the commodity (e. g. , warehouse receipts or shipping certificates). Futures contracts may be settled by delivery, but more often they are settled by offset or cash. Each futures exchange has specific procedures for delivery of a commodity.

Delivery month : The specified month within which a futures contract matures and can be settled by delivery. Also referred to as contract month.

Delivery point : A location where a commodity can be delivered to fulfill a futures contract.

DEM : Digital Elevation Model that depicts landscape elevation. The data are developed by the USGS at either 10-meter or 30-meter grid spacing. Often used in a GIS as a data layer.

Deme : A group of organisms in the same taxon.

Demineralize : To remove the mineral content (salts, ions) from a substance, especially water. Removal methods include distillation, electrodialysis and ion exchange.

Demodicosis generalized : Also called the pustular form. Many small focal areas of involvement or a diffuse generalized distribution. Lesions include generalized erythema, crusting, scaling and patchy to diffuse alopecia.

Demodicosis localized : Also called squamous. One or more well circumscribed areas of alopecia with mild scaling and erythema usually located on the forelimbs, face and on periocular skin.

Denatured : DNA Double-stranded DNA that has been converted to single strands by breaking the hydrogen bonds linking complementary nucleotide pairs. Often reversible. Usually achieved by heating.

Denatured protein : Altering the in vivo conformation of a protein by heat or salt treatment, thereby destroying its biological activity. Unlike denatured DNA, denatured proteins are seldom able to be renatured.

Denaturing Gradient Gel Electrophoresis (DGGE) : An electrophoresis method for separating similar sized DNA fragments on the basis of their sequence, by applying across the gel a gradient of increasingly denaturing conditions (usually by increasing the concentration of a denaturing chemical, such as formamide or urea). As the double-stranded molecules denature into a partially and eventually a fully single-stranded state, their electrophoretic mobility changes.

Dendrimer : A polymer that repeatedly branches until stopped by the physical constraint of having formed a complete, hollow sphere. These structures possess sites on their exterior surface to which DNA fragments can be attached, and are thus useful as carriers of DNA for transgenesis.

Denitrification : A chemical process in which nitrates in the soil are reduced to molecular nitrogen, which is released to the atmosphere.

Density gradient centrifugation : High-speed centrifugation in which molecules are separated on the basis of their different densities using a concentration gradient of caesium chloride or sucrose. The density gradient may either be formed before centrifugation by mixing two solutions of different density (as in sucrose density gradients) or it can be formed by the process of centrifugation itself.

Derepression : The process of "turning on" the expression of a gene or set of genes whose expression has been repressed (turned off), usually by the displacement of a repressor from a promoter, since, when attached to the DNA, the repressor prevents transcription.

Derivative : 1) Resulting from or derived from. 2) Term used to identify a variant during meristematic cell division.

Dermatomyositis : A immune-mediated, familial dermatopathy suggested to be a primary vasculopathy with secondary dermatitis and myositis. Breed predilection includes Collies and Shetland Sheepdogs.

Dermatophilosis : Pyoderma caused by the aerobic and facultative anaerobic actinomycete : Dermatophilus congolensis. Also called Streptotricosis, rain scald, and streptothricosis (horses).

Dermatophyte Test Medium (DTM) : Agar for growing fungi. Dermatophyte test media (DTM) contains phenol red as a pH indicator and substances to inhibit growth of saprophytic fungi and bacteria.

Descemetocele : Very deep ulcers right down to decemets membrane.

Descemet's membrane : A clear membrane forming the inner boundary of the cornea.

Desiccant : A chemical agent that absorbs moisture; desiccants can be used to control insect pests or mildew, and also to dry foliage before harvest (as with potatoes). Desiccants are regulated as pesticides under the Federal Insecticide, Fungicide, and Rodenticide Act.

Desiccation : Drying.

Designated uses of water : Water uses identified in state water quality standards that must be achieved and maintained as required under the Clean Water Act. Uses can include cold water fisheries, public water supply, irrigation, etc.

Desired future condition : Used to describe the future condition of federal rangeland resources that meet management objectives. Desired future condition is based on ecological, social, and economic considerations during the land and resource management planning process. Desired future condition is usually expressed as ecological status or management status of vegetation and desired soil qualities.

Desired plant community : The plant community that has been determined through a land use or management plan to best meet the plan's objectives for a site. A desired plant community is consistent with the site's capability to produce the required resource attributes through natural succession, management intervention, or a combination of both.

Desoxyribonucleic acid : Obsolete spelling of deoxyribonucleic acid.

Determination : Process by which undifferentiated cells in an embryo become committed to develop into specific cell types, such as neurons, fibroblasts or muscle cells.

Determined : Describing embryonic tissue at a stage when it can develop only as a certain kind of tissue.

Dethatch : The process of taking up dead grass and plant material that builds up under the grass making the soil easier to absorb nutrients.

Dextrose 5% (D5W) : 5% dextrose is hypotonic relative to extracellular fluid. It contains only dextrose, no electrolytes. 5% dextrose is a constituent of most maintenance solutions. It can be used a sole fluid for rehydration for animals who cannot tolerate the administration of sodium, such as those with cardiac disease. More commonly, it is used as part of the rehydration solution in these sodium intolerant animals, used in combination with lactated Ringer's or sodium chloride.

Dextrose hypertonic : Hypertonic dextrose is any percentage of dextrose which has an osmolality in excess of extracellular fluid. Dextrose is available in several commercial strengths. Any concentration of dextrose can be created by adding additional dextrose to a commercial solution. The predominant use of hypertonic dextrose solutions is as a calorie source in total parenteral nutrition solutions. There is also an indication to promote urine flow in patients with oliguric acute renal failure. TPN solutions containing 50% dextrose are extremely hypertonic and can cause an irritation to the blood vessel if given in a small peripheral vein, such as cephalic or saphenous. Hypertonic solutions are typically given in larger veins such as the jugular vein in which blood flow is faster to dilute the hypertonicity of the infused solution and reduce irritation to the lining of the blood vessel.

Diagnostic procedure : A test or assay used to determine the presence of a specific substance, organism or nucleic acid sequence alteration, etc.

Diagnostic tests : These are tests performed to find the cause of a pet's problem. Diagnostic tests may include analysis of blood, urine, and other body fluids; x-rays (the correct term is radiographs); biopsies, etc.

Diakinesis : A stage of meiosis at the end of prophase I, in which the contraction of the chromosomes is almost at a maximum, pairing configurations are well defined, the nucleolus normally disappears and the nuclear envelope is disrupted.

Diazotroph : An organism that can fix atmospheric nitrogen.

Dibble : A tool used to make holes for seeds or bulbs: a pencil end, dowel, or anything that works for the situation.

Dicentric chromosome : A chromosome having two active centromeres.

Dichogamy : The condition in which the male and the female reproductive organs of a flower (or certain hermaphroditic animals) mature at different times, thereby making self-fertilization improbable or impossible.

Dicot : Also dicotyledon; flowering plants with embryos that have two cotyledons.

Dicotyledon : A plant with two cotyledons. One of the two major classes of flowering plants (along with the monocotyledons). Examples include many crop plants (potato, pea, beans), ornamentals (rose, ivy) and timber trees (oak, beech, lime).

Dideoxynucleotide (didN) : A deoxynucleotide that lacks a 3' hydroxyl group, and is thus unable to form a 3'-5' phosphodiester bond necessary for chain elongation. Dideoxynucleotides are used in DNA sequencing and the treatment of viral diseases.

Di-deoxynucleotide : A synthetic deoxynucleotide that lacks a 3'-hydroxyl group, and is thus unable to form the 3'?5' phosphodiester bond necessary for chain elongation. Used as strand terminators in the Sanger DNA sequencing reaction and in the treatment of some viral diseases.

Dieback : A process caused by disease or pests. It is the death of the tips of branches and shoots. It will progress until the whole plant dies.

Diestrus : A stage of the female reproductive cycle that follows the period of receptivity.

Dietary scours : When the calf is getting so much nutrient intake they can not absorb it all and it is fermenting in the colon producing gassy, large volume, smelly diarrhea.

Diethylstibestrol (DES) : A synthetic estrogen hormone. DES was used widely in the United States as a growth promoter in cattle and sheep and as a treatment for estrogen-deficiency disorders in veterinary medicine, and for postcoital contraception. However, because of its carcinogenic properties and other adverse effects, the Food and Drug Administration has revoked all use of it in food-producing animals.

Differential centrifugation : A method for separating sub-cellular particles according to their sedimentation coefficients, which are roughly proportional to their size. Cell extracts are subjected to a succession of centrifuge runs at progressively faster rotation speeds. Large particles, such as nuclei or mitochondria, will be precipitated at relatively slow speeds; higher G forces will be required to sediment small particles, such as ribosomes.

Differential Global Positioning System (DGPS) : is a technique used to improve GPS accuracy.

Differentially permeable : Referring to a membrane, through which different substances diffuse at different rates. Some substances may be unable to diffuse through such a membrane, usually because they are too large to fit through the pores of the membrane.

Differentiation : A process as a result of which unspecialized cells develop structures and functions characteristic of a particular type of cell, typically during the process of development from one cell to many cells, accompanied by a modification of the new cells for the performance of particular functions. The process is generally irreversible in vivo in higher organisms. In tissue culture, the term is used to describe the formation of different cell types.

Diff-quik stain : A 3-step staining process to stain cytology samples.

Dihaploid : An individual which arises from a doubled haploid.

Dihybrid : An individual that is heterozygous for two pairs of alleles; the progeny of a cross between homozygous parents differing at two loci.

Dihydrotestosterone (DTH) : The form of testosterone used by the prostate gland.

Dimensions of pain : There are 3 dimensions of pain : sensory-discriminative, motivational-affective and cognitive-evaluative, which influence how an individual interprets and responds to a painful stimulus.

Dimer : 1) A molecule formed by the covalent combination of two monomers, generally accompanied by elimination of water. 2) The reversible association of two similar (or nearly similar) molecules. The active form of many enzymes is as a dimer between two non-active monomeric subunits.

Dimethyl Sulphoxide (DMSO) : A highly hygroscopic liquid and powerful solvent with little odour, colour or toxicity when pure. It is employed in small quantities to dissolve organic substances in tissue culture media preparation and has uses as a cryoprotectant and in promoting the passage of chemicals through skin.

Dimorphism : The existence of two distinctly different types of individuals within a species. An obvious example is sexual dimorphism in mammals.

Dinucleotide : A nucleotide dimer.

Diocecious : A plant which bears either male of female flowers.

Dioxin : Any of a group of toxic chlorinated compounds known chemically as dibenzo-p-dioxins (or the most toxic of these compounds, 2,3,7,8 tetrachloro dibenzo-p-dioxin). They are produced inadvertently as a by-product of chemical production or combustion and are widespread pollutants in the environment.

Diphenhydramine HCL : Benadryl. An antihistamine.

Diploid : The status of having two complete sets of chromosomes, most commonly one set of paternal origin and the other of maternal origin. Somatic tissues of higher plants and animals are ordinarily diploid in chromosome constitution, in contrast with the haploid gametes.

Diploid cell : A cell which contains two copies of each chromosome.

Diplonema : Stage in prophase I of meiosis following the pachytene stage, but preceding diakinesis, in which one pair of sister chromatids begin to separate from the other pair.

Direct embryogenesis : The formation in culture, on the surface of zygotic or somatic embryos or on explant tissues (leaf section, root tip, etc.), of embryoids without an intervening callus phase.

Direct export credit : A federal export promotion program (designated as GSM-5) operated by the Foreign

Agricultural Service. Loans are made directly by the Commodity Credit Corporation at market interest rates to foreign buyers of agricultural commodities. Through FY1980, government credit for agricultural exports was made available through the GSM-5 program. For budget austerity reasons, the program was replaced with federal export credit guarantees in FY1981. A more limited blended credit program was used in FY1983-85 that combined direct credit with guaranteed credit.

Directed Amplification of Minisatellite DNA (DAMD) : A polymerase chain reaction technique used for obtaining molecular markers in the region of minisatellites. To target these regions, one of the primers is directed to a VNTR core sequence.

Directed mutagenesis : The generation of changes in the nucleotide sequence of a cloned gene by one of several procedures. Undertaken to explore the relationship between nucleotide sequence and gene function, and to modify gene products.

Discharge : In water resources, the term refers to the flow of surface water in a stream or canal or the outflow of ground water from a flowing artisan well, ditch, or spring.

Discharge summary : A description of a patient's workup. May include an overview in client terms of what tests were performed and test results as well as a description of treatment and care for the patient.

Discoid Lupus Erythematosus (DLE) : A form of systemic lupus erythematosus which only onvolves the skin.

Disease triangle : Interactions between the host, the pathogen, and the environment.

Disease-free : A plant or animal certified through specific tests as being free of specified pathogens. Should be interpreted to mean "free from any known disease" as "new" diseases may yet be discovered to be present.

Distichiasis : An extra row of cilia or eyelashes grow from the meibomian gland openings on the eyelid margin.

Distichous : In two ranks or rows on opposite sides of an axis

Distillation : The process of heating a mixture to separate the more volatile from the less volatile parts, and then condensing fractions of the resulting vapour so as to produce a more nearly pure or refined substance.

Diuretics : Drugs that increase the amount of urine produced.

Diurnal : Referring to daytime; in reference to flowers, signifying those which open only during the day

Dizygotic twins : Two-egg twins, i. e. a pair of individuals that shared the same uterus at the same time, but which arose from separate and independent fertilization of two ova.

DNA diagnostics : The use of DNA polymorphisms to detect the presence of a specific sequence, which could indicate the presence of a contaminant, of a pathogen, or of a particular allele at a target gene. Most commonly utilises the polymerase chain reaction.

DNA fingerprint : The unique pattern of DNA fragments identified by Southern hybridization (using a probe that binds to a polymorphic region of DNA) or by polymerase chain reaction (using primers flanking the polymorphic region).

DNA helicase : An enzyme that catalyses the unwinding of the complementary strands of a DNA double helix.

DNA hybridization : The annealing of two single-stranded DNA molecules, possibly of different origin, to form a partial or complete double helix. The degree of hybridization varies with the extent of complementarity between the two molecules, and this is exploited to test for the presence of a specific nucleotide sequence in a DNA sample.

DNA ligase : An enzyme that catalyses a reaction to link two separate DNA molecules via the formation of a phosphodiester bond between the 3'-hydroxyl end of one and the 5'-phosphate of the other. Its natural role lies in DNA repair and replication. An essential tool in recombinant DNA technology, as it enables the incorporation of foreign DNA into vectors.

DNA polymorphism : One of two or more alternate forms (alleles) of a chromosomal locus that differ in nucleotide sequence or have variable numbers of repeated nucleotide units.

DNA topo-isomerase : An enzyme that catalyses the introduction or removal of supercoils in DNA.

DNA vaccine : A vaccine generated by the injection of specific DNA fragments to stimulate an immune response.

DNAse : Abbreviation for deoxyribonuclease. Any enzyme that catalyses the cleavage of DNA phosphodiester bonds. DNAse I is a digestive endonuclease secreted by the pancreas, that degrades DNA into shorter fragments. Many other endonucleases and exonucleases are involved in DNA repair and replication.

DO : Dissolved oxygen

Dockage : A factor in the grading of grains and oilseeds; i. e. , dockage in wheat is described as 'weed seeds, weed stems, chaff, straw, or grain other than wheat, which can be readily removed from the wheat by the use of appropriate sieves and cleaning devices; also, underdeveloped, shriveled and small pieces of wheat kernels removed in properly separating, properly rescreening, or recleaning. ' The term is also used to describe the amount of reduction in price taken because of a deficiency in quality.

Doctrine of prior appropriation : Water rights doctrine adopted by most western states, giving the first person to use water from a stream the first right to such water. If the first user does not consume all of the water, then the second and later users can appropriate water for their needs. The water right is not necessarily tied to land ownership.

Dolly : The first mammal (a sheep) to be created (via nuclear transfer) by the cloning of an adult cell (from the mammary tissue of a ewe). This showed that the process of differentiation into adult tissue is not, as previously thought, irreversible.

Domain : A portion of a protein or DNA molecule that has a discrete function or conformation. At the protein level, can be as small as a few amino acid residues or as large as half of the entire protein.

Domboro's solution : Aluminum acetate solution. A topical drying agent (astringent).

Domestic price : The price at which a commodity trades within a country, in contrast to the world price. For those commodities not benefitting from some form of price support, the domestic price is determined by supply and demand. For commodities that receive price support, the domestic price is usually set by the loan rate or some comparable support level that serves as a price floor in the marketplace working in conjunction with any import quota that may be in effect.

Dominance : Dominant genes affect the phenotype when present in either homozygous or heterozygous condition. A dominant gene need only be obtained from one parent to achieve expression.

Dominant gene : A gene whose phenotype is when it is present in a single copy.

Dominant marker selection : Selection of cells via a gene encoding a product that enables only the cells that carry the gene to grow under particular conditions. For example, plant and animal cells that express the introduced neor gene are resistant to neomycin and analogous antibiotics, while cells that do not carry neor are killed.

Dominant selectable marker : A gene that allows the host cell to survive under conditions where it would otherwise die.

Dominant(Acting) oncogene : A gene that stimulates cell proliferation and contributes to oncogenesis when present in a single copy.

Double cropping : The practice of consecutively producing two crops of either like or unlike commodities on the same land within the same year. An example of double cropping might be to harvest a wheat crop by early summer and then plant corn or soybeans on that acreage for harvest in the fall. This practice is only possible in regions with long growing seasons.

Double crossing-over : The formation of two chiasmata within a chromosome arm, leading to the generation of a double recombinant gamete with respect to genes located within the segment defined by the two genes concerned.

Double dig : A method of digging a garden bed which involves removing the soil to the depth of one spade blade and then digging down an equal distance, breaking up and mixing the soil.

Double digging : A method of deep cultivation.

Double fertilization : A process, unique to flowering plants, in which two male nuclei, which have travelled down the pollen tube, separately fuse with different female nuclei in the embryo sac. The first male nucleus fuses with the egg cell to form the zygote; the second male nucleus fuses with the two polar nuclei to form a triploid nucleus that develops into the endosperm.

Double flower : A flower that is full from overlapping petals.

Double helix : Describes the coiling of the antiparallel strands of the DNA molecule, resembling a spiral staircase in which the paired bases form the steps and the sugar-phosphate backbones form the rails.

Downer (Or downed animals) : Commonly used term for animals that are disabled due to illness or injury. A longstanding issue is whether these animals are treated humanely or inhumanely by shippers, stockyards, and packers while they are being moved or held for slaughter. Legislation periodically introduced in Congress would outlaw the sale or transfer of such animals, but livestock producer groups (who generally agree that livestock markets should not accept severely disabled animals) contend that their voluntary efforts to end harmful practices have already proven successful.

Down-regulate : To induce genetically a reduction in the level of a gene's expression.

Downstream : 1) With respect to DNA, the nucleotides that lie in the 3' direction from the point of reference, which is frequently the site at which transcription is initiated. This is generally designated +1, with downstream nucleotides numbered +2, +10 etc. 2) In chemical engineering, those phases of a manufacturing process that follow the biotransformation stage. Usually refers to the recovery and purification of the product of a fermentation process.

Downstream processing : A general term for biotechnological processes which follow the biology, i. e. fermentation of a micro-organism or growth of a plant. Particularly relevant to fermentation processes, which produce a large quantity of a dilute mixture of substances, products and micro-organisms. These must be separated, and the product concentrated, purified and converted into a useful form.

Downy mildew : A certain kind of mildew caused by a special fungi. Often confused with sooty mildew and powdery mildew. As with all mildews it is a problem in hot and humid weather. And, like many fungi it transports its spores. The plants affected will have fuzzy patches on the leaves.

Dowsing : Using a forked stick or wire to locate underground water.

Doxapram : A respiratory stimulant.

Drainage wells : Wells drilled to carry excess water off agricultural fields. Because they act as a funnel from the surface to the groundwater below, drainage wells can contribute to groundwater pollution.

Drawn : Referring to the structure of a plant, one that is too tall and has grown too weak. Caused by growing in too little light or too close together. Often is the case in flats in nurseries. Buyer beware.

DRES : Dietary Risk Evaluation System

Drift : A design term generally attributed to Gertrude Jekyll. To express a feeling in with plants. The technique is to plant flowers thicker in the center and further apart on the outskirts.

Drill : A farm implement for planting seeds which forms a small furrow, deposits the seed in dribbles, covers the seed, and packs soil over it. It can also deposit fertilizer, lime, or other amendments into the soil, alone or with the seed.

Drip irrigation : A method used to place irrigation water near plants' roots through pipes or tubes. This reduces water evaporation and runoff, but may not be cost effective for all crops.

Drip line : A line encircling a tree corresponding to the furthest extension of the branches of a tree.

Drosophila melanogaster : The fruit fly, used for many years as a model for eukaryotic genetics. Of the nearly 300 disease-causing genes in the human genome, more than half have an analogous gene in the Drosophila genome.

Drought : A prolonged period of dryness that can cause damage to plants.

Drug delivery : Method by which a drug is delivered to its site of action. For traditional drugs this is another name for formulation. However, biotechnology has allowed the development of a range of new therapeutic-agent delivery systems, such as liposomes and other encapsulation techniques, and a range of mechanisms that target a therapeutic agent to a particular cell or tissue.

Drupe : A type of fruit (i. e. plums, cherries, olives, peaches). Also considered stone fruits. The fruit wall is fleshy. The outside layer is generally juicy. The one seed fruit will not open up.

Dry cow : A cow that is not lactating.

Dry cow therapy : Antibiotic therapy given at the onset of the nonlactating period of the cow. It is intended to cure and protect against intramammary infection.

Dry matter : Feed residue left after all moisture has been removed by drying.

Dry matter basis : An expression of feed nutrient content after the moisture has been removed by drying.

Dry period : A period of 45-60 days when lactation is halted before the next lactation begins. The dry period is required for rejuvenation of secretory parenchyma.

Dryland farming : A system of producing crops in semi-arid regions (usually with less than 20 inches of annual rainfall) without irrigation. Dryland farmers often try to rebuild soil moisture by leaving the land fallow (unplanted) or mulched in alternate years, called summer fallowing.

Dual culture : A culture made of a plant tissue and one organism (such as a nematode) or an obligate parasite/ micro-organism (such as a fungus). Dual culture techniques are used for a variety of purposes, including assessing host-parasite interactions and the production of axenic cultures.

Dumping : Selling commodities in a foreign market at a lower price than in the domestic market. Under World Trade Organization rules, dumping occurs when the price to the importer is less than the normal price of the product charged to the buyer in the country of origin.

Duodenum : The portion of the intestine directly attached to the stomach.

Duplex dNA : Double-stranded DNA.

Durum wheat : A species of wheat distinct from wheat used to make bread and other bakery products. The hard, flinty kernels of durum wheat are specially ground and refined to obtain semolina, a granular product used in making pasta items such as macaroni and spaghetti. Most durum wheats are grown in Mediterranean countries, the former Soviet Union countries, North America, and Argentina.

Duty, import : A customs duty is a charge assessed by a government on an imported item at its point of customs entry into the country, and paid for by the importer; the term is now used interchangeably with tariff. In terms of assessing duties there are two basic types : an ad valorem duty is assessed in proportion to the value of the imported item, whereas a 'specific' duty is assessed on the basis of a measure other than value, such as the quantity of the product imported. In addition, a 'compound' or 'mixed' duty, which is a combination of an ad valorem and specific duty, is occasionally used in the Harmonized Tariff Schedules of the United States (HTSUS). Special duties such as anti-dumping duties or countervailing duties may also be levied on imports to offset the unfair price advantage of an imported article that is sold below normal value or subsidized by an exporting country.

DVD : A DVD is digital media source capable of storing large amounts of data. Is a common format for movies, but is also used for computer data storage.

Dwarf : Shorter than its normal growth. Each family of plants has a height recommendation for dwarfness.

Dysmature cria : A cria that has developed too slow inside the uterus. They are born weak and lacking vigor.

Dysphagia : Difficulty eating and swallowing.

E

Ecology : The study of the interactions of organisms with their environment and with each other.

Economic Trait Locus (ETL) : A locus influencing a trait that contributes to producer's income.

Economic value : The net return within a herd for making a pound or percentage change in the trait in question.

Economies of size : The concept that the average cost of production per unit declines as the size of the operation grows. One reason farms have been growing in size is to make more economical use of machines capable of covering more ground with less labor, to capture economies of size. Larger sized farms can typically get volume discounts on such inputs as chemicals and seed.

Ecosystem : A functioning community of nature that includes fauna and flora together with the chemical and physical environment with which they interact. Ecosystems vary greatly in size and characteristics; an ecosystem can be a mud puddle, a field or orchard, or a forest. An ecosystem provides a unit of biological study and can be a unit of management.

Ecotype : A population or a strain of an organism that is adapted to a particular habitat.

ECP : Emergency Conservation Program

Ectoparasites : They live outside of the body. Many of the arthropod parasites are ectoparasites; they land on your skin and cause an infestation.

Ectopic : Anomalous situation or relation, particularly with respect to pregnancy, where the foetus is implanted outside the uterus.

Ectopic cilia : Abnormal eyelashes originating from the upper lid on the conjunctival side, usually just a few millimeters in from the eyelid margin, about mid way along the upper lid.

Edema : The presence of abnormally large amounts of fluid in the interstitial tissue spaces of the body. Edema fluid may accumulate in the subcutaneous tissues, peritoneal cavity (ascites), pleural cavity (hydrothorax) or pericardial sac (hydropericardium).

EDF : Environmental Defense Fund

Edging plant : On the edge or border of a bed.

Edible vaccine : Edible antigen-containing material, that activates the immune system via gut-associated lymphoid tissues. A preferred route for vaccine administration, particularly in areas where the technological infrastructure needed for maintenance of vaccines is absent. The vaccine is synthesized in vivo in the edible parts of transgenic plants (e.g. grains, tubers, fruits, etc.) or eggs.

EDV : Abbreviation for essential derivation of varieties.

EFAP : Emergency Food Assistance Program (formerly TEFAP); Emergency Feed Assistance Program.

Effective progeny Number (EPN) : An indication of the amount of information available for estimation of expected progeny differences in sire evaluation. It is a function of number of progeny but is adjusted for their distribution among herds and contemporary groups and for the number of contemporaries by other sires. EPN is lesis than the actual number because the distribution of progeny is never ideal.

Effector cells : Cells of the immune system that are responsible for the production of cell-mediated cytotoxicity.

Ejaculate : The movement of semen through the urethra to outside the penis.

Ejaculation : The ejection of sperm from the penis.

Elastin : A fibrous protein that is the major constituent of the yellow elastic fibres of animal connective tissue.

Elderly and disabled : For food stamp purposes : 'elderly' persons are age 60 or older; and 'disabled' persons are beneficiaries of disability-based governmental assistance, such as social security disability payments and certain veterans disability payments.

Electro-blotting : The electrophoretic transfer of DNA, RNA or protein from a gel, in which they have been separated, to a support matrix, such as nitrocellulose. A transfer technique employed in Southern and northern blotting.

Electrocardiography (ECG) : A test that measures the electrical activity of the heart. ECG or EKG.

Electrochemical sensor : Biosensors, such as an enzyme electrode, in which a biological process is harnessed to an electrical sensor system. Other types couple a biological event to an electrical one via a range of mechanisms, including the reduction of oxygen or pH change.

Electroejaculation : Using an electrical stimulus to cause the male to ejaculate semen.

Electrolytes : A general term for sodium, potassium, chloride and magnesium.

Electron microscope (EM) : A microscope that uses an electron beam focussed by magnetic 'lenses'.

Electronic Benefit Transfer (EBT) systems : Under an EBT system, recipients are issued an 'ATM-like' card and a 'personal identification number' (PIN) instead of food stamp coupons. They access their food stamp benefits when purchasing food by using the card at an approved retailer : 'swiping' the card through a point-of-sale terminal and entering their PIN. This electronically debits a 'food stamp account' maintained for them (and is replenished monthly) and credits the retailer with the purchase amount. States are permitted to issue food stamp benefits through EBT systems, and, unless a waiver is granted, must use EBT systems by 2002.

Electrophoresis : A ubiquitous molecular biology technique, with many variants, used to resolve complex mixtures of macromolecules into their components. Its principle is to subject samples to an electric field applied across a porous matrix. Molecules will migrate under these conditions at a rate dependent on their net electric charge and/or their molecular weight.

Electroporation : A method for transforming DNA, especially useful for plant cells, in which high voltage pulses of electricity are used to open pores in cell membranes, through which foreign DNA can pass.

Electroretinography : A diagnostic technique used to evaluate the function of the photoreceptors, specifically used to diagnose retinal degeneration.

Element : A substance that cannot be separated into different substances. All matter is made of elements.

Elevator : A tall warehouse facility that uses vertical conveyors to raise or elevate grain, generally owned privately or by an agricultural cooperative, where grain is stored before being marketed.

ELISA : Abbreviation for enzyme-linked immunosorbent assay. An immunoassay, i.e. an antibody-based technique for the diagnosis of the presence and quantity of specific molecules in a mixed sample. It combines the specificity of an immunoglobulin with the detectability of an enzyme-generated coloured product. In one form, the primary antibody (specific to the test protein) is adsorbed onto a solid substrate, and a known amount of the sample is added; all the antigen in the sample is bound by the antibody. A second antibody (conjugated with an enzyme) specific for a second site on the test protein is added; and the enzyme generates a colour change in the presence of a substrate reagent.

Elite tree : A phenotypically superior tree in a tree breeding programme.

Elizabethan collar : A large plastic collar that is placed over the head of a dog or cat. It has a cone shape and is used to keep them from licking or chewing on themselves.

Elongation factors : Soluble proteins required for the elongation of polypeptide chains on ribosomes.

Embryo culture : The culture of embryos on nutrient media.

Embryo multiplication and Transfer (EMT) : The cloning of animal embryos and their subsequent transfer to recipients via artificial inembryonation. The cloned embryos can be derived from embryonic or adult tissue.

Embryo rescue : A sequence of tissue culture techniques utilized to enable a fertilized immature embryo resulting from an interspecific cross to continue growth and development, until it can be regenerated into an adult plant.

Embryo sac : The mature female gametophyte in angiosperms. Generally a seven-celled structure - two synergids, one egg cell, three antipodal cells (each with a single haploid nucleus) and one endosperm mother cell with two haploid nuclei.

Embryo sexing : The determination of the sex of an embryo prior to birth. Typically achieved by the polymerase chain reaction-mediated amplification of DNA extracted from a sample of embryonic tissue. Dependent on the availability of reliable markers for the differential sex chromosome.

Embryo splitting : The splitting of young embryos into several sections, each of which develops into an animal. A form of animal cloning, i.e. of producing animals that are genetically identical. In practice, the number of animals that can be produced from a single embryo is less than 10.

Embryo storage : Cryogenic preservation of animal embryos, allowing inembryonation or other manipulations long after embryo formation.

Embryo technology : Generic name for any modification of mammalian embryos. It encompasses embryo cloning, embryo splitting, embryo storage, and in vitro fertilization.

Embryo transfer : Removing fertilized ova, or embryos, from one cow (donor dam) and placing these embryos into other cows (host cows), usually accompanied by hormone-induced superovulation of the donor dam. More calves can be obtained from cows of superior breeding value by this technique. Only proven producers should become donor dams.

Embryogenesis : 1) (General) Development of an embryo. 2) (In plants) In vitro formation of plants from plant tissues, through a pathway closely resembling normal embryogeny from the zygote. Somatic cell embryogenesis is an alteRNAtive technique. The generation of embryos has two stages: initiation and maturation. Initiation needs a high level of the group of plant hormones called auxins; maturation needs a lower level.

Embryoid : Plant biotechnology term no longer commonly used. An embryo-like body developing in vitro, forming a complete, self-contained plantlet with no vascular connection with the callus.

Embryonic Stem cells (ES cells) : Cells of the early embryo that can give rise to all differentiated cells, including germ line cells.

Embryonic vesicle : The sac containing the embryo which later in pregnancy develops into a fetus.

Emergency conservation program : A program administered by the Farm Service Agency to help farmers to rehabilitate farmland damaged by natural disasters by sharing in the cost of rehabilitation.

Emergency feeding agency : This refers to an organization serving the food needs of the poor and unemployed that is designated by a state as eligible for commodities and administrative support to distribute commodities or operate a meal service program under the Emergency Food Assistance Program.

Emollient : A softening agent.

Encapsidation : Process by which a virus' nucleic acid is enclosed in a capsid.

Encapsulating agents : Anything which forms a shell around an enzyme or bacterium, common agents being polysaccharides such as alginate or agar. The agents are inert and allow nutrients and oxygen to diffuse readily into and out of the sphere, and are easy to convert from gel (solid) to sol (liquid) or solution form by altering the temperature or the concentration of ions.

Encapsulation : Any method packaging an enzyme or bacterium and maintaining its normal functions. Used to immobilize cells in a bioreactor.

Encephalitis : Inflammation of the brain.

Encode : The gene product specified by a particular nucleic acid sequence.

End Stage Renal Disease (ESRD) : Advanced, irreversible chronic renal disease. Also a non-specific histologic finding on renal biopsy that may be the end result of renal disease of any etiology.

Endemic : Describing an organism, often a disease or pest, that is always present in a stated area.

Endocytosis : The process by which materials enter a cell without passing through the cell membrane. The membrane folds around material outside the cell, resulting in the formation of a sac-like vesicle inside which the material is entrapped. This vesicle is then pinched off from the cell surface so that it lies within the cell.

Endoderm : The internal layer of cells of the gastrula, which develops into the alimentary canal (gut) and digestive glands of the adult.

Endodermis : The layer of living cells, with various characteristically thickened walls and no intercellular spaces, which surrounds the vascular tissue of certain plants and occurs in nearly all roots and certain stems and leaves. It separates the cortical cells from cells of the pericycle.

Endogenous : Derived from within; from the same cell type or organism.

Endomitosis : Duplication of chromosomes without division of the nucleus, resulting in a doubling (or more) in the chromosome number within a cell.

Endonuclease : An enzyme that cleaves a phosphodiester bond within a DNA strand, forming two smaller strands.

Endoparasites : They live within the animal.

Endophyte : A plant living within another plant. In turfgrasses, it is a fungus within the grass plant secreting substances that repel insect pests.

Endoplasmic Reticulum (ER) : A cytoplasmic net of membranes, adjacent to the nucleus, visible under the electron microscope. The sites of protein synthesis.

Endopolyploidy : The net result of endomitoses. The somatic chromosome number has doubled (or more), forming a polyploid cell line. If these differentiate into a germ line, then the gametic number will have also increased proportionately, giving rise to homogeneously polyploid individuals, termed endopolyploids.

Endoprotease : An enzyme that cleaves internal peptide bonds within a polypeptide molecule. Site of cleavage is usually specific to certain amino acid residues.

Endoreduplication : Chromosome reproduction during interphase. Four-chromatid chromosomes (diplochromosomes) are seen during this phase.

Endorphin : A morphine-like peptide that is produced in the brain and which binds to certain receptors to reduce the sensation of pain.

Endothelium : The epithelial cells lining the inside of a blood vessel.

Endotoxemia : A type of shock caused by absorbing endotoxin which is released from some types of bacteria in the intestine when those bacteria die.

Endotoxin : A component of the cell wall of gram-negative bacteria that elicits, in mammals, an inflammatory response and fever.

End-product inhibition : The inhibition of an enzyme by a metabolite. Typically, the enzyme is the first enzyme in a biosynthetic pathway, and the metabolite the product of the last step in the pathway.

End-tidal CO_2 : Monitoring CO_2 of exhaled gases provides information about the patient's approximate CO_2 levels and is an indirect indicator of cardiac output and blood flow.

Enophthalmos : Retraction of globe into the orbit resulting in a sunken eye.

Enteral : Delivery of drugs or nutrients to the intestianl tract by deposition in the mouth, stomach or jejunum.

Enteric : A pathogen that is related to E. coli.

Enteropatogenic e. coli : Specific strains of E. coli that attach very tightly to gut wall and secrete various toxins, causing both excess secretion and malabsorption as well as general systemic effects on the calf.

Enterotoxemia : A highly fatal disease related to the proliferation of gram negative organisms in the intestine of susceptible animals.

Enterotoxigenic e. coli : A specific strain K99 that attaches to intestinal cells and causes a hypersecretory diarrhea.

Enterotoxin : A bacterial protein that, following release into the intestine, causes cramps, diarrhoea and nausea.

Entomology : The study of insects and their environments.

Entropion : Inversion or turning inward.

Enucleated ovum : Egg cell from which the nucleus has been removed, usually as a preparatory step for nuclear transfer.

Enucleation : Removing the eye from the orbit : leaves most of the orbital contents behind.

Environmental Protection Agency (EPA) : An independent federal government agency established in 1970 and charged with coordinating effective governmental action concerning the environment, including setting standards, promulgating and enforcing regulations, and initiating and implementing environmental programs. Two areas of jurisdiction that most directly affect agricultural production are the registration of pesticides and enforcement of water quality laws.

Enzyme : A protein which, even in very low concentration, catalyses specific chemical reactions but is not used up in the reaction. Enzymes are classified into six major groups (1-6), according to the type of reaction they catalyse: 1) oxidoreductases; 2) transferases; 3) hydrolases; 4) lyases; 5) isomerases; 6) ligases. Generally enzymes are named by the addition of the suffix -ase to the name of their substrate, and are classified by a standard numerical system: the Enzyme Commission (EC) number.

Enzyme bioreactor : A reactor in which a chemical conversion reaction is catalysed by an enzyme.

Enzyme immunoassay : A range of immunoassay techniques employing enzymes, which includes ELISA.

Enzyme kinetics : The quantitative characteristics of enzyme reactions.

EPA : Environmental Protection Agency

Ephemeral : Lasting only one day when in flower

Ephemeral stream : A stream that flows only sporadically, such as after storms.

Epichil : The upper part of the jointed, complex lip of certain orchids, as in the genus Stanhopea

Epichile : Terminal lobe of labellum in certain orchids

Epidermal membrane : Also called the fourth membrane. A membrane that covers the cria entirely at birth.

Epidermis : 1) The outmost layer of cells of the body of an animal. In invertebrates the epidermis is normally only one cell thick and is covered by an impermeable cuticle. In vertebrates the epidermis is the thinner of the two layers of skin. 2) The outermost layer of cells covering a plant. It is overlaid by a cuticle and its functions are principally to protect the plant from injury and to reduce water loss. Some epidermal cells are modified to form guard cells or hairs of various types. In woody plants the functions of the shoot epidermis are taken over by the periderm tissues and in mature roots the epidermis is sloughed off and replaced by the hypodermis.

Epidural anesthesia : Injection of an anesthetic agent into the space outside the dura mater of the spinal cord.

Epigenesis : Describes the developmental process whereby each successive stage of normal development is built up on the foundations created by the preceding stages of development; an embryo is built up from a zygote, a seedling from an embryo, and so on.

Epigenetic variation : Non-hereditary and reversible variation;

often the result of a change in gene expression due to methylation of DNA.

Epilate : Removing hair.

Epinasty : A process by which the growth of branches or petioles is abnormally pointing downward. This phenomenon is caused by the more rapid growth of the upper side. Epinasty may result from either nutritional deficiencies or irregularities at the plant growth regulator level. Not to be confused with wilting, as epinastic tissues are turgid.

Epinephrine : A vasopressor drug which via alpha stimulation increases systemic vascular resistance and improves coronary and brain blood flow.

Epiphora : Excessive tearing.

Epiphyte : A plant that grows upon another plant, but is neither parasitic on it nor rooted in the ground.

Episome : A genetic extrachromosomal element (e.g. the F factor in Escherichia coli) which replicates within a cell independently of the chromosome and is able to integrate into the host chromosome. The step of integration may be governed by a variety of factors and so the term episome has lost favour and been superseded by the wider term plasmid.

Epistasis : Interaction between genes at different loci, e.g. one gene suppresses the effect of another gene that is situated at a different locus. Dominance is associated with members of allelic pairs, whereas epistasis describes an interaction among products of non-alleles.

Epistaxis : Bloody nose.

Epithelial cells : Cells that line the surface of an organ such as the epithelial cells lining the vagina.

Epitope : The site on a bacteria that specific antibody recognizes and binds to.

Epizootic : A disease simultaneously affecting a large number of animals.

Equational division : A chromosome division in which the two chromatids of each duplicated chromosome separate longitudinally, prior to being incorporated into two daughter nuclei. Seen at the mitotic-type second division of meiosis; also in somatic mitosis and the non-reductional division of meiosis. The number of chromosomes is the same at the end of the division as at the beginning.

Equilibrium density gradient centrifugation : A procedure used to separate macromolecules based on their density (mass per unit volume).

Equitainer : A container originally designed for shipping horse semen; also used to maintain temperature control of semen from other species.

Equivalence : A term applied by the Uruguay Round Agreement on the Application of Sanitary and Phytosanitary (SPS) Measures. WTO Member countries shall accord acceptance to the SPS measures of other countries (even if those measures differ from their own or from those used by other Member countries trading in the same product) if the exporting country demonstrates to the importing country that its measures achieve the importer's appropriate level of sanitary and phytosanitary protection.

Erlenmeyer flask : A conical flat-bottomed laboratory flask with a narrow neck, widely used for culturing micro-organisms.

Erose : With the margin irregularly notched, as if gnawed

Erosion : The wearing away of the land surface. Unconsolidated materials, such as soil, erode more rapidly than consolidated materials, such as rock. The most common causes of erosion are wind and moving water. The susceptibility of soil to erosion is quantified by the erosion index. Water causes sheet, rill, and gully erosion.

Erosion (Erodibility) Index (EI) : The erosion (sometimes called erodibility) index is created by dividing potential erosion (from all sources except gully erosion) by the 'T' value, which is the rate of soil erosion above which long term productivity may be adversely affected. The erodibility index is used in the conservation compliance and Conservation Reserve Programs. For example, one of the eligibility requirements for the CRP is that land have an EI greater than 8.

ERS : Economic Research Service

Erythema Multiforme (EM) : An acute, self-limiting eruption of the skin and mucous membranes characterized by distinctive gross lesions and a diagnostic sequence of pathologic changes.

Erythrocyte (RBC) : Red blood cell.

Escape rhythm : When the SA node is firing at an abnormally slow rate, another location in the heart takes over pacing the heart. This may be the AV node or a ventricular focus.

Escherichia coli : A commensal bacterium inhabiting the colon of many animal species, including human. E. coli is widely used as a model of cell biochemical function, and as a host for cloning DNA. In environmental studies, its presence is a key indicator of water pollution due to human sewage effluent. Some strains, notably E. coli 0157:H7, are significant pathogens.

Esophagus : A muscular tube leading from the mouth to the stomach.

Espalier : The method of training a tree or shrub as to grow in a pattern. Often pear trees, apple trees, or ornamentals.

Essential amino acid : An amino acid required for normal metabolism, but which cannot be synthesized by an organism. It therefore has to be supplied via feed or food.

Essential Derivation of Varieties (EDV) : Genotypes very similar to an originating cultivar, obtained, for example, by the selection of a mutant or a variant individual from plants of the initial variety, or by backcrossing or transformation.

Essential element : Any of a number of elements required by living organisms to ensure normal growth, development and maintenance.

Essential host : Humans are an essential element of the organisms life cycle.

Essential nutrient : Any substance required by living organisms to ensure normal growth, development and maintenance.

Essential requirement : In plant cell tissue culture, comprises inorganic salts, including all of the elements necessary for plant metabolism; organic factors (amino acids, vitamins); usually also endogenous plant growth regulators (auxins, cytokinins and often gibberellins); as well as a carbon source (sucrose or glucose).

Established : The state of a plant when it is adjusted to the site and thriving.

Established culture : 1) An aseptic viable explant. 2) A suspension culture subjected to several passages with a constant cell number per unit time.

Estimate : The process of calculating a particular value from data (verb). The value itself obtained from data (noun). The idea is that the true value is being obtained from the calculated value within limits of sampling variation.

Estimated Breeding Value (EBV) : Twice the expected progeny difference. The difference is doubled because breeding value is a reflection of all the genes of an individual, in contrast to progeny difference, which is a reflection of a sample half of an individual's genes. The predicted performance of the offspring of the mating between any two parents is the average of their EBVs (averaged because each parent makes an equal contribution to each offspring).

Estimated Crude Protein from Non-Protein Source (ECP from NPS) : Non-protein nitrogen sources such as urea or ammonia; used in ruminant diets in limited amounts to enhance dietary protein levels.

Estrogen : The hormone that makes a female receptive to the male.

Estrus : The time of receptivity, when the bitch accepts the male for breeding.

Estuary : Regions of interaction between rivers and near- shore ocean waters, where tidal action and river flow mix fresh and salt water. Such areas include bays, mouths of rivers, salt marshes, and lagoons. These brackish water ecosystems shelter and feed marine life, birds, and wildlife. Estuaries typically include adjoining wetlands.

ET : Abbreviation for embryo transfer.

Ethanol : Commonly used to disinfect plant tissues, glassware utensils and working surfaces in tissue culture manipulations; to precipitate aqueous solutions of nucleic acids; and to dissolve water-insoluble components of culture media.

Ethephon : A synthetic compound commonly used as a source of ethylene, a gaseous plant growth regulator.

Ether extract laboratory test : A test to measure the total fat content of a feed.

Ethidium bromide : A fluorescent dye which can intercalate between base pairs of double-stranded DNA, and hence is much used to stain DNA in gels. The dye fluoresces when exposed to UV light. It is a known to be a strong mutagen and is also possibly both a carcinogen and a teratogen.

Ethyl lactate : A topical agent that alters follicular environment to reduce bacterial flora.

Ethylene : A gaseous plant growth regulator acting on various aspects of vegetative growth, fruit ripening and abscission of plant parts.

Ethylenediamine Tetraacetic Acid (EDTA) : A chelating compound. Used to keep nutrients, such as iron, bound in a soluble form that leaves them still available to the plant cells in vitro. Also a potent inhibitor of DNase activity and therefore used as an additive for long-term storage of dissolved DNA.

Etiolation : An abnormal increase in stem elongation, accompanied by poor (if any) leaf development. Physiological etiolation is caused by a lack of chlorophyll, and is typical of plants growing under low light intensity or in complete darkness. It can also be induced by some fungal pathogens.

EUP : Experimental use permit

Euploid : An organism or cell having a chromosome number that is an exact multiple of the haploid number. Terms used to identify different levels in an euploid series are diploid (2x), triploid (3x), tetraploid (4x) etc. Opposite: aneuploid.

Eutrophication : The process by which a body of water acquires a high concentration of plant nutrients, especially nitrates or phosphates. This nutrification promotes algae growth that, when it dies, can lead to the depletion of dissolved oxygen, killing fish and other aquatic organisms. While eutrophication is a natural, slow-aging process for a body of water, human activities can greatly accelerate the process.

Evapotranspiration : The loss of water from the soil both by evaporation and by transpiration from the plants growing in the soil.

Everblooming : Those flowers that will bloom all season.

Evergreen : A plant that will bear foliage throughout the year.

Evergreen plants : Plants that do not drop the current season's leaves at the end of the growing season.

Evergreen tree : A tree that retains some or most of its leaves, or needles, throughout the year.

Everlasting : Flowers that have been grown for drying and preserving.

Evolution : The long-term process through which a population of organisms accumulats genetic changes that enable its members to successfully adapt to environmental conditions and to better exploit food resources.

Ewe : A female sheep of any age.

Ex vivo gene therapy : The delivery of a gene or genes to the isolated cells of an individual, with the intention of alleviating a genetic disorder. After culturing, the transformed cells are re-introduced into the individual by transfusion, infusion or injection.

Excess land : Irrigable land, other than exempt land, owned by any landowner in excess of the maximum acreage limitation (ownership entitlement) under the applicable provision of reclamation law.

Excinuclease : The endonuclease-containing protein complex that excises a segment of damaged DNA during excision repair.

Excision : 1) The natural or in vitro enzymatic removal of a DNA segment from a chromosome or cloning vector. 2) The cutting out and preparation of a tissue, organ, etc., for culture. 3. The removal of adventitious shoots from callus tissue.

Excision repair : DNA repair processes that involve the removal of a damaged or incorrect segment of one strand of double-stranded DNA and its replacement by the synthesis of a new segment using the complementary strand of DNA as template.

Excitation wavelength : The specific wavelength of light required to stimulate a fluorescent molecule, such as a labelled probe, to emit light at the (lower) emission wavelength.

Excoriation : Superficial loss of the epidermis caused by physical damage such as scratching.

Exocrine gland : An animal gland that secretes through a duct.

Exogenous : DNA DNA that has been derived from one organism, and is to be introduced into a cell a different species. Also referred to as foreign DNA or heterologous DNA.

Exon : A segment of a eukaryotic gene that is transcribed as part of the primary transcript and is retained, after processing, with other exons to form a functional mRNA molecule. Many eukaryotic genes are composed of a mosaic of exons and introns.

Exon amplification : A procedure that is used to amplify exons.

Exotic : Plants that are native to other parts of the world and have been introduced here. Watch out. honeysuckle and purple loosestrife are invasive exotic pests.

Exotic species : A non-native plant or animal species introduced by humans, either deliberately or accidentally.

Exotoxin : A toxin released by a bacterium into the medium in which it grows.

Explant : A portion of a plant aseptically excised and prepared for culture in a nutrient medium.

Explant donor : The plant from which an explant has been taken.

Explantation : The removal of cells, tissues or organs of animals and plants for observation of their growth and development in appropriate culture media.

Explosion method : A technique for the genetic transformation of cells, in which the transgene is driven into the target (plant) cells by the sudden vaporization (effected by the application of a pulse of high voltage) of a water droplet containing the DNA and gold particles.

Export : The removal of a compound from a cell by active transport.

Export licenses : A government document authorizing the export of specific goods in specific quantities to a particular destination. Licenses may be required to export to some countries for most or all goods, and for other countries only under special circumstances. The Office of Export Administration in the Department of Commerce administers the export licensing system under the authority of the Export Administration Act.

Expressed sequence Tag (EST) : Partially sequenced cDNA clone. Because the read length of a standard DNA sequencing reaction is shorter than the majority of cDNA clones, full length sequence can only be obtained by further manipulations. For the purposes of 1) assigning putative function to a cDNA and 2) designing PCR primers to extract the genomic DNA equivalent to the cDNA, full length sequence is usually unnecessary. By restricting sequencing to a single run, large numbers of cDNAs can be characterized at the EST level.

Expression library : A cDNA library that has been inserted into a bacterial host cell engineered to express transgenes.

Expression system : Combination of host and vector which provides a genetic context for making a cloned gene functional, i.e. produce peptide, in the host cell.

Expression vector : A cloning vector that has been constructed in such a way that, after insertion of a DNA molecule, its coding sequence is properly transcribed and the mRNA is translated. The cloned gene is put under the control of a promoter sequence for the initiation of transcription, and often also has a transcription termination sequence at its end.

Expressivity : Degree of expression of a trait controlled by a particular gene. The gene may show different degrees of expression in different individuals.

Ex-situ conservation : The conservation of components of biological diversity outside their natural habitats.

Extra-Long staple (ELS) cotton : Also called American Pima, this cotton has a staple length of 1-3/8" or more, is characterized by fineness and high fiber strength, and is used in high-value products such as sewing thread and expensive apparel. It is grown chiefly in west Texas, New Mexico and Arizona.

Extranuclear genes : Genes residing elsewhere than in the nucleus.

Exude : Slowly discharge liquid material through pores or cuts, or by diffusion into the medium.

Eyelid agenesis : Born without part of the upper eyelids.

F

Family : 1) A group of plants or animals that have some common characteristics. For example acacia and albizia trees are members of the same family, mimosaceae. 2) The offspring of a single tree after open pollination, or of a single pair of trees after controlled pollination.

Family farm : An agricultural business which 1) produces agricultural commodities for sales in such quantities so as to be recognized as a farm rather than a rural residence; 2) produces enough income (including off-farm employment) to pay family and farm operating expenses, to pay debts and to maintain the property; 3) is managed by the operator; 4) has a substantial amount of labor provided by the operator and family; and 5) may use seasonal labor during peak periods and a reasonable amount of full-time hired labor.

Fan design : A type of design for plant-spacing studies in which the plants are arranged at systematically increasing distances along radii and arcs.

Fao : Food and agricultural organization of the united nations

Farm : An area of land that is devoted to agriculture.

Farm Animal Genetic Resources (ANGR) : Those animal species that are used, or may be used, for the production of food and agriculture, and the populations within each of them. These populations within each species can be classified as wild and feral populations, landraces and primary populations, standardized breeds, selected lines, and any conserved genetic material.

Farm credit system : The Farm Credit System (FCS) is a nationwide farmer-owned system of lending institutions and affiliated service organizations that provides credit and related services to farmers, farm-owned supply, marketing and processing cooperatives, including agribusinesses, agricultural and aquatic cooperatives, rural utilities and certain foreign or domestic entities.

Farm enterprise : An individual crop or animal production function within a farming system, the smallest unit for which analysis of resource use and cost return is normally carried out.

Farm forestry : Growing trees for timber, poles, fuelwood on farmland. This may be done in small woodlots or as boundary plantings.

Farm household system : A group of people, usually related, who individually or jointly provide management, labour, capital, land and other inputs for the production of crops and livestock, and who consume at least part of the farm produce.

Farmer : A person who raises livestock and/or cultivates crops.

Farmer cooperative : A business whose membership is limited to persons producing agricultural and aquacultural products that are marketed by the co-op. They provide business related services, sell farm production supplies, and can process farm products for sale.

Farming system : 1) A unique and reasonably stable arrangement of farming enterprises that a household manages according to well-defined practices in response to the physical, biological and socioeconomic environments, and in accordance with the household's goals, preferences and resources. These factors combine to influence output and production methods. More commonality will be found within the system than between systems. The farming system is part of larger systems and can itself be divided into subsystems, such as those providing food or cash. 2) A decision-making unit comprising the farm household and cropping and livestock systems, which produces crop and animal products for consumption and sale. The farming system is a subsystem of a higher level land-use system such as village or watershed. That in turn forms a component of the agricultural sector of the regional system.

Farmland : Land that is part of farm units, including cropland, pasture, small woodlots, and areas used for small farm roads and buildings.

Farmyard manure : The partly decomposed excreta of domestic animals mixed with straw or other litter.

Fasciculate : Bundled; radiating from a central growing point.

Fast-growing tree : A tree species that matures quickly and is usually not long lived. Can often be highly productive on fertile sites : 15-20 t ha-1 of wood products per annum or more. Some, for example, leguminous species in the mimosaceae and papilionaceae families and actinorrhizal plants such as the genus alnus, may also be nitogen fixing. Among the many genera included are calliandra, gliricidia, leucaena and sesbania.

Fat : A term used in a general sense to refer to both fats and oils. Fat supplied 2.25 times as much energy as carbohydrates. Both fats and oils share the same general structure and chemical properties, but have different physical properties, i.e., oils are liquid at room temperature.

Fauna : A book listing, with descriptions and illustrations, all animals that live in a given area. [jvg]

Fc : A product of hydrolysis of an IgG antibody, consisting of parts of the constant regions of two heavy chains held together by a disulphide bridge, but excluding the antigen-binding regions, and also excluding the light chains.

Fdiu : Field Disease Investigative Unit.

Fecundity : A measurement of the egg-producing ability of a fish. Fecundity may change with the age and size of the fish.

Fed (or fat) cattle : Cattle that have been finished, usually in the feedlot, and are ready for slaughter.

Feed conversion : Units of feed consumed per unit of weight gained. Also the production (meat, milk) per unit of feed consumed.

Feed efficiency : A ratio describing the amount of feed required per unit of production (grain, milk, eggs).

Feed grade : Term to describe the quality of feedstuffs suitable for animal, but no human, consumption.

Feed processing : Physical or chemical changes in feedstuffs which influence their nutritional value.

Feed wheat : Although wheat traditionally is used as food for human consumptions, large amounts of wheat are fed to livestock and poultry, especially in years when prices of lower quality wheat are competitive with those of coarse grains.

Feeder cattle : Cattle past the calf stage that have weight increased making them salable as feedlot replacements.

Feedlot : A confinement facility where cattle are fed to produce beef for the commercial trade. May be under a roof or outdoors.

Feedstuff : An edible material that contributes nutrients to animals' diets.

Feminization : A male showing signs of being under the influence of the female hormone, estrogen.

Fenoxycarb : An insect growth regularor recently withdrawn from the market.

Fentanyl patches : A sticky patch impregnated with the narcotic fentanyl which is applied topically for sustained release and absorption of the drug.

Fermentation : The anaerobic breakdown of complex organic substances, especially carbohydrates, by micro-organisms, yielding energy. Often misused to describe large-scale aerobic cell culture in specialized vessels (fermenters, bioreactors) for secondary product synthesis.

Fermentation substrates : Materials used as food for growing micro-organisms. The fermentation substrates and the trace materials needed, together with chemicals added to make the fermentation easier, form the culture medium.

Fertile : Capable of breeding and reproduction.

Fertilization : The union of two gametes from opposite sexes to form a zygote. Typically, each gamete contains a haploid set of chromosomes. Hence the zygotic nucleus contains a diploid set of chromosomes. Several categories can be distinguished: 1) Self-fertilization (selfing): fusion of male and female gametes from the same individual. 2) Cross-fertilization (crossing): fusion of male and female gametes from different individuals. 3) Double fertilization; restricted to flowering plants, in which the fusion of one male gamete with the ovum occurs at about the same time as the second male gamete nucleus fuses with the female polar nuclei (or secondary nucleus) to form the endosperm.

Fertilization rate : The percentage of females bred that get pregnant. A 90% fertilization rate means that 9 out of 10 females bred get pregnant.

Fertilize(RS) : The act of or the actual substance added to soil to provide additional nutrients for plants. May also be used to describe the pollination process flowers undergo with the help of bees and other insects. There are organic and chemical fertilizers.

Fertilizer : Any substance that is added to soil in order to increase its productivity. Fertilizers can be of biological origin (e.g. composts), or they can be synthetic (artificial fertilizer).

Fertilizer burn : The browning and in extreme cases, killing of plants from exposure to excessive nitrogen.

Fertilizer spreaders : They spread fertilizer on the field.

Fetal : Refers to a puppy or kitten before birth.

Fibroblasts : Irregularly shaped, branching cells distributed throughout vertebrate connective tissue. A cell type which is readily cultured in vitro.

Fibrosis : Scarring.

Fibrous root : Root system in which both primary and lateral roots have approximately equal diameters.

Fibro-vascular Membranes (PIFMS) : Cats with uveitis form fibro-vascular membranes due to chronic inflammation. Chronic uveitis that smolders for a long time causes these membranes to form on the iris and they eventually block the drainage angle causing glaucoma.

Field : 1) A set of alphanumeric characters comprising a unit of information. 2) A location in a data record in which a unit of information is stored.

Field capacity : 1) The amount of water a soil will hold against gravity when given reasonable time to drain. Commonly taken as one-third atmosphere tension for clays, and one-tenth atmosphere for sands. 2) The total amount of water remaining in a freely drained soil after the excess has flowed into the underlying unsaturated soil unit.

Field corn : Any variety of corn that is grown extensively in large fields primarily for livestock feed, as contrasted with the horticultural varieties, such as sweet corn or popcorn. Most field corn is of the dent variety.

Field grown : Grown in the field, as opposed to root cuttings which are grown in pots in greenhouses.

Field layer : The vegetation at ground level in a forest or woodland.

Field prescriptions : Applications of inputs at variable rates based on data obtained through yield monitors, crop scouting, remote sensing and soil sampling.

Field trial : Tests of the ability of a new crop variety to perform under normal cultivation conditions.

FIFRA : The Federal Insecticide, Fungicide, and Rodenticide Act.

Filament : The part of the stamen that holds the anther in position for pollen dispersal.

Fillet : A portion of flesh taken from either side of a fish, cut parallel to the central bones. The main bones, fins and belly flaps are usually removed from finished fillets.

Filly : A female horse less than three years old.

Filter bioreactor : A cell culture system, in which cells are grown on a fine mesh of an inert material, which allows the culture medium to flow past it but retains the cells. This is similar in idea to membrane and hollow fibre reactors, but can be much easier to set up, being similar to conventional tower bioreactors, but with the mesh replacing the central reactor space.

Filter sterilization : Process of removing microbial contaminants from a liquid by passing through a filter with pores too small to allow the passage of micro-organisms and spores.

Filter strip : A strip of permanent vegetation of sufficient width and vegetative density above farm ponds, diversion terraces and other structures to retard flow of runoff water, causing it to deposit soil, thereby preventing silting of a storage structure or reservoir.

Filtration : 1) Separation of solids from liquids by using a porous material that only allows passage of the liquid or of solids smaller than the pore size of the filter. The material passing the filter forms the filtrate. 2) Removal of cell aggregates to obtain a filtrate of single cells that can be utilized as plating inocula.

Final crop : In forestry, the trees that remain after successive thinnings and are finally felled at maturity.

Financial mechanism : As defined by the convention on biological diversity, its role is to provide under the guidance of the cop financial resources to help developing countries implement the convention; the gef is operating the mechanism on an interim basis.

Finishing stage (in swine operations) : It is the growth stage leading up to market. Pigs remain here until they reach market weight, typically 240 to 275 pounds.

Finnan haddie : A headed and gutted haddock, split and lightly salted in brine, then cold smoked. Traditionally cooked in butter or cream, the dish originated in findon, scotland, where it was known as findon haddock, which evolved to finnan haddie.

Fipronil : Trade name is Frontline. A phenylpyrazole insecticide which acts as a neurotoxin.

Fire : Used in forestry and range management to carry out a burn in a controlled manner and to dispose of unwanted vegetation. A headfire is where the fire is lit at the bottom of a slope and allowed to burn quickly to the top. A backfire is lit at the top and burns slowly downhill. Flankfires are lit at the sides; jackpot fires are where only piled slash is burned. A wildfire is a burn occurring spontaneously (that is, an uncontrolled fire).

Firebreak : 1) In forestry, an existing barrier, or one constructed before a fire occurs, from which flammable materials have been removed, designed to stop or check creeping or running fires. Also serves as a line from which to work and to facilitate the movement of men and equipment in fire suppression. 2) A form of fire protection, usually against uncontrolled fires, where either (a) a zone of trees and any other woody vegetation is removed so that only a limited amount of flammable material is present or (b) tree species that are relatively less flammable are planted (for example, broadleaved) so as to separate more flammable species (for example, resinous conifers).

First-last grazing : A method of utilising two or more groups of animals, usually with different nutritional requirements, to graze sequentially on the same land area. If more than two groups of animals are grazed sequentially, this would be described as first, second, and last grazing.

Fish : Defined as finfish, crustaceans, mollusks, and amphibians and reptiles which spend the majority of their life cycle in water, and any part, egg, offspring, or dead body of any of these species.

Fish biomass : The weight of living fish in a pond.

Fish habitat : The structural component of the environment on which fish depend for feeding, breeding, and growth to maturity. These environments include waters from freshwater rivers and streams to saltwater seas.

Fish steak : A thick, cross-section cut of a large fish that includes a piece of the backbone.

Fish sticks : Rectangles of fish cut from a frozen block and breaded or battered.

Fishery : Defined in the magnuson-stevens fishery conservation and management act as "one or more stocks of fish which can be treated as a unit for purposes of conservation and management and which are identified on the basis of geographical, scientific, technical, recreational, and economic characteristics; and...any fishing for such stocks."

Fishery dependent data : Data collected on a fish or fishery from sport fishermen, commercial fishermen, and seafood dealers.

Fishery Management Plan (FMP) : A plan developed by a regional fishery management council and the secretary of commerce to manage a fishery resource pursuant to the magnuson-stevens fishery conservation and management act.

Fishing capacity : The quantity of fish that can be taken by a particular fishing unit, for example, an individual, a community, a vessel or a fleet.

Fishing community : Defined in the magnuson-stevens fishery conservation and management act as "a community which is substantially dependent on or substantially engaged in the harvest or processing of fishery resources to meet social and economic needs, and includes fishing vessel owners, operators, and crew and united states fish processors that are based in such community."

Fishing effort : 1) The total fishing gear in use for a specified period of time. When two or more kinds of gear are used, they must be adjusted to some standard type. 2) Effective fishing effort.

Fishing intensity : 1) Effective fishing effort. 2) Fishing effort per unit area 3) Effectiveness of fishing.

Fishing mortality (F) : A measurement of the rate of removal of fish from a population by fishing. Fishing mortality can be reported as either annual or instantaneous. Annual mortality is the percentage of fish dying in one year. Instantaneous is that percentage of fish dying at any one time. The acceptable rates of fishing mortality may vary from species to species.

Fishing mortality : Deaths in a fish stock caused by fishing.

Fishing power : Represents the ability of a gear or vessel to catch fish during a certain time interval. Larger vessels with greater horsepower that catch more fish have a greater fishing power than smaller vessels. Improvements in a vessel or gear, such as a fish finder, can increase fishing power.

Fix : A single position calculated by a GPS receiver with latitude, longitude, altitude, time, and date.

Fixation : The situation in which only one allele for a given gene/locus is present in a population. This can occur as a result of direct selection where the allele delivers a greater level of fitness; because of indirect selection, where the locus is linked to a gene that is subject to direct selection; or because of genetic drift.

Flaming : A technique for sterilizing instruments, to remove live micro-organism contaminants. The instrument is dipped in alcohol, and the alcohol remaining on the instrument is ignited, thereby heat-sterilizing the surface.

Flanking region : The DNA sequences extending on either side of a specific locus or gene.

Flask : A glass container used in the germination of orchid seeds and new seedlings.

Flasking : This is the process of sowing orchid seeds in a flask or transplanting seedlings into a flask.

Flat : A shallow wooden box or plastic tray used to start cuttings or seedlings. Annuals may be purchased in a flat.

Fleece : The wool coat of a sheep.

Flehmen : A curling of the upper lip or open mouth behavior which is a normal mating behavior in the male alpaca and llama.

Flexibility : The degree to which a plant genotype confers the ability for the plant to establish and maintain itself in more than one ecological niche.

Flocculant : A chemical agent that causes small particles to aggregate (flocculate).

Floricanes : On raspberries and blackberries, two-year-old canes which bear fruit and then die.

Floriculture : The cultivation and management of ornamental and flowering plants.

Floriferous : Free-flowering; easily brought into flower

Flower : Strictly, an angiospermous reproductive structure bearing pistils or stamens or both, and usually sepals and petals. The so-called 'flower' of conifers is the male or female strobilus before and during pollination.

Flower induction : Stimulation of plants to produce flowers.

Fluid milk : Milk that is prepared for consumption as milk.

Fluid therapy : Fluid therapy is broadly defined to include the administration of many types of fluids including crystalloids and colloids. Fluid therapy may be given to prevent or correct fluid deficits or electrolyte abnormalities. Correct water imbalance from excessive fluid loss or inadequate intake Hemorrhage Vomiting Diarrhea Polyuria Expand blood volume - shock Correct electrolyte imbalance(s) Correct acid-base imbalance Supply blood components Supply calories and nutrients Renal disease - promote renal blood flow.

Fluorescence In Situ Hybridization (FISH) : Hybridization of cloned, fluorescently labelled DNA or RNA, to intact biological materials, notably chromosome spreads and thin tissue sections. The technique allows the visualization of the physical location of nucleic acid sequences homologous to the probe, and is used for the placement of genes on chromosomes and for the spatial and temporal pattern of gene expression of specific mRNA molecules.

Fluorescence-Activated Cell Sorting (FACS) : A flow cytometry method in which targets (cells, individual chromosomes etc.) are labelled with a fluorescent dye, which is excited by a laser beam. Differences in the fluorescence signal emitted are used as a criterion for sorting the material. A specific application is in sperm sexing.

Fluorescent probe : A probe which is labelled with a fluorescent dye, so that the signal emitted can be captured by photometric methods.

Fluoroscopy : A type of radiograph (x-ray) in which motion can be seen.

Flushing : Increasing the feed amount and/or quality (energy intake) prior to mating to increase the ovulation rate.

Fmax : The rate of fishing mortality for a given exploitation pattern rate of growth and natural mortality, that results in the maximum level of yield per recruit. This is the point that defines growth overfishing.

Foal : A young horse of either sex, less than one year old.

Fodder : Plants or plant parts eaten by browsing or grazing animals. Fodder trees include species of acacia, leucaena, prosopis and many others. Normally, fodder refers to the green parts of the tree, for example, leaves or sometimes flowers and pods. Often fodder is collected and stored for future consumption.

Foetid : With a disagreeable odour

Foiliar fertilizer : A liquid, water soluble, fertilizer applied to a plant's foliage in a fine spray so that the plant can absorb the nutrients through its leaves.

Fold-back : The structure of a double-stranded DNA molecule formed when a molecule containing an inverted repeat sequence is denatured and then allowed to re-anneal at low DNA concentrations. Under these conditions, the repeated sequence self-anneals to form a double-stranded region within each of the separated strands of the original molecule.

Folded genome : The condensed state of the chromosomal DNA of a bacterium. The DNA is segregated into domains, and each domain is independently negatively supercoiled.

Follicle Stimulating Hormone (FSH) : A hormone, secreted by the anterior pituitary gland in mammals, that stimulates the ripening of the specialized structures in the ovary (Graafian follicles) that produce ova in female mammals; and in males, the formation of sperm in the testis. FSH is a major constituent of fertility drugs.

Follicular cycle : The series of events that occur when the ovary produces a follicle (an egg) and the follicle goes through a series of changes.

Folliculitis : Superficial bacterial dermatitis associated with the hair follicle.

Fomite : A vector of disease transmission that has no part in the pathogen's life cycle. A contaminated milking towel that spreads disease from cow to cow with each subsequent use is a fomite.

Food chain : A sequence of organisms in a community in which each member of the chain feeds on the member below it, as in fox, rabbit and grass.

Food guide pyramid : A graphic design used to communicate the recommended daily food choices contained in the dietary guidelines for americans. The information provided was developed and promoted by the u.s. Department of agriculture and the u.s. Department of health and human services.

Food processing enzyme : Enzyme used to control food texture, flavour, appearance, or nutritional value. Amylases break down complex polysaccharides to simpler sugars; proteases tenderize meat proteins. A prominent target of food biotechnology is to develop novel food enzymes which can improve the quality of processed foods.

Food security : The condition of having both physical and economic access to the basic food that people need to function normally.

Food web : An abstract representation of the feeding relationships of organisms within a community or an ecosystem.

Foot and Mouth Disease (FMD) : A highly infectious viral disease in cattle, pigs, sheep and goats, characterised by the development of blisters in the mouth and on the feet resulting in lameness. Death is not usual but animals cease gaining weight and milk production drops.

Forage allowance : The relationship between the weight of forage dry matter per unit area and the number of animal units or forage intake units at any point in time; a forage-to-animal relationship. The inverse of grazing pressure. May be expressed as forage mass per animal unit or forage intake unit (forage mass/animal unit at a specific time). This definition can be appropriately altered to be specific to herbage or browse by substituting these terms in place of forage.

Forage crop : A crop of cultivated plants or plant parts, other than separated grain, produced to be grazed or harvested for use as feed for animals.

Forage forestry : Growing close-planted, fast-growing tree species that can be mechanically harvested, such as by a forage harvester in agriculture, for wood products such as woodchips.

Forage harvester : A machine powered by a tractor or self propelled which lifts a swath of wilted grass and chops it finely before delivering it to a following trailer. It is ensiled in a clamp

Forage mass : The total dry weight of forage per unit area of land, usually above ground level and at a defined reference level. This definition can be appropriately altered to be specific to herbage or browse by substituting these terms in place of forage.

Forage wagon : It is used to carry haylage in from the field. It is a wagon with 2 solid walls, a back, and a mechanical unloader.

Foreign : DNA Exogenous DNA that is incorporated into a host genome.

Forest : A continuous stand of trees > 10 m high, with interlocking crowns. There are many kinds of forests and ways to classify them, for example, by ecozone, vegetation type, climate, dominant species, conformation.

Forest garden : A land-use form on private lands outside the village in which planted trees and sometimes additional perennial crops occur.

Forestry : The science, art, and practice of managing and protecting tree and forest resources for human benefit.

Fork length : The length of a fish as measured from the tip of its snout to the fork in the tail.

Form : In forestry, the general shape of a tree. Trees with good form are straight, more or less cylindrical, with fine branches, and do not taper rapidly.

Forskolin : A medicinal, diterpenoid, compound exclusive to plant roots and used in the preparation of drugs for the treatment of cardiomyopathy, glaucoma and certain cancers.

Fortify : To add strengthening components or beneficial ingredients to a nutrient medium.

Forward contracting : A method of selling crops before harvest, by which the buyer agrees to pay a specific price to a grower for a portion, or all, of the grower's crop.

Forward mutation : A mutation from the wild type to the mutant type.

Foundation seed : Seed stock produced from breeder's seed by or under the direct control of an agricultural experiment station. Foundation seed is the source of certified seed, either directly or through registered seed.

Founder animal : An organism that carries a transgene in its germ line and can be used in matings to establish a pure-breeding transgenic line, or one that acts as a breeding stock for transgenic animals.

Founder effect : The loss of genetic diversity when a new colony is formed (e.g. On an oceanic island) by a very small number of individuals from a larger population elsewhere.

Founder principle : The possibility that a new, isolated population, initiated by a small number of individuals taken from a parent population, may be genetically different from the parent population, because the founding individuals might not be typical of the parent population.

Four-base cutter : A type II restriction endonuclease with a four-nucleotide recognition site. Because any particular sequence of four bases occurs more frequently by chance than one of six bases, four-base cutters cleave more frequently than six-base cutters, and therefore generate, on average, smaller restriction fragments.

Fourth membrane : Also called epidermal membrane. A membrane that covers the cria entirely at birth.

Fractionation : The separation in components of a complex mixture of molecules.

Fracture : Break in a bone.

Fragmentation : The breaking up of extensive landscape features into disjunct, isolated, or semi-isolated patches as a result of land-use changes.

Frame score : A score based on subjective evaluation of height or actual measurement of hip height. This score is related to slaughter weights at which cattle will grade choice or have comparable amounts of fat cover over the loin eye at the 12th to 13th rib.

Frameshift mutation : A mutation that changes the reading frame of a DNA, either by the insertion or the deletion of nucleotides. Because of the triplet nature of codons, this occurs if the number of nucleotides involved is not a multiple of three.

Free mating : Free mating Also called paddock mating. A single male is introduced with a band of females.

Free on Board (FOB) : The seller's price only includes the cost of the grain up to and including delivery of the goods at the end of the loading spout to an ocean going vessel provided by the buyer at the named port of shipment.

Freeze-dry : The removal of water as vapour from frozen material under vacuum. Used to measure water content and to preserve samples, particularly spores. Unlike oven-drying, bound water remains associated with the specimen.

Frenulum : A piece of tissue that maintains adhesion between the penis and prepuce.

Fresh frozen plasma : Plasma that has been separated from the RBC shortly after blood collection and then frozen. Coagulation factors are preserved in this blood product.

Fresh weight : The weight, including the water content, of a specimen.

Freshening : Parturition, calving.

Frost : The freezing and condensation of moisture in the air. Frost dates are important to know for your zone or area.

Frost hardy : Plants that are able to survive winter frosts without damage to their leaves (i.e. evergreens) or damage to dormant stems, buts or roots (i.e. deciduous plants). Very much relative to geographic areas.

Frost pocket : A depression in the terrain into which cold air drains, but cannot escape.

Frost tender : These plants will be damaged or killed by even the lightest of winter frosts. Most evident would be tropical plants stretched to a cooler zone.

Frozen plasma : Plasma that has been separated from RBC after blood collection but not with the intent of preserving the labile coagulation factors. Used primarily to provide plasma protein in hypoproteiemic patients.

Fruit fly : A small insect pest that will lay its eggs beneath the surface of developing fruits. The larvae will then grow quickly and exit through holes in the fruit or vegetable causing rot.

Fumigation : Application of a pesticide or chemical to a cargo in order to rid the cargo of insects. The most common type of fumigant is phosphine gas, which is applied, in several different methods, to grain while in the elevator or vessel or barge. A firm licensed by the government should handle fumigant, which can be toxic.

Functional food : A foodstuff that provides a health benefit beyond basic nutrition, demonstrating specific health or medical benefits, including the prevention and treatment of disease.

Functional genomics : The field of research, that aims to determine patterns of gene expression and interaction in the genome, based on the knowledge of extensive or complete genomic sequence of an organism.

Fungi : Saprophytic and parasitic organisms that lack chlorophyll and include molds, rusts, mildews, smuts, mushrooms and yeast; singular, fungus.

Fungus : A primitive form of plant life. It is not vascular, and non-photo synthetic organism : powdery mildew, sooty mold, mushrooms.

Fusion protein : A polypeptide translated from a chimeric gene. The different genes are joined so that their coding sequences are in the same reading frame, and the resulting construct is transcribed and translated as a single gene, producing a single protein. These are used for a number of purposes, including: 1) To add an affinity tag to a protein; 2) To produce a protein with the combined characteristics of two natural proteins; 3) To produce a protein where two different activities are physically linked.

Fusion toxin : A fusion protein that consists of a toxic protein domain plus a cell receptor binding domain. The latter delivers the toxin directly to the target cell, thus sparing other healthy tissues from the effect of the toxin.

G

Gametophyte : The phase of the plant life cycle that carries the gamete producing organs. In flowering plants, the pollen grain is the male gametophyte and the embryo sac is the female gametophyte.

Gametophytic incompatibility : A phenomenon in plants, in which a pollen grain is genetically incapable of fertilizing a particular egg, because both gametes carry the identical allele at an incompatibility locus. This is a mechanism for forcing crossfertilization.

Gap : A missing section on one of the strands of double-stranded DNA. The DNA will therefore have a single-stranded region.

Gapped : DNA A double-stranded DNA molecule with one or more internal single-stranded regions.

Garden designer : A person who professionaly will create plans for a home or public space. Many are self-taught, and not generally licensed by the state. Not to be confused with garden architects who are specifically trained and licensed. Garden designers sometimes are referred to as landscape designers.

Gas chromatograph / mass spectrometer : An analytical technique for identifying the molecular composition and concentrations of various chemicals in water and soil samples.

Gas transfer : The rate at which gases are transferred from gas into solution, an important parameter in fermentation systems because it controls the rate at which the organism can metabolize. Efficient gas transfer can be achieved in several ways, including the use of small bubbles, from which gas dissolves faster than from larger ones, due to their larger surface area per unit of volume; or spreading the liquid out, for example in a thin sheet, or in a thin permeable tube, as in hollow fibre bioreactor.

Gasohol : Registered trade name for a blend consisting of 90% unleaded gasoline and 10% fermentation ethanol. Gasohol emissions contain less carbon monoxide than those from gasoline.

Gel : A jelly-like solid, used widely as a matrix for the electrophoresis of macromolecules, for encapsulation, and to solidify media for cell cultures.

Gel filtration : A method of protein or DNA purification, where differences in size are used to separate the components of a complex mixture.

Gelatin : A glutinous, proteinaceous gelling and solidifying agent. Gelatin is produced by the partial hydrolysis (via boiling) of collagen, found in the connective tissues of many farm animals. Used to gel or solidify nutrient solutions for tissue culture, and as a food additive.

Gelatinization : The swelling of starch when added to hot water. Hydrolysis causes the molecule to lose structure, and technically gelatinization is not complete until there is no structure left at all.

Gelding : A castrated male horse.

GelriteTM : The brand name of a Pseudomonas-derived refined polysaccharide used as a gelling agent and agar substitute.

GEM : A genetically engineered microorganism.

Gene (Resources) conservation : The conservation of species, populations, individuals or parts of individuals, by in situ or ex situ methods, to provide a diversity of genetic materials for present and future generations.

Gene : The unit of heredity transmitted from generation to generation during sexual or asexual reproduction. More generally, the term is used in relation to the transmission and inheritance of particular identifiable traits. The simplest gene consists a segment of nucleic acid that encodes an individual protein or RNA.

Gene addition : The addition of a functional copy of a gene to the genome of an organism.

Gene amplification : The presence of multiple genes. Amplification is one mechanism through which proto-oncogenes are activated in malignant cells.

Gene bank : 1. The physical location where collections of genetic material in the form of seeds, tissues or reproductive cells of plants or animals are stored. 2. Field gene bank: A facility established for the ex situ storage and maintenance, using horticultural techniques, of individual plants. Used for species whose seeds are recalcitrant, or for clonally propagated species of agricultural importance, e.g. apple varieties. 3. A collection of cloned DNA fragments from a single genome. Ideally the bank should contain cloned representatives of all the DNA sequences in the genome.

Gene cloning : The synthesis of multiple copies of a chosen DNA sequence using a bacterial cell or another organism as a host. The gene of interest is inserted into a vector, and the resulting recombinant DNA molecule is amplified in an appropriate host cell.

Gene conversion : A process, often associated with recombination, during which one allele is replicated at the expense of another, leading to non-Mendelian segregation ratios.

Gene imprinting : The differential expression of a single gene according to its parental origin.

Gene insertion : The addition of one or more copies of a normal gene into a defective chromosome.

Gene interaction : The modification of the action of one gene by another, non-allelic gene.

Gene linkage : The hereditary association of genes located on the same chromosome.

Gene modification : The chemical repair of a gene's defective DNA sequence.

Gene pool : 1) The sum of all genetic information in a breeding population at a given time. 2) In plant genetic resources, use is made of the terms 'primary', 'secondary' and 'tertiary' gene pools. In general, members of the primary gene pool are inter-fertile; those of the secondary can be crossed with those in the primary gene pool under special circumstances; but to introgress variation from the tertiary gene pool, special techniques are required to achieve crossing.

Gene regulation : The process of controlling the synthesis or suppression of gene products in specific cells or tissues.

Gene replacement : The incorporation of a transgene into a chromosome at its normal location by homologous recombination, thus replacing the copy of the gene originally present at the locus.

Gene splicing : Combining genes from different organisms into one organism.

Gene therapy : The proposed treatment of an inherited disease by the transformation of an affected individual with a wild-type copy of the defective gene causing the disorder. In germ-line (or heritable) gene therapy, reproductive cells are transformed; in somatic-cell (or non-inheritable) gene therapy, cells other than reproductive ones are modified.

Generalized System of Preferences (GSP) : First authorized by the Trade Act of 1974, GSP allows some 140 developing countries to ship more than 3,000 products to the United States duty free. This helps developing countries to generate foreign exchange needed to purchase import commodities. The United States and 18 other industrialized nations began GSP programs in the mid-1970s to promote the economic growth of developing nations.

Generation interval : Average age of the parents when the offspring destined to replace them are born. A generation represents the average rate of turnover of a herd.

Generative nucleus : In many flowering plants, shed pollen is two-celled (in others it is three-celled or has a variable number). Before pollen is shed, the male gametophyte divides mitotically to give a generative and a vegetative nucleus. The former is the progenitor of the sperm cells.

Generic : Of or pertaining to a genus

Generic advertising and promotion : The promotion of a particular commodity without reference to a specific producer, brand name, or manufacturer. Because individual producers of nearly homogeneous agricultural commodities cannot easily convince consumers to choose one egg or orange or a single cut of beef over another, they join together to use generic advertising to expand total demand for the commodity, thereby helping their own sales as well. Activities are intended to expand both domestic and export demand; examples include advertising, nutrition education, research to improve product quality and appeal, market research studies, and technical assistance. These activities are often self-funded through assessments on marketings called check-off programs.

Genes : The basic units of heredity that occur in pairs and have their effect in pairs in the individual, but which are transmitted singly (one or the other gene at random of each pair) from each parent to offspring.

Genet : The individual(s) descended vegetatively from a single sexually produced zygote, including all entities derived from it. All these individuals are genetically identical to one another (barring mutation).

Genetic correlations : Correlations between two traits that arise because some of the same genes affect both traits. When two traits are positively and highly correlated to one another, successful selection for one trait will result in an increase in the other trait. When two traits are negatively and highly correlated to one another, successful selection for one trait will result in a decrease in the other trait.

Genetic disease : A disease that has its origin in changes to the genetic material, DNA. Usually refers to diseases that are inherited in a Mendelian fashion, although noninherited forms of cancer also result from DNA mutation.

Genetic distance : A measure of the genetic similarity between any pair of populations. This is measured on the basis of variation in a combination of phenotypic traits, allele frequencies or DNA sequences. For example, the genetic distance between two populations having the same allele frequencies at a particular locus, and based solely on that locus, is zero.

Genetic diversity : The heritable variation within and among populations which is created, enhanced or maintained by evolutionary or selective forces.

Genetic drift : Change in allele frequency from one generation to another within a population, due to the sampling of finite numbers of genes that is inevitable in all finite-sized populations. The smaller the population, the greater is the genetic drift, with the result that some alleles are lost, and genetic diversity is reduced. Thus minimization of genetic drift is an important consideration for conservation of genetic resources.

Genetic engineering : The genetic modification of organisms by recombinant DNA or other specific molecular gene transfer or exchange techniques. USDA's Agricultural

Research Service does in-house research in this field, and the Animal and Plant Health Inspection Service regulates the release of genetically engineered organisms for field experiments.

Genetic equilibrium : The maintenance of a steady state with respect to allele frequencies in a group of interbreeding organisms.

Genetic erosion : The loss over time of allelic diversity, particularly in farmed organisms, caused by either natural or man-made processes.

Genetic gain : The increase in productivity achieved following a change in gene frequency effected by selection.

Genetic heterogeneity : Occurs where the genetic determination of a given phenotype differs between individuals.

Genetic immunization : Delivery to a host organism of a cloned gene that encodes an antigen. After the cloned gene is expressed, it elicits an antibody response that protects the organism from infection by the relevant pathogen.

Genetic information : Information contained in a nucleotide base sequence in chromosomal DNA or RNA.

Genetic linkage map : A linear map of the relative positions of genes along a chromosome. Distances are established by linkage analysis, which determines the frequency at which two gene loci become separated during chromosomal recombination.

Genetic map : The linear array of genes on a chromosome, based on recombination frequencies (linkage map) or physical location (physical or chromosomal map).

Genetic marker : A DNA sequence used to identify a particular location (locus) on a particular chromosome.

Genetic pollution : Uncontrolled spread of genetic information (frequently referring to transgenes) into the genomes of organisms in which such genes are not present in nature.

Genetic relatedness : A quantitative estimate of the proportion of genes, ®, shared between the genomes of any two individuals, groups or populations, e.g. r = 0.5 for full siblings and parent offspring pairs.

Genetic selection : The process of selecting genes, cells, clones, etc., within populations or between populations or species. Genetic selection usually results in differential survival rates of the various genotypes, reflecting many variables, including the selection pressure and genetic variability present in populations.

Genetic Use Restriction Technology (GURT) : A proposed technology applying transgenesis to genetically compromise the fertility or the performance of saved seed of a cultivar or of second generation animals. The intention is to protect the market for the seed producer or to prevent undesired escape of genes. Two types of GURTs have been patented: variety-level GURT (V-GURT), which produces sterile progeny, and trait-specific GURT (T-GURT), in which only the added value transgenic trait is genetically protected.

Genetically modified food : Foods and food ingredients consisting of or containing genetically modified organisms, or produced from such organisms.

Genetically modified Organism (GMO) : An organism produced from genetic engineering techniques that allow the transfer of functional genes from one organism to another, including from one species to another. Bacteria, fungi, viruses, plants, insects, fish, and mammals are some examples of organisms the genetic material of which has been artificially modified in order to change some physical property or capability. Living modified organisms (LMOs), and transgenic organisms are other terms often used in place of GMOs.

Genetics : The science of heredity.

Genomic library : A clone library specifically constructed from restriction fragments of the genomic DNA of an organism.

Genus : Used when naming plants. Genus is the plant equivalent of our surnames. When followed by the name of the "species" you have it's botanical name. Almost always in Latin.

GEO : Abbreviation for genetically engineered organism.

Geographic coordinate system : A reference system using latitude and longitude to define the locations of points on the surface of a sphere or spheroid.

Geosynchronous satellite : A satellite moving west to east whose orbital period is equal to the earth's rotational period. If the orbit is circular and lies in the plane of the equator, the satellite will remain over one point. Otherwise it will appear to make a figure eight once a day between the latitudes that correspond to its angle of inclination over the equator. The constellation for GPS is geosynchronous.

Germ cell : A member of a cell lineage (the germ line) leading to the production of gametes. In mammals, germ cells are found in the germinal epithelium of the ovaries and testes.

Germ cell gene therapy : The repair or replacement of a defective gene within the gamete-forming tissues, resulting in a heritable change in an organism's genetic constitution.

Germ layer : The layers of cells in an animal embryo at the gastrula stage, from which the various organs of the animal's body will be derived.

Germ line : A lineage of cells which, during the development of an organism, are set aside as potential gamete-forming tissues. The location, nature and time of formation of potential gamete-forming tissues are species specific, and may vary greatly from one species to another.

Germinate : The sprouting of a seed.

Germination : 1) The initial stages in the growth of a seed to form a seedling. 2) The growth of spores (fungal or algal) and pollen grains.

Germplasm : Germplasm is living tissue from which new plants can be grown--seed or another plant part such as a leaf, a piece of stem, pollen or even just a few cells that can be cultured into a whole plant. Germplasm contains the genetic information for the plant's heredity makeup.

Germs : Microscopic organisms that can cause disease. May include bacteria and viruses.

Gestation : The period between conception to parturition (birth) spent in utero by the foetus of viviparous animals.

Gibberellins : A class of plant growth regulators which are active in the elongation, enhancement of flower, fruit and leaf size, germination, vernalization and other physiological processes.

Gilt : Sexually mature female hog, prior to having her first litter.

Gingiva : The gums.

Gingivitis : Inflammation and swelling of the gums surrounding the teeth. The gingiva are normally pink and become red when inflamed.

Girdling : The choking of a branch by a wire, rope, or other inflexible material which usually occurs most often in woody stemmed plants that have been tied down too tightly without regard for growth.

GIS (Geographic information system) : A computer based system that is capable of collecting, managing and analyzing geographic spatial data. This capability includes storing and utilizing maps, displaying the results of data queries and conducting spatial analysis.

Glabrous : Without hair or down.

Glade : An open space in a woodland area.

Gland : A specialized group of cells or a single cell in animals or plants that secretes a specific substance. The two types of animal glands are: endocrine, which secrete directly into the blood vessels; and exocrine, which secrete through a duct or network of ducts into a body cavity or onto the body surface.

Glandular : With glands, secreting organs, often tiny, which usually make the plant sticky.

Glasshouse : our friends the British use this in reference to a greenhouse.

Glaucoma : Increased fluid accumulation in the eye causing increased pressure, pain and leading to blindness if untreated.

Glaucous : A surface with a waxy, white coating. In most cases, this waxy covering can be rubbed off.

Gleaning : Collecting unharvested crops from fields or obtaining unused agricultural products from farmers, processors, or retailers, usually for distribution to food banks and charitable feeding organizations.

Glen : A very romantic term meaning a narrow valley.

Globulins : Common class of proteins in blood, eggs and milk, and seeds. Characterized by their slight solubility in water but are freely soluble in dilute salt solutions. Gamma-globulins are defined further by their electrophoretic behaviour, and include the immunoglobulins.

Glochids : Tiny, still hairs with barbs found in cacti. Don't let them get you.

Glomerular basement Membrane (GBM) : One component of the filtration barrier of the glomerulous, interposed between the lumen of the glomerular capillary and the urinary space.

Glomerular Filtration rate (GFR) : The rate at which the glomeruli form filtrate from blood in glomerular capillaries. GFR correlates with renal function and to renal blood flow. Kidney disease and dehydration both result in a decrease in GFR.

Glomerulonephropathy (GN) : Disease that begins in the glomerulus.

Glomerulus : The microscopic functional unit of the kidney. Disease of the glomeruli causes protein to leak into the urine.

Glucocorticoid : A general term for drugs that act like the hormone, cortisol. Also called a corticosteroid.

Glucose invertase : An enzyme that catalyses the hydrolysis of sucrose into its component monosaccharides, glucose and fructose.

Glucose isomerase : An enzyme that catalyses the interconversion of the two sugars, glucose and fructose. As fructose is a lower energy compound compared with glucose, a mixture of glucose and fructose with the enzyme will end up almost entirely as fructose.

Glucosinolates : A class of molecules produced in the seeds and green tissue of a range of plants, in particular brassicas. Their natural role is thought to be involved in plant-insect interactions. Their importance in plant breeding is largely because of their negative influence on taste and their positive effect on the prevention of cancers of the alimentary tract.

Gluten : A mixture of two seed storage protein classes, gliadin and glutenin, found in the endosperm of cereal (particularly wheat) grain. High levels of gluten impart elasticity to dough, and thus the composition of wheat glutens largely determines whether a specific flour is suitable for biscuit or bread making. Sensitivity of the lining of the intestine to gluten in some humans results in coeliac disease, a condition that requires a gluten-free diet.

Glycoalkaloids : A group of modified alkaloids, including solanine and tomatine, having a range of toxic effects in humans and other species. They are of particular significance in food plants from the Solanaceae.

Glycoform : One of several structures possible for a given glycoprotein, determined by the type and position of attachment of the component oligosaccharide(s). Certain glycoforms may exhibit different biological activities from one another because the oligosaccharide units mediate interactions with other cell components.

Glycolysis : The sequence of reactions that converts glucose into pyruvate, with the concomitant production of ATP.

Glycoprotein : A protein molecule modified by the addition of one or several oligosaccharide groups.

Glycoprotein remodelling : The use of restriction endoglycosidases to enzymatically remove oligosaccharide branches from glycoprotein molecules. Removal of one or more oligosaccharide branches can lessen or abolish the antigenicity of the glycoprotein, so allowing its injection for pharmaceutical purposes without incurring an unwanted immune response.

Glycosylation : The covalent addition of sugar or sugar-related molecules to other classes of molecule, including proteins or nucleic acids.

Glyphosate : An active ingredient in some herbicides, killing plants by inhibiting the activity of plant enolpyruvyl-shikimate 3-phosphate synthase.

Golden rice : A biotechnology-derived rice, which contains large amounts of beta carotene (a precursor of vitamin A) in its seeds. Achieved by inserting two genes from daffodil and one from the bacterium Erwinia uredovora.

Golgi apparatus : An assembly of vesicles and folded membranes within the cytoplasm of plant and animal cells that stores and transports secretory products (such as enzymes and hormones) and plays a role in formation of a cell wall (when this is present).

Gonad : One of the (usually paired) animal organs that produce reproductive cells (gametes). The most important gonads are the male testis, which produces spermatozoa, and the female ovary, which produces ova (egg cells). The gonads also produce hormones that control secondary sexual characteristics.

Gonadotropin Releasing Hormone (GNRH) : This hormone is secreted from the hypothalamus and stimulates the release of follicle stimulating and luteinising hormones (FSH/LH) from the pituitary gland. LH is believed to be involved in testicular descent into the scrotum.

Gonioscopy : A technique used to evaluate the iridocorneal angle to help judge the risk for glaucoma in an eye.

Good Laboratory Practice (GLP) : Written codes of practice designed to reduce to a minimum the chance of procedural or instrument problems which could adversely affect a research project or other laboratory work.

Good manufacturing Practice (GMP) : Codes of practice designed to reduce to a minimum the chance of procedural or instrument/manufacturing plant problems which could adversely affect a manufactured product.

GPCP : Great Plains Conservation Program

GPRA : Government Performance and Results Act

GPS (Global Positioning system) : Global Positioning System is a constellation of 24 satellites, developed by the U.S. Department of Defense, which are used to calculate your position anywhere on earth.

Grade : Not your A, B, C's in class, but the degree or direction of a slope, generally. Real important with house construction and ground placement.

Grade A milk : Milk produced under sufficiently sanitary conditions to qualify for fluid (beverage) consumption. Also referred to as fluid grade milk. Only Grade A milk is regulated under federal milk marketing orders. Grade B milk (also referred to as manufacturing grade) does not meet fluid grade standards and is used only in manufactured products. More than 90% of all milk produced nationally is Grade A. Therefore, much of the Grade A milk supply is used in manufactured dairy products.

Grade A pasteurized milk ordinance : Minimum standards and requirements for Grade A milk production and processing are outlined in the Grade A Pasturized Milk Ordinance (PMO) published by the Food and Drug Administration. Grade A standards are recommended by the National Conference on Interstate Milk Shipments (NCIMS), which is comprised of voting representatives from state and local regulatory agencies, and non-voting representatives of the dairy industry and FDA. As a general rule, FDA accepts the Conference recommendations and incorporates them into the revised PMO. The state regulator (which is usually either the State Department of Agriculture or the State Health Department) adopts the PMO standards as a minimum, and in many cases requires more stringent standards.

Grade cow : A cow that is not registered.

Grades and standards ; The segregation, or classification, of agricultural commodities into groupings that share common characteristics. Grades provide a common 'trading language,' or common reference, so that buyers and sellers can more easily determine the quality (and therefore value) of those commodities.

Grading certificates : A formal document setting forth the quality of a commodity as determined by authorized inspectors or graders.

Graft 1 : Verb. To place a detached branch or bud (scion) in close cambial contact with a rooted stem (rootstock) in such a manner that scion and rootstock unite to form a single plant. 2. Noun.

Graft chimera : A plant which is a mosaic of two sorts of tissue differing in genetic constitution and assumed to have arisen as the result of a nuclear fusion following grafting.

Graft hybrid : An individual formed from graft (2) and stock showing the characteristics of both progenitors.

Graft inoculation test : A test based on the use of a suspected viral carrier which is grafted to an indicator plant. If symptoms appear in the indicator plant, the viral assay is positive.

Graft union : The point at which a scion from one plant is joined to a rootstock from another plant.

Grafting : This is a method of propagation. The process of joining a desirable stem or bud of one plant (known as the scion) on to the less desirable, but hardier, stem of another (known as the stock). This will give a stronger root system than the scion would have normally had. Commonly done in roses, fruit trees and in some ornamentals.

Graft-versus-host disease : The rejection of transplanted organs by the recipient's immune system, due to attack of the recipient's T lymphocytes on the transplanted organ caused by differences in major histocompatibility complex proteins.

Grain cubic : The capacity of a vessel, measured in cubic feet available for cargo shipped in bulk which is free to flow between the frames and beams.

Grain flow dynamics : Refers to the grain flow through the harvest machine. Grain flow dynamics result in errors relating to grain mixing, delayed measurement and resulting positional errors in yield mapping systems.

Grain reserve : A phrase that might refer to the food security commodity reserve, food security wheat reserve, the farmer-owned grain reserve, or the strategic grain reserve.

Gram staining : A technique to distinguish between two major bacterial groups, based on whether or not their cell wall retains the Gram stain. Gram-positive bacteria are stained dark purple, while Gram-negative bacteria are only faintly coloured. Stain retention is determined by the structure of the cell wall.

Granular fertilizer : A fertilizer that is dry and is a tiny pellet form. It is spreadable and should be measured. A granular fertilizer can come in both a natural and synthetic form.

Granum : Structure within the chloroplasts, appear as green granules with the light microscope and as a series of parallel lamellae with the electron microscope. They contain the chlorophyll and carotenoid pigments directly involved in photosynthesis.

GRAS : Generally Recognized As Safe

Grasscycling : Leaving grassclippings on your lawn to break down and add nutrients. You must mow a little more often so only short clippings are left on the lawn. Take a look at the City of Seattle's Natural Lawn Care site.

Grassed waterway : A generally broad and shallow depression planted with erosion-resistant grasses, which is used to convey surface waters off of or across cropland.

Grasshoppers : Many varieties throughout the state. Problem on New Mexico rangeland because the insects eat grass.

Gratuitous inducer : A substance that can induce transcription of a gene or genes, but is not a substrate for the induced enzyme(s).

Grazing permit/License/Lease : Official written permission to graze a specific number, kind, and class of livestock for a specified time period on defined federal rangeland.

Grazing preference : The status of qualified holders of grazing permits acquired by grant, prior use, or purchase, that entitles them to special consideration over applicants who have not acquired preference.

Grazing privilege : The benefit or advantage enjoyed by a person or company beyond the common advantage of other citizens to graze livestock on federal lands. Privilege may be created by permit, license, lease, or agreement.

Greasy wool : The wool as it comes off the sheep. It contains yolk (wool grease lanolin) suint (sweat) and dirt and vegetable fiber.

Green box : Domestic or trade policies that are deemed to be minimally trade-distorting and that are excluded from reduction commitments in the Uruguay Round Agreement on Agriculture. Examples are domestic policies dealing with inspection and grading, environmental and conservation programs, disaster relief, crop insurance, domestic food assistance, and direct payments not linked to production. Trade measures or policies such as export market promotion are also exempt.

Green Fluorescent Protein (GFP) : A protein derived from a species of jelly fish, that fluoresces when exposed to ultra violet light.

Green manure : A crop (such as rye grass) that is grown and then incorporated into the soil to increase soil fertility or organic matter content. Usually turned over into the soil a few weeks before new planting begins.

Green revolution : Name given to the dramatic increase in crop productivity during the third quarter of the 20th century, as a result of integrated advances in genetics and plant breeding, agronomy, and pest and disease control.

Greenhouse : A house that is green. One would think, but this is a structure that can be build out of glass, plastic, or fiberglass. This building will be controlled in its temperature and humidity. Greenhouses are used for public display, cultivation, and in general protection of plants. Greenhouse comes in hobby sizes and as commercial usage.

Greenhouse effect : The hypothesized warming of the Earth's atmosphere as a result of increasing atmospheric levels of carbon dioxide and other gases that trap infrared radiation emitted from the earth's surface. While the increase in such gases is well documented, the effect on climate remains debatable. Estimates of the temperature effect range from zero to an increase of several degrees average global temperature by 2050; changes in temperature would affect rainfall patterns. Significant climate change would inevitably affect agricultural practices.

Greens : The term "greens" is used to denote organic materials high in nitrogen, more specifically, materials whose carbon to nitrogen ratio is lower than 30:1. Achieving a carbon-to-nitrogen ratio of about 30:1 is one factor in creating favorable conditions for backyard pile composting.

Greensand : A sediment composed of grains of glauconite mingled with clay or sand used as an organic fertilizer. It contains about twenty-two trace minerals including potash, silica, iron oxide, magnesia, lime, and phosphoric acid. Mined in Florida, once the ocean floor. Roses and tomatoes love it. The material will prolong fruiting and loosen heavy clay soils.

Gregarious : Growing together in clusters or colonies

Grex : A Latin word meaning "group" or. "flock"; the name used to describe a group of offspring of any given hybrid cross. When a grex name is registered, All additional identical crosses, plants produced from seeds of that cross or any asexual divisions of the cross all have the same grex name.

Griseofulvin : Oral treatment for dermatophytes.

Gro-luxä : A wide-spectrum fluorescent lamp suitable for artificial light for plant growth.

Gross Domestic Product (GDP) : Gross domestic product is a measure of the total production and consumption of goods and services in the United States. The Bureau of Economic Analysis constructs two complementary measures of GDP, one based on income and one based on expenditures. It is measured on the product side by adding up the labor, capital, and tax costs of producing the output. On the expenditure side, GDP is measured by adding up expenditures by households, businesses, government and net foreign purchases. Theoretically, these two measures should be equal. However, due to problems collecting data, there is often a discrepancy between the two measures. The GDP price deflator is used to convert output measured at current prices into constant-dollar GDP.

Gross farm income : The monetary and non-monetary income received by farm operators. Its main components include cash receipts from the sale of farm products, government payments, other farm income (such as income from custom work), value of food and fuel produced and consumed on the same farm, rental value of farm dwellings, and change in value of year-end inventories of crops and livestock.

Gross National Product (GNP) : A measure of the market value of goods and services produced by the labor and property of a nation. Includes receipts from that nation's business operations in foreign countries, as well as the share of reinvested earnings in foreign affiliates of domestic corporations.

Gross Processing Margin (GPM) : This refers to the difference between the cost of a commodity and the combined sales income of the finished products that result from processing the commodity. Various industries have formulas to express the relationship of raw material costs to sales income from finished products.

Growing habit : A direction or shape a plant takes as it grows.

Growing point : The area where the new growth occurs. When a plant is pinched and the new shoots then develop, this is the growing point.

Growing season : The time period, usually measured in days, between the last freeze in the spring and the first frost in the fall. Varies for crops as different plants have different freezing thresholds. It also is an important component in defining wetland areas.

Growth cabinet : An enclosed space in which environmental conditions can be controlled. The degree of control over temperature, light and humidity is a function of the quality of the cabinet.

Growth inhibitor : Any substance inhibiting the growth of an organism. The inhibitory effect can range from mild inhibition (growth retardation) to severe inhibition or death (toxic reaction). The concentration of the inhibitor, the length of exposure to it, and the relative susceptibility of the organisms exposed to the inhibitor, are all important factors which determine the extent of the inhibitory effect.

Growth phase (Curve) : The characteristic periods in the growth of a bacterial culture, as indicated by the shape of a graph of viable cell number versus time.

Growth rate : Change in an organism's mass per unit of time.

Growth substance : Any organic substance, other than a nutrient, that is synthesized by plants and regulates growth and development. They are usually made in a particular region, such as the shoot tip, and transported to other regions, where they take effect.

Grub : Short, fat, worm-like larva, especially of beetles.

Guanine (G) : One of the bases found in DNA and RNA.

Guano : Manure, i.e., excretions, of bats and birds. Can be purchased after being dried and composted.

Guanosine : The (ribo)nucleoside resulting from the combination of the base guanine (G) and a D-ribose sugar. The corresponding deoxyribonucleoside is called deoxyguanosine.

Guaranteed export credit : A Commodity Credit Corporation guarantee of commercial export credit is available through several export credit guarantee programs.

Guard cell : Specialized epidermal cells found in pairs around a stoma. Their function is to control the opening and closing of the stoma through changes in turgor.

GUS : Abbreviation for beta-glucuronidase.

Gus gene : An E. coli gene that encodes for production of beta-glucuronidase (GUS). Because this activity is absent in plants, the gene is commonly utilized as a reporter gene to detect the occurrence of transformation events.

Gymnosperm : A class of plant (e.g. conifers) whose ovules and the seeds into which they develop are borne unprotected, rather than enclosed in ovaries, as are those of the flowering plants, the (angiosperms).

Gynandromorph : An individual in which one part of the body is female and another part is male; a sex mosaic.

Gynogenesis : Female parthenogenesis: after fertilization of the ovum, the male nucleus is eliminated and the haploid (gynogenetic) individual possesses the maternal genome only.

H

Hairy root culture : A culture consisting of highly branched roots of a plant. A plant tissue is treated with the bacterium Agrobacterium rhizogenes containing the Ri plasmid, which causes the explant to grow highly branched roots from the sites of infection. Transgenes engineered into the plasmid can be expressed in these cultures.

Hairy root disease : A disease of broad-leaved plants, where a proliferation of root-like tissue is formed from the stem. Hairy root disease is a tumorous state similar to crown gall, and is induced by the bacterium Agrobacterium rhizogenes, when containing an Ri plasmid.

Half-hardy : Just as the word depicts, not completely hardy. Good examples re pansies, snapdragons, sweet alyssum. They will tolerate some light frost and cold nights.

Half-sibs : Individuals having the same sire or dam. Half-brothers and/or half-sisters.

Halophyte : A plant species adapted to soils containing a concentration of salt that is toxic to most plant species.

Hand breeding : Also called hand mating. The females are completely supervised during the mating process and the male is led to the female and controlled during the breeding process.

Handler : Generally, the first buyer of a farmer's commodity destined for fresh market use (in contrast to processing).

Under marketing orders, handlers are defined as anyone who receives the commodity from producers, grades and packs it, and sells it to someone else for further marketing. Usually, the requirements spelled out in marketing orders technically apply to handlers, although producers absorb their effects.

Handy vessel : Is a type of ocean vessel with cargo capacities between 20,000 to 40,000 metric tons. The handy-sized vessels are used to service shallow water ports that have lower draft restrictions and for lower volume trade routes.

Haploid : A cell or organism containing one of each of the pairs of homologous chromosomes found in the normal diploid cell.

Haploid cell : A cell containing only one set, or half the usual (diploid) number, of chromosomes.

Hardening off : Adapting glasshouse or controlled environment grown plants to outdoor conditions by reducing availability of water, lowering the temperature, increasing light intensity, or reducing the nutrient supply. The hardening-off process conditions plants for survival when transplanted outdoors.

Hardiness : When a plant has the ability to withstand low temperatures or frost.

Hard-pad disease : Crusty, dry footpads that may occur as a consequence of canine distemper infection.

Hardpan : Compacted soil, sometimes new, created by construction. Water will run off and plant roots can not penetrate the layer. Can be broken up.

Hardscape : Includes any garden feature that is not a plant. Like birdbaths, deck, fences, trellises, benches, and patios.

Hardwood : A term describing broadleaf trees, usually deciduous, such as oaks, maples, cottonwood, ashes, and elms.

Hardwood cutting : A mature, woody piece of a woody plant that is removed to asexually propagate a new individual plant.

Harvested acres : The cropland actually harvested for a particular crop, usually somewhat smaller at the national level than planted acres due to weather damage or abandonment because of low market prices.

Harvesting : Removing compost from the composting environment for use in the landscape, lawn or garden.

Hastate : Spear shaped, with the basal lobe turned outward

Hay : Stems of grass. Most popular feed for horses and cattle, however gardeners are always looking for "spoiled hay" or "mulch hay". This is hay that has rotted or gotten moldy. It is great for compost piles and using as a mulch. Beware of weed seeds and compost well.

Hay additives : Organic acids or acid-forming compounds designed to allow hay to be harvested at higher than normal moisture contents by preventing the microbial activity responsible for spoilage.

Hazard : The likelihood or the probability that a substance, i.e., the poison, will induce a disease state under conditions of use.

Hazard Analysis And Critical Control Point (HACCP) : A production quality control system now being adopted throughout much of the food industry as a method for minimizing the entry of foodborne pathogens into the food supply in order to protect human health. Under a HACCP system, potential hazards are identified and risks are analyzed in each phase of production; critical control points for preventing such hazards are identified and constantly monitored; and corrective actions are taken when necessary.

Hazmat : Hazardous materials

Headwaters : The source, or upper part, of a stream. Often used in discussing water rights related to wilderness or other federal land designations.

Heart rot : most commonly heard of in reference to trees. The center merely has rotted out. Can also happen in root vegetables.

Heat : Period of fertility when the cow is receptive to the male. It only lasts 24 hours in the bovine.

Heat Shock Protein (HSP) : A class of protein chaperones which are typically over-expressed as a response to heat stress. Two such proteins - HSP 90 and HSP 70 - have a role in ensuring that crucial proteins are folded into the correct conformation.

Heat synchronization : Causing a group of cows or heifers to exhibit heat together at one time by artificial manipulation of the estrous cycle.

Heave : The partial lifting of a plant out of the soil as a result of alternating freezing and thawing of the soil.

Heaving : When there is a climate change from frost to warming of the soil, it often causes the soil to buckle upward. Sometimes called frost heaves.

Heavy metals : The heavy metals of concern to gardeners are lead, zinc, nickel, arsenic, copper and cadmium. These metals can be toxic to plants when they accumulate to high levels in the soil.

Hectare : A metric unit of area equal to 10,000 square meters, or 2,471 acres.

Hedge : Suitable trees, shrubs, or bushes planted relatively close together so that the branches will intertwine to provide a barrier fence for a windbreaker or privacy. Hedges can be any height or width depending on the plant material used. Generally they are long lived species.

Hedge row : Just as it reads - a row of plant material (shrubs and trees) that are suitable for hedges.

Heifer : Young bovine female starting her first lactation having calved for the first time. Age at first calving should be 2 years.

Heirloom plant : Plants that have been around for 50 years or more. Not all people will consider the same plant an heirloom.

Heirloom vegetables : Cultivars that were popular a generation or more ago.

HEL : Highly-Erodible Land

Helix : A structure with a spiral shape. The normal state of double-stranded DNA is in the form of a double helix.

Helminth : A class of parasitic worms, especially those which are internal parasites of man and animals.

Helper cell : T cells that assist in stimulating B and T lymphocytes to develop into antibody-producing plasma cells and killer T cells, respectively.

Helper plasmid : A plasmid that provides a function or functions to another plasmid in the same cell.

Helper virus : A virus that provides a function or functions to another virus in the same cell.

Hemangiosarcoma : A cancer of blood vessels. This cancer usually occurs in the spleen, skin or sometimes the heart.

Hematology : The study of blood.

Hemizygous : The condition in which genes are present only once in the genotype and not in pairs. Occurs for all genes in haploids, for all genes located in the differential segments of the sex chromosomes in diploids, and in various aneuploids and deletion mutant heterozygotes.

Hemocytometer : A piece of equipment that is used to count white blood cells and can also be used to count sperm.

Hemoglobin : The substance contained in red blood cells that carries oxygen to parts of the body.

Hemostat : A surgical instrument used to pinch small blood vessels to stop bleeding (hemostasis is to stop bleeding). Hemastats may be used in non-surgical procedures, for example to pluck hair from the ear canals.

HEPA filter : Abbreviation for high efficiency particulate air filter. A filter capable of excluding particles larger than 0.3ìm. HEPA filters are used in laminar air flow cabinets to ensure that the air is pathogen-free.

Hepatitis : Inflammation of the liver.

Herb : A plant grown for its medicinal or flavoring qualities, or its scented foliage.

Herbaceous : A plant with a non-woody stem. The upper parts will die back at the end of the growing season. It generally refers to perennials. Gertrude Jekyll invented the term.

Herbicide resistance : The ability of a plant to remain unaffected by the application of a herbicide.

Herbicide-Tolerant (HT) crops : The insertion of a herbicide tolerant gene enables farmers to spray wide-spectrum herbicides on their fields killing all the plants but the HT crop. . The most common herbicide-tolerant crops (cotton, corn, soybeans, and canola) are tolerant to glyphosateand to glufosinate-ammonium, which are the active ingredients of common wide spectrum herbicides. There are also HT rapeseed and cotton which are tolerant to bromoxynil.

Herbivores : Macroorganisms that eat plants. Includes insect and beetle larva, grub, mouse, slug, snail, termite, woodchuck.

Herd summary : Summary statistics for herd production, reproduction, health, and demographic factors.

Hermaphrodism : A condition where reproductive structures of both the male and the female are in one body.

Hermaphrodite : 1) An animal that has both male and female reproductive organs, or a mixture of male and female attributes. 2) A plant whose flowers contain both stamen and carpels.

Hernia : The abnormal protrusion of part of an organ or tissue through the structures that normally contain it. Also called a rupture.

Hetastarch : A colloid solution of hydrolyzed amylopectin containing a range of particle sizes, from 10,000 daltons to over 3 million daltons.

Heteroduplex analysis : The use of the electrophoretic mobility of heteroduplex DNA to estimate the degree of non-homology between the sequences of the two strands. Gel mobility tends to be reduced as the amount of sequence divergence increases, because the effective size of a fully complementary pair of strands is smaller than that of a partially complementary structure.

Heterogametic : Producing unlike gametes with regard to the sex chromosomes. In mammals, the XY male is heterogametic, and the XX female is homogametic.

Heterogeneous Nuclear RNA (hnRNA) : Large RNA molecules, which are found in the nucleus of a eukaryotic cell and the precursors of mRNA and other RNA molecules.

Heteroploid : Cells with nuclei containing chromosome numbers other than diploid.

Heteropyknosis : The property of certain chromosomes, or of their parts, to remain more dense during the cell cycle and to stain more intensely than other chromosomes or parts.

Heterosis (Hybrid vigor) : Amount by which measured traits of the crossbreds exceed the average of the two or more purebreds that are mated to produce the crossbreds.

Heterotroph : Organism non capable of self-nourishment utilizing carbon dioxide or carbonates as the sole source of carbon and obtaining energy from radiant energy or from the oxidation of inorganic elements, or compounds such as iron, sulphur, hydrogen, ammonium and nitrites.

High Oil Corn (HOC) : Corn varieties that contain a higher oil content than typical yellow feed corn.

High shade : Always a difficult gauge but generally it is the shade beneath trees that have been "limbed up" or pruned to get some light in.

High throughput screening : Automated systems designed to process large numbers of assays, especially in the context of genotyping.

High/Low string : High/low producing cows are split into feeding groups to optimize ration inputs for milk output.

High-Fructose Corn Syrup (HFCS) : Produced from converting to fructose a portion of naturally occurring glucose in starch produced from corn. A natural sweetener, HFCS production expanded during the 1980s as a substitute for higher-cost sugar used in soft drinks. HFCS-55 (55% fructose), which is as sweet as sugar, has almost completely replaced liquid sugar in beverages. HFCS-42 (42% fructose) is roughly 90% as sweet as sugar, and is mainly used in cereal, baking, dairy, and processed foods.

Highly Erodible Land (HEL) : Land that is very susceptible to erosion, including fields that have at least 1/3 or 50 acres of soils with a natural erosion potential of at least 8 times their 'T' level. More than 140 million acres are classified as HEL. Farms cropping highly erodible land and under production flexibility contract must be in compliance with a conservation plan that protects this cropland.

Hill planting : Grouping plants in a cluster, not necessarily on an elevated mound.

Hill up : It sounds like an old fashion term but means to pull the soil around the stem of a plant for support.

Histone : Group of water-soluble proteins rich in basic amino acids, closely associated with DNA in plant and animal chromatin. Histones are involved in the coiling of DNA in chromosomes and in the regulation of gene activity.

HLA : Abbreviation for human-leukocyte-antigen system.

hnRNA : Abbreviation for heterogeneous nuclear RNA.

Hog/Corn ratio (Corn-hog ratio) : Number of bushels of corn equal in value to 100 pounds of live hogs (feed ratio). Put another way, the price of hogs, per hundredweight, divided by the price of corn per bushel. Since corn is a major input cost to hog producers, the higher the price of hogs relative to corn, the more profit there is in feeding hogs.

Hollow fibre : A tube of porous material, with an internal diameter of a fraction of a millimetre, making its ratio of surface area to internal volume very large. Employed as filters or in bioreactors as a method of retaining cells while allowing the easy removal of spent medium and/or products.

Holometabolous : An insect that undergoes complete metamorphosis to the adult from a morphologically distinct larval stage.

Home range : The area within which the activities of an animal are confined. The boundaries may be marked, such as by scent marking, and also may be defended, depending on the species.

Homeobox : A highly conserved 180 bp DNA sequence that controls body part-, organ- or tissue-specific gene expression, most particularly involved in segmentation in animals (e.g. development of antennae or legs of Drosophila melanogaster), but also in a variety of other eukaryotes. It encodes a DNA-binding region, the homeodomain, which acts as a transcription factor.

Homodimer : A protein comprising two identical polypeptide chains, or a dimer of identical residues.

Homoduplex : DNA A double-stranded fully complementary DNA molecule.

Homoeologous : Referring to chromosomes which are descended from a common progenitor, but which have evolved to be no longer fully homologous. Homoeologous chromosomes have similar gene content to one another, but are structurally altered in subtle ways to inhibit, and sometimes completely prevent their pairing with one another at meiosis.

Homogametic : Producing similar gametes with regard to the sex chromosomes. In mammals, the female is homogametic (XX), and the male is heterogametic (XY).

Homogenization : The process of physically reducing the particle size of fat in milk, thus enabling even distribution of fat throughout the milk.

Homologous chromosomes : Chromosomes that have the same linear arrangement of genes--a pair of matching chromosomes in a diploid organism.

Homologous recombination : The exchange of DNA fragments between two DNA molecules or chromatids of paired chromosomes (during crossing over) at the site of identical nucleotide sequences.

Homology : 1) The degree of identity between individuals, or characters. 2) The degree of identity of sequence (nucleotide or amino acid) between a number of DNA or polypeptide molecules.

Homomultimer : A protein consisting of a number of identical subunits.

Homonym : A taxonomic designation rejected because the identical term has been used to disignate another group of the same rank.

Homoplasmy : The condition in which all copies of an organelle in a cell are genetically identical.

Homopolymer : A polymer (nucleic acid, polypeptide, etc.) which contains only one kind of residue.

Homozygote : An individual that has two copies of the same allele for a given gene on its two homologous chromosomes. The condition is termed "homozygous".

Homozygous : Genes of a specific pair (alleles) are alike in an individual.

Honey dew : The sweet and sticky syrup secreted by aphids and other sap-sucking insects. It then sometimes gets moldy fungus on it. Should be washed off with a soapy water rinse.

Horizontal transmission : Disease transmission from one animal to another.

Hormone : A specific chemical, produced in one part of a plant or animal body, and transported to another part where, at low concentrations, it promotes, inhibits or quantitatively modifies a biological process.

Horn fly : Small black fly that is a blood-sucking pest of cattle.

Horner's syndrome : Loss of sympathetic innervation resulting in miosis, ptosis and enopthalmos.

Horticulture : The art and science of gardening. Commercial horticulture would include fruit, flower and small scale vegetable growing including the nursery industry. Agriculture covers broad acre farming of plants.

Host-specific toxin : A metabolite, produced by a pathogen, and which is responsible for the adverse effects of the pathogen. The toxin has a host specificity equivalent to that of the pathogen. Utilized for in vitro selection experiments to screen for tolerance or resistance to the pathogen.

Hot cap : Cones that are used a lot in cooler zones to protect newly planted seedlings from cold weather and birds. Usually made of plastic or a very heavy translucent waxed paper.

Hot composting, hot pile : Optimum conditions for compost piles, including 30:1 Carbon-to-Nitrogen ratio, 1" or smaller particles of various sizes and textures, moisture, air, volume of 3 cubit feet, produce an environment that will attract psychrophilic, mesophyllic, and then thermophilic bacteria. As the thermophilic bacteria work, the compost pile will reach as high as 170 degrees F. This is the fastest method of creating compost from a backyard pile, and can take as little as 3 weeks if the pile is monitored and turned each time the temperature starts to fall.

Hot house : Another term for a greenhouse sometimes found in earlier garden writings.

Hot nursery : A nursery where piglets are raised until they are 4 weeks old and the ambient temperature is very warm.

Hot spot : Acute moist dermatitis or pyotraumatic dermatitis. A surface pyoderma.

Hotbed : A bed of soil enclosed by a structure with a top of glass, heated, often by manure, for forcing or raising seedlings.

Hotz- celsus technique : A surgical procedure for correction of lower lid entropion.

Hotz-celsus : A surgical technique used to repair entropion.

House fly : A two-winged fly that can carry many diseases. Problem in the state's dairies.

House plants : Plants that are grown in containers inside the home.

Household (Foodstamp) : A food stamp household is composed of all those who purchase food and prepare meals in common. All related co-residents must apply as a single food stamp household, no matter how they purchase and prepare food : except for elderly persons who are medically certified as unable to purchase and prepare meals separately. Other co-residents may apply separately if they purchase and prepare food separately, and residents in certain eligible institutional settings (e.g., shelters for battered women, residential drug treatment programs) may apply as separate households no matter how they purchase and prepare food.

HSI : Habitat suitability index

Human albumin : A colloidal solution prepared from pooled human plasma and heated to kill many types of blood borne diseases.

Human Artificial Chromosome (HAC) : Analogous to yeast artificial chromosome, a construct comprising a human centromere and telomeres, which would allow for the cloning of very large fragments of DNA, and their transfer into human cells for the purpose of gene therapy. Not yet established as a working technology, although some partial success has been reported.

Human Chorionic Gonadotropin stimulation test (HCG stimulation) : A stimulation test which measures testosterone in response to HCG administration. Used to detect retained testicles.

Human genome project : A project coordinated by the National Institutes of Health (NIH) and the Department of Energy (DOE) to determine the entire nucleotide sequence of the human chromosomes.

Human Growth hormone (HGH, somatotrophin) : A protein produced in the pituitary gland that stimulates the liver to produce somatomedins, which stimulate growth of bone and muscle.

Humidity : The amount of moisture in the air.

Humoral : Immunity mediated via antibody.

Humoral immunity : Antibody produced by the B-cells to fight a specific antigen.

Humus : Decomposed organic matter. Healthy soil will consist of about 3.5 to 5% of this organic matter. Humus is soft, sweet-smelling, shapeless dark and crumbly and smells like the forest floor (more correctly, the forest floor smells like humus because that is what is naturally there). It is this stage of the decomposition process which provides nutrients for plant life. It contains about 30% each of lignin, protein, and complex sufars. It contains 3 - 5% nitrogen and 55 - 60% carbon. Humus is the slow-release food source for microorganism development. It is constantly being transformed into acids, enzymes and minerals and, therefore, must be constantly replenished for proper vegetative nutrition.

Hybrid arrested translation : A method used to identify what protein(s) are encoded by a particular cloned DNA sequence. A total mRNA preparation, which contains many different mRNAs, is hybridized with cloned DNA, so that those mRNA molecules homologous to the cloned DNA will anneal to give DNA/RNA heteroduplexes. The non-annealed mRNA molecules can be translated in vitro and this is then compared to translation products from the untreated mRNAs.

Hybrid dysgenesis : Infertility and an increased incidence of chromosome mutations thought to be caused by the activation of transposons.

Hybrid released translation : A method used to identify the gene product of a cloned gene. The cloned DNA is immobilized and hybridized with a mixed mRNA sample, so that only mRNA sequences homologous to the cloned DNA will be retained. These mRNA molecules are subsequently removed and translated in vitro.

Hybrid seed : 1) Seed produced by crossing genetically dissimilar parents. 2) In plant breeding, used colloquially for seed produced by specific crosses of selected pure lines, such that the F1 crop is genetically uniform and displays hybrid vigour. As the F1 plants are heterozygous with respect to many genes, the crop does not breed true and so new seed must be purchased each season.

Hybrid selection : The process of choosing individuals possessing desired characteristics from among a hybrid population.

Hybrid vigour : The extent to which a hybrid individual outperforms both its parents with respect to one or many traits. The genetic basis of hybrid vigour is not well understood, but the phenomenon is widespread, particularly in inbreeding plant species.

Hybridization : 1. The process of forming a hybrid by cross pollination of plants or by mating animals of different types. 2. The production of offspring of genetically different parents, normally from sexual reproduction, but also asexually by the fusion of protoplasts or by transformation. 3. The pairing of two DNA strands, often from different sources, by hydrogen bonding between complementary nucleotides.

Hybridoma : A synthetic hybrid cell, derived by fusing a B lymphocyte with a tumour cell. The former secretes a single antibody, while the latter confers the property of growing indefinitely in tissue culture. The underlying technology behind the monoclonal antibody.

Hydric soil : Soil that, in its undrained state, is flooded long enough during a growing season to develop anaerobic conditions that support the growth and regeneration of hydrophytic vegetation.

Hydrocephalous : The accumulation of fluid in the ventricles of the brain. The head may appear to be large and dome shaped. Many small breeds of dogs have a degree of hydrocephalous that is normal for the breed. Severe hydrocephalous damages brain tissue.

Hydrogen bond : A relatively weak bond formed between a hydrogen atom (which is covalently bound to a nitrogen or oxygen atom) and a nitrogen or oxygen with an unshared electron pair.

Hydrolysis : A chemical reaction in which water is added across a covalent bond, often cleaving the molecule into two. Occurs for example when polynucleotides, polypeptides, and polysaccharides are broken into their component monomers. Thus sucrose can be hydrolysed to glucose and fructose; and proteins to individual amino acids.

Hydrolyzed : Breaking a compound into smaller and simpler compounds by a chemical reaction with water.

Hydrophobic interaction : An interaction between a hydrophobic ('water-hating') part of a molecule and an aqueous environment. Particularly significant in establishing the conformation of molecules in solution, and thus their biological activity. Many enzymes have a structure where the polypeptide chain is folded to form a hydrophobic core and a hydrophilic ('water-loving') surface.

Hydroponics : The growing of plants without soil by using an inert medium such as sand, peat, or vermiculite and adding a nutrient solution containing all the essential elements needed by the plant for its normal growth and development. Water culture, when plant roots are suspended in a liquid medium containing the nutrient solution while their crowns are supported in a thin layer of inert medium, is true hydroponics. Often called soilless culture, it also includes aeroponics where plant roots are suspended in a dark chamber and sprayed with the nutrient solution.

Hygromycin : An antibiotic used as selective agent in bacterial and transgenic plant cell cultures.

Hymen : A thin membrane partially occluding the opening to the vagina in a virgin.

Hypercalcemia : Elevated blood calcium. The most common cause is the production of a biochemical substance by tumors, resulting in the retention of calcium. This is called pseudohyperparathyroidism, most commonly occurring in patients with lymphoma or tumors of the apocrine anal sac. Pseudohyperparathyroidism has been reported associated with other tumor types. Primary hyperparathyroidism occurs uncommonly.

Hyperchloremia : Elevated blood chloride.

Hyperesthesia : Increased sensitivity to stimulation. Is most commonly seen with peripheral nerve diseases, such as, tumors and polyradiculoneuritis.

Hyperglycemia : Elevation of blood glucose. There are numerous causes of hyperglycemia including diabetes mellitus, hyperadrenocorticism, excitement and the administration of glucose or glucocorticoids.

Hyperkalemia : Elevated blood potassium.

Hyperkeratosis : Increased thickness of the horny layer of the epidermis.

Hypermagnesemia : Elevated blood magnesium.

Hypernatremia : Elevated blood sodium. Hypernatremia is uncommon in dogs and cats and most often is iatrogenic from the repetitive administration of high sodium containing solutions. Animals who have severe hypernatremia in excess of 170 meq/L show nervous system signs of depression progressing to coma.

Hyperosmolarity : An increase in the osmotic concentration of the blood. Hyperosmolarity of the blood can draw water from RBC's causing lysis or from neurons causing neurologic signs such as coma.

Hyperosmotic agents : Drugs such as mannitol and glycerine which draw water to themselves. Used to control edema and swelling.

Hyperphosphatemia : Elevated phosphorus.

Hypersensitive site : Regions in the DNA that are highly susceptible to digestion with restriction endonucleases.

Hypersensitivity type IV : An exagerated reaction of the cellular components of the immune system.

Hypertension : Elevated blood pressure.

Hypertensive : Elevation in blood pressure.

Hypertensive retinopathy : Retinal damage caused by edema or hemorrhages beneath the retina causing it to detach. Systemic hypertension is the cause of the detachment.

Hyperthyroidism : Increased production of thyroid hormone. Hyperthyroidism occurs commonly in geriatric cats but is rare in dogs.

Hypertonic : A fluid that contains a ratio of electrolytes to water that is greater than extracelluar fluid. A fluid that contains a concentration of electrolytes greater than extracellular fluid.

Hypervariable region : The parts of both the heavy and light chains of an antibody molecule that enable it to bind to a specific site on an antigen.

Hypervariable segment : A region of a protein that varies considerably between strains or individuals.

Hyperventilation : Fast breathing. Also called hyperpnea.

Hyphae : A threadlike filament possessed by many fungi that function in nutrient absorption and transfer.

Hyphema : Blood in the anterior chamber.

Hypo : This prefix is used in conjunction with many terms and means a decrease, for example, hypothermia means a decrease in temperature.

Hypoalbuminemia : Low concentration of blood albumin.

Hypomorph : A mutation that reduces, but does not completely abolish gene expression.

Hyponatremia : Low blood sodium. The most common cause is Addison's disease or iatrogenic from the administration of electrolyte free solution, such as 5% dextrose.

Hypoplasia : Smaller or softer than normal due to loss of normal tissue.

Hypoplastic : Defective and reduced growth or development (e.g. dwarfing and stunting in plants) resulting from an abnormal condition, for example disease or nutritional stress.

Hypoploid : The situation in which a particular chromosome or chromosome segment is present in less than the normal number.

Hypothalamus : A part of the brain. some hormones associated with reproduction are produced or stored in the hypothalamus.

Hypothyroid : Low function of the thyroid gland.

Hypotonic : A fluid that contains a ratio of electrolytes to water that is less than extracelluar fluid. A fluid that contains a concentration of electrolytes less than extracellular fluid.

Hypotonic dehydration : Dehydration that develops after a hypertonic fluid is lost from the body. The fluid lost from the body contains a ratio of electrolytes to water that is greater than extracelluar fluid. The osmolality of ECF is hypotonic after the electrolyte-rich fluid is lost. The best example of this type of dehydration is hypoadrenocorticism.

I

Imaginal disc : A mass of cells in the larvae of Drosophila melanogaster and other holometabolous insects that gives rise to particular adult organs, such as antennae, eyes or wings.

Imbibition : 1) The absorption of liquids or vapours into the ultramicroscopic spaces or pores found in materials. 2) The initial water uptake by seeds prior to germination.

Imidocloprid : Advantage, Bayer) is a neurotoxin available as a topical "pour-on" for use in dogs and cats over 4 months of age.

Immediate early gene : A viral gene that is expressed promptly after infection.

Immobilized cells : Cells entrapped in matrices such as alginate, polyacrylamide and agarose, for use in membrane and filter bioreactors.

Immortalization : The genetic transformation of a cell type into a cell line which can proliferate indefinitely.

Immortalizing oncogene : A gene that upon transfection enables a primary cell to grow indefinitely in culture.

Immunity : The lack of susceptibility of an animal or plant to infection by a particular pathogen, or to the harmful effects of their toxins.

Immunization : The production of immunity in an individual by artificial means. Active immunization involves the introduction, either orally or by infection, of specially treated bacteria, viruses or their toxins so as to stimulate the production of antibodies.

Immunoaffinity chromatography : A purification technique in which an antibody is bound to a matrix and is used to isolate a protein from a complex mixture.

Immunosensor : A biosensor having an antibody as the biological element.

Immunosuppression : The suppression of the immune response. Necessary following organ transplants from a genetically different donor in order to prevent the host rejecting the grafted organ.

Immunosuppressor : A substance, an agent or a condition that prevents or diminishes the immune response.

Immunotherapy : The use of an antibody or a fusion protein containing the antigen binding site of an antibody to cure a disease or enhance the well-being of a patient.

Immunotoxin : Protein drugs consisting of an antibody joined to a toxin molecule. Made by either chemically linking the molecules, or by fusing the genes for the toxin and the antibody, and expressing a fusion protein. The antibody portion of the molecule targets the toxin.

In silico : In a computer file. In the present context, the use of data bases of DNA and protein sequence to help answer biological questions. This is growing area of biology as the amount of genomics and proteomics data continues to grow.

In situ : In the natural place or in the original place. 1) Experimental treatments performed on cells or tissue rather than on extracts from them. 2) Assays or manipulations performed with intact tissues.

In situ colony hybridization : A procedure for screening bacterial colonies or plaques growing on plates or membranes for the presence of specific DNA sequences by the hybridization of nucleic acid probes to the DNA molecules present in these colonies or plaques.

In situ hybridization : The visualization of in vivo location of macromolecules (particularly polynucleotides and polypeptides) by the histological staining of tissue sections or cytological preparations via labelled probes/antibodies.

In vitro : Outside the organism, or in an artificial environment. Applied for example to cells, tissues or organs cultured in glass or plastic containers.

In Vitro Embryo production (IVEP) : The combination of ovum pickup, in vitro maturation of ova, and in vitro fertilization. A potential means of overcoming the variability between donors in number of ova collected in embryo-transfer programmes.

In Vitro Fertilization (IVF) : A widely used technique in human and animal science, whereby the egg is fertilized with sperm outside the body before re-implanting into the uterus.

In Vitro Maturation (IVM) : Culture of immature ova in the laboratory, usually until they are ready for in vitro fertilization.

In vitro transcription : The cell-free synthesis from DNA of RNA in the test tube.

In vitro translation : The synthesis of proteins from isolated mRNA molecules in the test-tube.

In vivo : The natural conditions in which organisms reside. Refers to biological processes that take place within a living organism or cell under normal conditions.

In vivo gene therapy : The delivery of a gene or genes to a tissue or organ of a complete living individual to alleviate a genetic disorder.

Inactivated agent : A virus, bacterium or other organism that has been treated to prevent it from causing a disease.

Inbreeding depression : The reduction in vigour over generations of inbreeding. This affects species which are normally outbreeding and highly heterozygous.

Incidence : The proportion of sampled animals that develop a condition of interest over a defined period of time. It is the measure of the occurrence of disease over time in a defined group of susceptible animals. Incidence can also be applied to measuring the occurrence of new cases of disease in an ever-changing population over time.

Incisions : A wound made by something sharp like glass fragments or a scalpel blade, that penetrates all layers of the skin.

Incisors : The front teeth.

Incompatibility : 1) Genetically or physiologically determined prevention of intermating. 2) A physiological interaction resulting in graft rejection or failure. 3) A function of a related group of plasmids. Incompatible plasmids share similar replication functions, and this leads to the exclusion of one or the other plasmid if they are present in the same cell. Plasmids belonging to one incompatibility group are very closely related.

Incompatibility group : Plasmids must belong to different incompatibility groups to co-exist within the same cell. A plasmid cloning vector should always belong to an incompatibility group different from that of the host bacterium's endogenous plasmids.

Incomplete dominance : A condition where a heterozygous offspring has a phenotype that is distinctly different from, and intermediate to, the parental phenotypes.

Incomplete metamorphosis : Gradual growth of an arthropod that involves change in size, but not form.

Incubation : 1) The hatching of eggs by means of heat, either natural or artificial. 2) Period between infection and appearance of symptoms induced by a pathogen. 3) The culture of cells and organisms.

Incubator : An apparatus in which environmental conditions (light, photoperiod, temperature, humidity, etc.) are fully controlled; used for hatching eggs, multiplying micro-organisms, culturing plants, etc.

Indehiscent : Describing a fruit or fruiting body that does not open to release its seeds or spores when ripe.

Indemnity payment : The payment that eligible producers receive if they realize a qualifying crop loss under crop insurance, revenue insurance, or any insurance program.

Independent assortment : The random distribution during meiosis of alleles (at different genes) to the gametes that is the case when the genes in question are located on different chromosomes or are unlinked on the same chromosome.

Indeterminate : Being able to grow for an indefinite period of time (i. e. many tomatoes.)

Indeterminate growth : The condition in which the terminal bud persists and produces successive lateral branches over an indefinite period.

Indirect lifecycle : There are multiple hosts and so the parasite is actually required to pass from one host to another host, and sometimes to another host, before it comes back to the original host in this lifecycle.

Indirect organogenesis : Plant organ formation on callus tissues derived from explants.

Indirect transmission : A mode of disease transmission where the environment is somehow part of the transmission cycle; i. e. contaminated water in a water trough spreads the disease.

Indolent ulcer : Ulcerative lesions found most frequently on the upper lips, but also seen in the skin elsewhere or in the oral cavity.

Induced ovulator : An animal such as the queen that requires vaginal stimulation in order to ovulate.

Inducer : A low-molecular-weight compound or a physical agent that associates with a repressor protein to produce a complex that can no longer bind to the operator. Thus, the presence of the inducer turns on the expression of the gene(s) controlled by the operator.

Inducible : A gene or gene product whose transcription or synthesis is increased by exposure of the cells to an inducer or to a condition, e. g. heat.

Inducible enzyme : An enzyme that is synthesized only in the presence of the substrate that acts as an inducer.

Inducible gene : A gene that is expressed only in the presence of a specific metabolite, the inducer.

Inducible promoter : The activation of a promoter in response to either the presence of a particular compound, i. e. the inducer, or to a defined external condition, e. g. elevated temperature.

Induction : The act or process of causing some specific effect to occur; for example the transcription of a specific gene or operon, or the production of a protein by an organism after it is exposed to a specific stimulus.

Induction media : 1) Media used to induce the formation of organs or other structures. 2) Media causing variation or mutation in the tissues exposed to it.

Industrial crops : Crops that primarily have industrial applications in contrast to food or livestock feed uses. Industrial uses account for a relatively small but a growing and potentially much larger share of the market for farm commodities.

Inert ingredient : Pesticide components such as solvents, carriers, dispersants, and surfactants that are not active against target pests. Inert ingredients may be toxic and may be subject to testing under the Federal Insecticide, Fungicide, and Rodenticide Act.

Infertility : Inability to conceive and bear offspring.

Infiltrate : The entry of liquid into pores or other spaces.

Infiltration : The downward entry of water into soil. Also called percolation. A high rate of infiltration means that soil moisture for crops will be higher. Many conservation practices, such as conservation tillage, reduce rates of runoff and increase infiltration rates.

Inflammation : Redness, swelling, heat and pain of a body part.

Inflorescence : The "flower-cluster";Technically, it's "a general arrangement and disposition of the flowers on an axis" There are many types of inflorescences based on the form of the flower cluster and the manner/sequence of flower blooming. The major orchid inflorescence forms include Spike, Raceme and Scape. Other less common forms seen in orchids include Cyme, Corymb, and Umbel.

Inheritance : The transmission of genes and phenotypes from generation to generation.

Inhibitor : 1) Any substance or object that retards a chemical reaction. 2) A metabolite or modifier gene that interferes with a reaction or with the expression of another gene.

Initial : Cells in a meristem that remain permanently capable of differentiation, and which develop into tissues of particular structure and function.

Initial database : The initial information collected on a patient when the patient is first seen. The minimum amout of information that will be collected should be defined in advance and may differ for different types of patients.

Initial problem list : A listing of problems identified from history and physical examination. This list becomes more specific as the results of diagnostic tests become available.

Inoculate : Deliberately introduce, in contrast to contamination. 1) In bacteriology, tissue culture, etc. , placing an inoculum into (or onto) medium to initiate a culture. 2) In immunology, to carry out immunization. 3) In plant pathology, application of pathogen spores etc. on to plants under conditions where infection should result in the absence of resistance.

Inoculation : The introduction of a pathogen to a host.

Inoculation cabinet : Small room or cabinet for inoculation (of tissue or micro-organism cultures) operations, often with a current of sterile air to carry contaminants away from the work area.

Inorganic : A chemical or fertilizer which is not obtained from a source which is or has been alive.

Inorganic compound : Historically, chemicals that could not be derived from living processes. In modern usage, chemicals that do not contain carbon, although carbonates and a few other simple carbon compounds are generally regarded as inorganic.

Inositol : A cyclic acid (hexahydroxycyclohexane) that is a constituent of certain cell phosphoglycerides. It is a nutrient frequently referred to as a "vitamin" in plant tissue culture. Also acts as a growth factor in some animals and micro-organisms.

Insensible fluid loss : Insensible routes of fluid loss are those that are not readily observed and include the loss of fluid through the respiratory tract during respiration and loss of fluid by sweating. Dogs and cats sweat minimally through their foot pads so most insensible losses are through the respiratory tract. The fluid lost during breathing is close to pure water and does not contain many solutes (a hypotonic loss). The basal loss of water through breathing is about : 10-15 ml/lb/day. High environmental temperatures, fever and activity result in increased insensible losses.

Insert : 1) To incorporate a DNA molecule into a cloning vector; also used as a noun to describe such a DNA molecule. 2) To introduce a gene or gene construct into a new genomic site or into a new genome.

Insertion element : Generic term for DNA sequences found in bacteria capable of genome insertion. Postulated to be responsible for site-specific phage and plasmid integration.

Insertion mutation : Changes in the base sequence of a DNA molecule resulting from the random integration of DNA from another source.

Insertion site : 1) A unique restriction site in a vector DNA molecule into which foreign DNA can readily be inserted. This is achieved by treating both the vector and the insert with the relevant restriction endonuclease and then ligating the two different molecules, both having the same sticky ends.

Insitu : The act of sowing seeds or cuttings in the ground where they are to grow.

In-situ conservation : The conservation of ecosystems and natural habitats and the maintenance and recovery of viable populations of species in their natural surroundings and, in the case of domesticated or cultivated species, in the surroundings where they have developed their distinctive properties.

Instability : A lack of consistent phenotype, usually as a result of uncontrolled genetic changes. These may be due to transposon activity, or in cell lines, to changes in karyotype.

Instar : The stage in the life of an arthropod between molts.

Instream use : Water use taking place within the stream channel. Examples are hydroelectric power generation, navigation, fish propagation and use, and recreational activities. Often used in discussions concerning water allocation and/or water rights.

Integration : The combination (under the management of one firm) of two or more identical (horizontal) or successive (vertical) stages in the production or marketing process of a particular product. Generally the stages are capable of being operated as separate businesses. The firm that has management responsibility is called the integrator. The poultry industry, for example, is vertically integrated, from production through processing and distribution. Diversification, on the other hand, is the production of two or more products by one firm or farmer.

Integration-Excision region (I/E) : The portion of bacteriophage lambda (ë) DNA that enables ë-DNA to be inserted into a specific site in the E. coli bacteriophage lambda chromosome or excised from this site.

Integument : One of the layers that enclosed the ovule, and is the precursor of the seed coat.

Intellectual property Rights (IPR) : The legal framework, which includes patenting and plant variety protection, by which inventors control the commercial application of their work.

Intensifying screen : A plastic sheet impregnated with a rare-earth compound, such as calcium tungstate, which reacts to radiation by emitting light. When placed on one side of a piece of X-ray film with a radioactive sample on the other side, the intensifying screen will capture some of the radioactive energy which has passed through the film, exposing the X-ray film and so enhancing the sensitivity of the detection. Often used in Southern and northern blotting procedures.

Intercalary : 1) Meristematic tissue or growth not restricted to the apex of an organ, i. e. growth at nodes. 2) Referring to internal segments of a chromosomes (i. e. not at the ends).

Intercalary growth : A pattern of stem elongation typical of grasses. Elongation proceeds from the lower internodes to the upper internodes through the differentiation of meristematic tissue at the base of each internode.

Interfascicular cambium : Cambium that arises between vascular bundles.

Interference : The effect of one crossing over event in altering the probability of another crossing over event occurring at a nearby location. This probability can be either increased (positive interference) or decreased (negative interference), but the latter is the more usual.

Interferon : One of a group of small proteins synthesized by certain T cells of vertebrates, which inhibit virus replication. There are three types of interferon in humans.

Intergeneric : Term usually used when referring Cross breeding different species from different genera producing new hibrids. Genera are always genetically related members of the same taxonomic Tribe.

Intergeneric cross : A hybrid made between parents belonging to two different genera.

Intergenic regions : Non-coding DNA located between genes; this comprises a variable but considerable proportion of all eukaryotic genomic DNA, and its function is largely unknown.

Intergenic Spacer (IGS) : Non-coding DNA separating tandemly arranged copies of a repeated gene sequence (typically ribosomal DNA). Of particular interest because, unlike the coding sequence itself, the spacers show high levels of interspecific sequence polymorphism, and are thus useful as assays for species identification.

Interleukins : They are also referred to as cytokines. These are regulatory proteins that are secreted primarily by lymphocytes to help the interaction between the lymphocyte and a macrophage.

Intermediate host : A host where maturation of the parasite or asexual reproduction takes place, in other words, reproduction where there is division and amplification of the parasite, but there is no sex involved.

Internal Transcribed Spacer (ITS) : Non-coding regions separating the individual components of the ribosomal DNA units. These regions show much more sequence polymorphism than the genic regions themselves, and therefore, like the intergenic spacers, are useful a source of genetic markers for the ribosomal DNA locus.

International treaty on plant genetic resources for food and agriculture : The international treaty resulting from the revision of the International Undertaking on Plant Genetic Resources was adopted by the 2001 FAO Conference as a binding international instrument to enter into force after ratification by 40 states. Its objectives are the conservation and sustainable use of plant genetic resources for food and agriculture and equitable sharing of the benefits of this use.

International undertaking on plant genetic resources : The first comprehensive voluntary, international agreement dealing with plant genetic resources for food and agriculture. Designed as an instrument to promote international harmony in matters regarding access to plant genetic resources for food and agriculture. Following extensive negotiations to revise the Undertaking in harmony with the Convention on Biological Diversity, the binding International Treaty on Plant Genetic Resources for Food and Agriculture was adopted by the 2001 FAO Conference.

International Unit (IU) : A standard unit of potency of a biological agent. Example : vitamin, hormone, antibiotic, antitoxin. Also called a USP unit.

International wheat agreement : Replaced in 1995 by the International Grains Agreement.

Interspecific cross : A hybrid made between parents belonging to two different species.

Interstate Shellfish Sanitation Conference (ISSC) : The federal-state-industry cooperative body which manages the National Shellfish Sanitation Program.

Interstem : An intermediate stem piece that is grafted between the scion and the stock.

Interstitial cell tumor : A testicular tumor that usually displays benign biologic behavior.

Interstitial Cystitis (IC) : A condition of the bladder resulting in hematuria and pollakiuria that resembles the condition in humans with the same name.

Intracardiac route : The administration of drugs directly into the heart through the chest wall.

Intracellular : Occurring within a cell.

Intracellular fluid : Fluid located within cells.

Intracellular fluid (ICF) : Fluid located inside cells. Comprises 2/3 of total body water.

Intracellular parasites : Parasites that reside with in the hosts cells.

Intralipid : A solution of lipids available in 10 or 20% solution that can be administered IV.

Intra-mammary antibiotics : Antibiotics instilled directly into the mammary gland.

Intramedullary : A route of drug or fluid administration into the bone marrow cavity which is considered to be confluent with the vascular space. Fluids or drugs administered via this route, enter the blood stream very rapidly.

Intraocular Pressure (IOP) : The pressure within the globe. IOP is increased in glaucoma.

Intraosseous : A route of drug or fluid administration into the bone marrow cavity which is considered to be confluent with the vascular space. Fluids or drugs administered via this route, enter the blood stream very rapidly.

Intraspecific : Within a species, such as an intraspecific cross, or intraspecific variation.

Intraspecific cross : A hybrid made between parents belonging to the same species.

Intratracheal route : The administration of drugs into the trachea usually using a catheter placed near the tracheal bifurcation.

Intravascular (IV) : Given directly into the blood stream.

Intravascular space : The vascular space. Space located in the blood vessels.

Intravenous : Giving a drug or other substance into a vein for a rapid effect.

Invasiveness : Ability of a plant to spread beyond its introduction site and become established in new locations where it may provide a deliterious effect on organisms already existing there.

Inversion : A chromosome re-arrangement, which involves the re-orientation of a segment so that the order of a linear array of genes within it is reversed.

Inverted repeat : Two sequences of nucleotides occurring in one strand, where, relative to the first sequence, the second has complementary bases but in the inverted order. Under appropriate conditions this allows formation of a hairpin loop in the single strand.

Involution : The return of an organ to its normal size or condition after enlargement, as of the uterus after parturition. A decline in size or activity of other tissues; the mammary gland tissues normally involute with advancing lactation.

IPM : Integrated Pest Management. A method by which gardeners can learn to manage and eradicate pests by choosing appropriate plants providing good growing conditions and minimizing pests rather than annihilating them.

IPR : Abbreviation for intellectual property rights.

IPTG : Isopropyl-3-D-thiogalactopyranoside. A synthetic inducer of beta-galactosidase activity in many bacteria. Used in combination with the synthetic chromogenic substrate Xgal to differentiate recombinant from non-recombinant bacterial colonies in cloning strategies using plasmid vectors containing the lacZ gene: blue coloured colonies are produced when ?-galactosidase activity is not disrupted by an insert; but when it is disrupted, the colonies are white. Hence white colonies are indicative of recombinant plasmids, and blue colonies of non-recombinant ones.

Iridencleisis : Treatment for glaucoma in which a window is made in the sclera and the iris pulled through and sutured under the conjunctiva.

Iron chelate : This is often recommended when plants are showing signs of chlorosis. It is a form of iron, being readily absorbed by plants, especially in alkaline soils.

Irradiation : The process of exposing food or other items to radiation of wavelengths shorter than those of visible light (gamma, x-ray, or ultraviolet) in order to destroy contamination from microorganisms or other undesirable organisms. It is approved and now used for some food products.

Irrigation return flow : Part of artificially applied water that is not consumed by plants or evaporation, and that eventually 'returns' to an aquifer or surface water body, such as a lake or stream. Commonly used when discussing water conservation techniques and measurement.

Irrigation water management : Limiting irrigation applications based on the water-holding capacity of the soil and the need of the crop. The water is applied at a rate and in such a manner that the crop can use it efficiently and resource losses are minimized. Irrigation efficiency is the ratio of the amount of water stored in the crop root zone compared to the amount of water applied. Water conservation has become more important as costs have risen and demands have grown for wildlife and urban uses.

IS element : Abbreviation for insertion sequence element. A short (800-1400 nucleotide pairs) DNA sequence found in bacteria that is capable of transposing to a new genomic location; DNA sequences contained within an IS element can be transposed along with the IS itself.

Isoallele : Multiple similar copies of a gene, usually located at independent positions in the genome, which encode similar gene products and produce the same, or a very similar phenotype.

Isogenic : A group of individuals that possesses the same genotype, irrespective of their being homozygous or heterozygous.

Isogenic stock : Strains of organisms that are genetically nearly identical, except with respect to identified genes. Generally produced by repeated backcrossing, or by transformation.

Iso-ionic : Iso-ionic refers to a similar concentration of a particular electrolyte in a solution compared to extracellular fluid; therefore solutions which are iso-ionic with regard to sodium will have sodium concentrations comparable to the sodium concentration of extracellular fluid and plasma, which is approximately 145 mEq/l in the dog and cat.

Isolating mechanism : The properties of an organism that prevent interbreeding (and therefore exchange of genetic material) between members of different species that inhabit the same geographical area.

Isolation medium : An optimum plant tissue culture medium suitable for explant survival, growth and development.

Isotonic : Solutions with the same osmotic potential, as a result of being of the same molar concentration. For protoplasts to avoid losing or gaining water, the medium they are suspended in must be isotonic with them.

Isotonic dehydration : Dehydration characterized by the loss of water and electrolytes in a ratio similar to extracellualar water. Dogs and cats most often have isotonic dehydration as water and electrolytes are lost.

Isotope : One of two or more forms of an element that differ in the number of neutrons carried by the nucleus. Radioactive isotopes (radio-isotopes) are used as probes in many biochemical analyses.

Isotretinoin : (Accutane-Roache. A retinoids which is a synthetic derivatives of vitamin A.

Isozyme : A genetic variant of an enzyme. Isozymes for a given enzyme share the same function, but may differ in level of activity, as a result of minor differences in their amino acid sequence. Electrophoretic separation of isozymes has been used to distinguish between individuals and varieties.

J

J-cut : A method of removing pinbones that also removes the nape. J-cut fillets are more expensive than other fillets.

Jejunum : The longest part of the small intestinal tract.

Jen chung : An acupunture technique also referred to as governing vessel 26 which causes sympathetic stimulation.

Jennys : Female pacific salmon that mature precociously (earlier than other fish in its age-class).

Jigging : a method of fishing using lures on a vertical line that is moved up and down, or jigged. It is used to catch squid and may be carried out by hand-operated spools, or by automatic machines. The rotation of the spool as the line is wound creates the jigging action.

Jimmy : A male blue crab.

Johnsongrass : Perennial grass that is a problem in many crops. Introduced and tested as a forage species. Didn't produce well as forage plant but became a nuisance.

Joining : Putting the rams and ewes together for mating. Tupping is the same thing.

Joining segment (J) : A small DNA segment that links genes in order to yield a functional gene encoding an immunoglobulin.

Joint products : Commodities which are produced in such a way that a change in the output of one of them necessarily involves a change in the output of the other.

Joint ventures : Collaborative fishing operations, usually involving two companies from different countries.

JPEG : JPEG is a standardized image compression mechanism used to reduce file size. JPEG stands for Joint Photographic Experts Group. JPEG is designed for compressing either full-color or gray-scale images. Often used for internet delivery of aerial photography.

JPW : JPEG World file (JPW) contains coordinate information used to position an image with respect to a coordinate system. JPEG World File format is supported by most GIS software packages. However, the JPW file does not contain projection information and care should be taken to ensure that the coordinate system is the same as other data layers in a GIS system.

Juvenile cellulitis : Moist juvenile Pyoderma or Puppy strangles. Lesions of erythema, draining tracts, alopecia, and edema of the chin, lips, ears and eyelids seen in puppies less than 6 months old. Lesions are located on the muzzle and head, although abdominal, axillary and inguinal regions can be affected.

Juvenile in Vitro Embryo Technology (JIVT or JIVET) : A technology involving collection of immature eggs from young animals, their in vitro maturation and fertilization, and the transfer of the resultant embryos into recipient females. The method is designed to achieve rapid generation turnover.

Juvenile leaf : Referring to a leaf of young a plant or shoot from the base of an older plant, particularly when this leaf differs in shape from leaves of mature plants. For example, in eucalyptus, the first leaves formed after the cotyledons and before the formation of subsquent types of leaves.

Juvenile salmon : Young, non-mature salmon.

K

Kentucky bluegrass : A cool-season turfgrass that spreads by rhizomes. It is the most popular species for high-quality lawns in Ohio. It is very winter hardy.

Keratic precipitates : Clusters of inflammatory cells on the back (endothelial surface) of the cornea.

Keratin : A cystine rich protein produced by the epithelial cells.

Keratinization disorders : Cutaneous disorders characterized by scaling.

Keratitis : Inflammation of the clear part of the eye, the cornea.

Keratoconjunctivitis Sicca (KCS) : Dry eye which may be a consequence of prior exposure and infection with canine distemper virus.

Keratotomy : Removal of part of the thickness of the cornea.

Kernel : The edible part of nut.

Ketoacidosis (DKA) : A form of diabetes mellitus in which the pet has increased amounts of acids in the blood and is very sick.

Ketoconazole : Nizoral-Janssen. An oral treatment for dermatophytes.

Key species : 1) species that, because of their importance, must be considered in a management program; or 2) forage species whose use shows the degree of use of associated species.

Khot ail : Tent group in mongolia.

Kid : A baby goat.

Killed vaccine : A vaccine that contains antigen of the infectious agent that has been killed by chemical or physical means and does not replicate in the host.

Killer T cell : T cells that kill cells displaying recognized antigens.

Kilning : Drying wood under controlled temperature and humidity.

Kinetics : Dynamic processes involving motion. Often used as a suffix to indicate studies involving movement or rates of reactions.

Kinetochore : Structure at the centromere of eukaryotic chromosomes. The kinetochore consists of inner and outer electron dense plates and a central zone containing repetitive DNA elements. Kinetochores are involved in the control of chromosome movement in cell division.

Kinetosome : Granular cytoplasmic structure which forms the base of a cilium or flagellum.

King salmon : Another name for chinook salmon.

Kinin : A substance promoting cell division. In plant systems, the prefix cyto- has been added (cytokinin) to distinguish it from kinin in animal systems.

Kipper : Fish, or the process of curing fish (herring, salmon, etc.), By cleaning, salting and drying or smoking.

Klenow fragment : A truncated form of DNA polymerase I from E. coli, used extensively for the production of synthetic DNA molecules as it retains polymerase and 3'-exonuclease activities, but not 5'-exonuclease activity.

KM : A dissociation constant that characterizes the binding of an enzyme to a substrate. The smaller the value of Km, the tighter the binding of the enzyme to the substrate. Also called the Michaelis constant.

Knockout : A mutant individual, in which a single functional gene has been replaced by a non-functional form of the gene. Used to understand gene function via the comparison of the phenotypes of wild type and knockouts.

Knot garden : A very carefully planned garden of small dwarf shrubs or even herbs. Planned in a pattern and kept in order by constant pruning and trimming.

Kochia : Same family as tumbleweed and has the same characteristics.

Kriging (Creeging) : An interpolation technique for obtaining statistically unbiased estimates of spatial variation of known points such as surface elevations or yield measurements utilizing a set of control points.

K-selection : Selective conditions that favour longevity of individuals at expense of reproductive capacity. A 'k-strategist' is a species adapted to maximum survival of individuals at expense of reproductive capacity. See also r-selection

L

Lactation : The time between calving that a cow produces milk, usually 10 months.

Lactation curve : A graphic plot of days in milk vs. pounds of milk produced.

Lactogenic immunity : A form of local immunity in milk (post colostrum) that bathes the intestinal tract and prevents colonization by virulent bacteria and neutralized viruses passing through the gut.

Lactose : A disaccharide sugar produced in milk, composed of one unit each of glucose and galactose.

Lag phase : 1) The state of apparent inactivity preceding a response to a treatment; also called a latent phase. 2) The initial growth phase, during which cell number remains relatively constant, prior to the onset of rapid cell division.

Lagging strand : The strand of DNA that is synthesized discontinuously during replication.

Lagophthalmos : Inability to fully close the eyelids over the eyeball.

Lamb : A young sheep, less than one year old.

Laminar air-flow cabinet : Cabinet designed for cell or tissue culture manipulations requiring a sterile environment. Achieved by a continuous, non-turbulent flow of filter-sterilized air over the working area.

Laminarin : A storage polysaccharide of the brown algae.

Lampbrush chromosome : Large diplotene chromosomes present in oocyte nuclei, and particularly conspicuous in amphibians. These chromosomes have extended regions called loops, which are active sites of transcription.

Land management services contracts : A proposed national forest timber sale contract where purchasers would be required to perform activities, other than those directly related to timber cutting and removal, in or near the sale area, in exchange for a reduction in the stumpage price. Pilot tests of this contract arrangement have been conducted, but its general use is not authorized.

Land treatment : Any activity or project to improve conservation of soil, water, or other resources and improve production.

Land use plan : A coordinated collection of data, programs, and activities related to existing and potential uses of land and resources within a defined area. Commonly associated with local units of government trying to anticipate and organize uses of space so as to meet defined goals. For producers, conservation plans are a type of land use plan.

Landrace : In plant genetic resources, an early, cultivated form of a crop species, evolved from a wild population, and generally composed of a heterogeneous mixture of genotypes.

Landscape architect : A very good professional to consider when creating a garden. They are licensed by the state and know the mechanics of major construction, grading, drainage, and will advice solutions to problems.

Landscape fabric : Probably one of your best solutions against weeds for beds. This can be a variety of materials: newspaper, plastic, porous fibers, burlap. It provides a barrier for weeds to germinate. This is then dressed with mulch of any kind.

Laparotomy : A surgical procedure to open the abdominal (belly) cavity.

Latent agent : A pathogen, usually a virus, present in a host organism without producing any symptoms.

Latent bud : An inactive bud not held back by rest or dormant period, but which may start growth if stimulated.

Lateral bud : Smaller buds on the sides of stems, responsible for growth of leaves and side branches.

Lateral meristem : A meristem giving rise to secondary plant tissues, such as the vascular and cork cambia.

Lateral recumbant : Laying down on the side.

Lawn : A uniform and uninterrupted laver of bacterial growth, in which individual colonies cannot be observed.

Layering : A method of propagation in which adventitious roots form before the new plant is severed from the parent plant.

Leach : To dissolve in water and wash away.

Leachate : Liquid "run-off". Leachate from the compost pile contains nutrients generated in the composting process. In contrast, as groundwater and rain flow through a landfill, they pick up weak acids created by decaying organic matter. As these acids react with other garbage, the leachate can become toxic which may contaminate streams and groundwater unless the landfill is properly constructed to contain the run-off.

Leaching : The process by which chemicals are dissolved and transported through the soil by percolating water. Pesticides and nutrients from fertilizers or manures may leach from fields, areas of spills, or feedlots and thereby enter surface water, groundwater, or soil. Leaching from concentrated sources such as waste sites and loading areas vulnerable to spills can be prevented by paving or containment with a liner of relatively impermeable material designed to keep leachate inside a treatment pond, landfill, or a tailings disposal area. Liner materials include plastic and dense clay.

Lead compound : A chemical that has demonstrated promising biological activity in preliminary assays.

Leader : The main growing shoot of a sapling, it eventually will become the trunk of the tree.

Leaf bud cutting : A cutting that includes a short section of stem with attached leaf.

Leaf cutting : A method of propagation. A leaf is removed and is placed in vermiculite or perlite for future baby plants.

Leaf margin : The edge of a leaf.

Leaf mold : Partially decayed leaves used in some potting mixtures. It must be sieved and sterilized before use. Great for outdoor use in beds.

Leaf primordium : A lateral outgrowth from the apical meristem, which will become a leaf when fully developed and expanded.

Leaf roll : A symptom of some virus diseases, characterized by curling of the leaves. Can also occur as a response to water stress.

Leaf roller : Different moths that will roll leaves when larvae. Cannas often get a lot of leaf rollers.

Leaky mutant : A mutant in which the gene product still retains some biological activity.

Lecithin : Phospholipids found widely in animals and plants,(e.g. egg yolk) that have emulsifying, wetting, and antioxidant properties.

Lectin : A group of plant proteins that can bind to specific oligosaccharides on the surface of cells, causing the cells to clump together.

Leggy : This is tall and spindly growth, not usual to the growth habit of the plant. It is seen because of the lack of light.

Legume : A family of plants, including many valuable food and forage species, such as peas, beans, soybeans, peanuts, clovers, and alfalfas. They can convert nitrogen from the air to build up nitrogen in the soil.

Legumes : A family of plants, including many valuable food, forage and cover species, such as peas, beans, soybeans, peanuts, clovers, alfalfas, sweet clovers, lespedezas, vetches, and kudzu. Sometimes referred to as nitrogen-fixing plants, they can convert nitrogen from the air to build up nitrogen in the soil. Legumes are an important rotation crop because of their nitrogen-fixing property.

Lens : Structure in the eye which functions to transmit and focus incoming light rays directly on the retina; this is facilitated by accommodation - the subtle change in lens shape brought about by contraction and relaxation of the ciliary body; the accommodative ability of the lens is limited in domestic species.

Less Developed Countries (LDCs) : Countries with low per capita incomes. Also known as third world, poor, under-developed, lesser developed, developing, or economically emerging countries.

Lethal allele : A mutant form of a gene that, in the homozygous state, is fatal.

Lethargy : Malaise or inactivity.

Leukocyte : White blood cell, up to 0.02 mm in diameter, of which there are normally 4-11 million per millilitre of human blood. There are several kinds, all involved in the body's defence mechanisms. Granulocytes have granules in their cytoplasm; monocytes ingest and feed on bacteria and other micro-organisms that cause infection; lymphocytes include the B cells that are involved with the production of antibodies.

Leukocytosis : High white blood cell count.

Leukopenia : Low white blood cell count.

LIBOR : London Interbank Offered Rate

Library : A collection of cells, usually bacteria or yeast, that have been transformed with recombinant vectors carrying DNA inserts from a single species.

Lichen : A combined growing condition of algae and fungus. It looks crusty, and comes in many colors: gray, green, bluish, or browns.

Lichenification : Thickening, hardening and often hyperpigmentation of the skin.

Lidocaine : A drug used as a local anaesthetic and as an antiarrhythmic agent in treatment of certain cardiac arrhythmias such as ventricular fibrillation.

Life cycle : The sequence of events from a given developmental stage in one generation to the same stage in the following generation. In sexually reproduced organisms, the starting point is the fusion of gametes to form the zygote.

Ligate : The process of joining two or more DNA fragments.

Ligate, ligation : The joining of two linear double-stranded DNA fragments by the formation of phosphodiester bonds.

Lightbar : Is a navigation tool coupled with a GPS designed to keep the driver on-course. Applications include planting and fertilizer applications to reduce skips and overlaps. Typically, guidance is provided through as series of LED lights.

Lignification : The thickening and strengthening of a plant cell wall with lignin.

Lignin : A group of high-molecular-weight amorphous polymers of phenylpropanoid compounds, giving strength to certain tissues. A major component of wood.

Lignocellulose : The combination of lignin, hemicellulose and cellulose that forms the structural framework of plant cell walls.

Limbic system : A group of brain structures which exert an important influence on the endocrine and autonomic motor system's and which influence (emotion) mood states.

Limbing up : Pruning off the lower limbs of trees, usually for ease of walking underneath or admitting sunlight.

Limbus : Junction between conjunctiva and cornea.

Lineage : A group of individuals, related by common descent, e.g. an in vitro cell line derived from a single cell.

Linear : Narrow and comparatively long, with parallel margins

Linear immunoglobulin a dermatosis : Clinically presents as subcorneal pustules, epidermal collarettes, etc. generally truncal in distribution. Most often seen in the dachshund.

Linear phase : The growth phase during cell culture when cell number increases arithmetically. The linear phase follows a period of exponential growth.

Linearized vector : A covalently closed circular DNA vector (typically a plasmid) which has been opened by restriction digestion to convert it to a linear molecule. In molecular cloning, DNA to be cloned is mixed with the linearized vector, and treated with ligase to join and recircularize the resulting hybrid molecule.

Linkage : The tendency of a set of genes to be inherited together more often than would be expected if they were assorting independently. exists between two genes when they are located sufficiently close to one another on the same chromosome that a proportion of gametes is produced without crossing-over occurring between them.

Linkage map : A linear or circular diagram that shows the relative positions of genes on a chromosome as determined by recombination fraction.

Linked gene, linked marker : A gene or marker that is linked to another gene or marker.

Linker : A synthetic double-stranded oligonucleotide that carries the recognition sequence for one or more restriction endonucleases. The ligation of a linker to each end of a DNA fragment facilitates the preparation of the fragment for cloning into a vector.

Linters : The short fibers that remain on cottonseed after ginning. They are used mainly for batting, mattress stuffing, and as a source of cellulose.

Lipase : A class of enzymes which break down lipids into their component fatty acids and glycerol. Lipases used in biotechnology are generally digestive, with a role in the break-down of fats in food into their components, so that these can be used to make other materials.

Lipids : Any of a group of fats or fat-like compounds insoluble in water and soluble in fat solvents. Substances found in plant and animal tissues that are insoluble in water, but soluble in benzene or ether. Includes fats, oils, glycolipids, phosphoglycerides, waxes and steroids.

Lipofection : Delivery into eukaryotic cells of DNA, RNA or other compounds that have been encapsulated in liposomes.

Liquefaction : Enzymatic digestion (often by alpha-amylase) of gelatinized starch to form lower molecular weight polysaccharides.

Liquid medium : Culture solution, without a solidifying agent, for in vitro cell growth.

Liquid membrane : Thin films made up of liquids (as opposed to solids) which are stable in another liquid (usually water). Thus the liquid must not dissolve in the water, but nevertheless must be prevented from collapsing into small droplets.

Liquid nitrogen : Nitrogen gas condensed to a liquid with a boiling point of about -196 °C. Commonly used as a medium for long-term storage of biological materials.

Lithophyte : Plants that grow on rocks or other areas that do not need soil. They will receive their nourishment from the air. i.e. orchids and lichens.

Litmus paper : A pH indicator paper. It turns red in acidic and blue in alkaline solutions.

Live recombinant vaccine : A vaccine created by the expression of a pathogen antigen in a non-pathogenic organism.

Live vaccine : A living, non-virulent form of a pathogenic micro-organism or virus used to elicit an antibody response for the protection against infection by a virulent form of the same pathogen.

Live weight : The weight of live animals purchased or sold by a producer.

Living Modified Organism(LMO) : According to Biosafety Protocol Any living organism that possesses a novel combination of genetic material obtained through modern biotechnology. A living organism is biological entity capable of transferring or replicating genetic material.

Loan deficiency payments : A commodity payment program authorized by the Food Security Act of 1985 giving USDA discretion to provide direct payments, equal to marketing loan payments, to wheat, feed grain, upland cotton, rice, or oilseed producers who agree not to obtain nonrecourse loans, even though they are eligible. Loan deficiency payments continue to be available under the FAIR Act of 1996 for all loan commodities except extra-long staple cotton.

Loan forfeiture : Under commodity program rules, a producer or processor who pledges a stored commodity as collateral to the Commodity Credit Corporation to obtain a nonrecourse loan can settle the repayment obligation by forfeiting the commodity without any penalty. This happens, by design, if forfeiture is more profitable than selling the commodity in the marketplace. In this way the loan program serves a price support function.

Loan forfeiture level, sugar : The lowest market price that a processor must receive before concluding that forfeiting pledged sugar to the Commodity Credit Corporation is a more profitable than selling the sugar. USDA calculates the loan forfeiture level to be equal to the loan rate, plus transportation costs to a refinery (applicable only for raw cane sugar) plus interest expenses on a nonrecourse loan minus a sugar loan forfeiture penalty.

Loan rate : The price per unit (bushel, bale, pound, or hundredweight, depending on the commodity) at which the government will provide nonrecourse or recourse loans to farmers (or others), enabling them to hold their commodities for later sale.

Lobe : A part of a segment that represents a division to about the middle

Lochia : Green colored post-partum discharge. The appearance of lochia before delivery indicates placental separation and impaired blood flow to the fetuses.

Locoweed : Mostly perennial plant from the legume family. Occurs mostly on rangeland and is poisonous to livestock.

Locus : A specific location or site on a chromosome.

Lod score : The logarithm of the odds of linkage between two loci. Used to measure the statistical support for linkage.

Log phase : Abbreviation for logarithmic phase.

Logarithmic phase : The steepest slope of the growth curve--the phase of vigorous growth during which cell number doubles every 20-30 minutes.

Long : 1) One who has bought a futures contract or option to establish a market position; 2) a market position that obligates the holder to take delivery; 3) one who owns an inventory of commodities.

Long Interspersed Nuclear Element (LINE) : Families of common DNA elements, of average length 6.5 kb, which are dispersed at numerous locations within the genome.

The human genome contains over 500,000 LINEs (representing ca. 16% of the genome). They appear to represent degenerate copies of transposable elements.

Long template : A DNA strand, synthesized during PCR, which has a primer sequence at one end but is extended beyond the site that is complementary to the second primer at the other end.

Long Terminal Repeat (LTR) : A characteristic sequence of nucleotides that occurs at each end of a retrovirus element that has become integrated into the host genome. Involved in the integration process.

Long-day plant : A plant that requires a night shorter than its critical dark period, usually 12 hours or less, to develop flowers.

Longitude : An east/west measurement of position in relation to the Prime Meridian, an imaginary circle that passes through the north and south poles.

Loop bioreactor : Fermenters in which material is cycled between a bulk tank and a smaller tank or loop of pipes. The circulation helps to mix the materials and to ensure that gas injected into the fermenter is well distributed in the liquid. Particularly useful for photosynthetic fermentations, where the photosynthesizing organisms are passed through a system of many small transparent pipes, which allow the access of light.

Loratidine : Claritan. An antihistamine.

Lot : a plot of land.

Low-flow irrigation systems : These systems (drip, trickle, and micro sprinklers) provide water in small volumes and generally provide water to plants with less waste than furrow irrigation. Drip and trickle systems apply water through small holes in small diameter tubes placed on or below the surface of the field. Another type of system, micro sprinklers, supplies water from low-volume sprinkler heads located above the surface. Low flow systems are expensive and their use is generally limited to high-value crops such as vegetables, fruits, and vineyards.

Lox : mild-cured salmon (soaked in brine for long periods, then soaked to remove the salt) that has been cold smoked.

Luxury consumption : Nutrient absorption by an organism in excess of that required for optimum growth and productivity.

Lyase : Any of a class of enzymes that catalyse either the cleavage of a double bond and the addition of new groups to a substrate, or the formation of a double bond.

Lymphocyte : White blood cells that are important components of the immune system of vertebrates.

Lymphoid organs : Organs that regulate the production and differentiation of lymphocytes. The main lymphoid organ are the salivary glands, the thymus, the spleen, and the bone marrow.

Lymphokine : Generic name for proteins that are released by lymphocytes to act on other cells involved in the immune response. The term includes interleukins and interferons. A sub-class of cytokines.

Lysogenic : A type or phase of the virus life cycle during which the virus integrates into the host chromosome of the infected cell, often remaining essentially dormant for some period of time.

Lysosome : A membrane-bound sac within the cytoplasm of animal cells that contains enzymes responsible for the digestion of material in food vacuoles, the dissolution of foreign particles entering the cell and, on the death of the cell, the breaking down of all cell structures. The digestive system of the cell.

Lysozyme : A naturally occurring enzyme extracted from egg white protein and other animal and plant sources, which attacks the cell wall of gram-positive bacteria leading to cell lysis and death.

M

Macroclimate : The climate of a region.

Macroevolution : Large-scale evolution, entailing major changes in biological traits.

Macromolecule : Any high molecular weight molecule.

Macronutrient : A chemical element necessary in large amounts (usually > 50 ppm in the plant) for the growth of plants. Includes c, h, o, n, p, k, ca, mg, s. 'Macro' refers to quantity and not to essentiality of the element.

Macroorganism : Living organisms in the soil which are large enough to be seen with the naked eye. Includes mite, millipede centipede, snail, slug, spider, ant, beetle, cut worm, earthworm, rodent.

Macrophage : Large white blood cells that ingest foreign substances and display on their surfaces antigens which are recognized by other cells of the immune system.

Macropropagation : Production of plant clones from growing parts.

Macule : A circumscribed, flat (not raised or depressed) change in the color of the skin. Large macules are patches.

Mad cow disease : The common term used for bovine spongiform encephalopathy (BSE).

Magenta : A type of plastic container frequently used for plant micropropagation and tissue culture.

Magnetic Resonance Image (MRI) : A diagnostic technique that produces computerized images of internal body structures. MRI uses a large magnet to polarize hydrogen atoms in the tissues and then monitors the spinning energies within cells.

Maiden ewe : A ewe lambing for the first time.

Maiden female : A female that has not been bred.

Main effect : The response to different levels of a treatment factor, measured independently of other factors. In a balanced design such as a randomized complete block, the main effects of levels of a treatment factor are estimated by averaging the corresponding responses over all levels of every other factor.

Maintenance phase : A phase of acute renal failure following initiation during which oliguria persists. Whether an ARF patient is oliguric or polyuric reflects the severity of insult which caused ARF. The majority of ARF dogs and cats become oliguric although some ARF patients are never oliguric. In those patients which can repair the renal damage, the oliguric phase lasts 1-2 weeks. Many animals die or are euthanized during the oliguric phase because of the poor prognosis. The most life-threatening consequences of the oliguric phase include hyperkalemia and overzealous fluid therapy resulting in overhydration.

Maintenance solutions : Maintenance solutions are hypotonic compared to extracellular fluid. They have more potassium than extracellular fluid and less sodium than extracellular fluid. Maintenance solutions can be purchased or "created" from other cystalloid solutions.

Major histocompatibility antigen : A cell-surface protein or glycoprotein that allows the immune system to distinguish foreign or "non-self" from "self". A better term is histoglobulin. These are the antigens that must be matched between donors and recipients during organ and tissue transplants to prevent rejection.

Major Histocompatibility Complex (MHC) : The large cluster of genes that encode the major histocompatibility antigens in mammals.

Major Land Resource Area (MLRA) : Major land resource areas are geographically associated land resource units delineated by the Natural Resources Conservation Service and characterized by a particular pattern that combines soils, water, climate, vegetation, land use, and type of farming. There are 204 MLRAs in the United States, ranging in size from less than 500,000 acres to more than 60 million acres.

Make allowance (or milk manufacturing marketing adjustment) : The margin between the government support price for milk and the CCC's purchase price for butter, nonfat dry milk, and cheese. This margin is administratively set to cover the costs of 'making' milk into butter, nonfat dry milk, or cheese to reach the desired level of prices for milk in manufacturing uses.

Malassezia pachydermatis : A budding yeast considered part of the normal flora of the external ear canal. M ay become pathologic in certain situations. Formerly called Pityrosporum canis.

Malignancy : Cancer.

Malignant : A cancer that has high possibility for spread.

Malt extract : A mixture of organic compounds prepared from malt, used as a culture medium additive.

Malting : Enzymatic reduction of starch to sugars in germinating grain, used in brewing.

Mangroves : 1) Open or closed stands of trees and bushes occurring in the tropics in intertidal zones, usually around the mouths of rivers, creeks and lagoons where soils are heavy textured and have a fluctuating salt content and soil level. 2) A name used collectively for the assemblage of plants, as well as to refer to individual genera or species, for example, woody members of the rhizophoraceae, combretaceae and verbenaceae. These have knee-like roots that are 'pneumatophores' (roots with air spaces). Grown for wood and tannins.

Mangrove forest : A community of salt-tolerant trees, with associated shrubs or vines and other organisms, that grows in a zone roughly coinciding with the intertidal zone along protected tropical and subtropical coasts.

Manila declaration : The manila declaration concerning the ethical utilization of biological resources, developed at the asomps vii meeting in manila, philippines, 2-7 february 1992.

Man-made conveyance : Although not defined by ohio law, a man-made conveyance is interpreted as a means to intentionally pass pollutants or water in and/or out. Examples are tile, pipes, ditches and spillways. The term "manmade" means constructed by man for the purpose of transporting wastes or water.

Mannitol : A sugar alcohol widely distributed in plants. Commonly used as a nutrient and osmoticum in suspension media for plant protoplasts.

Manure remover : There are several kinds-stackers, pumps, gravity flow. They are used to move manure out of the barn.

Manure spreader : It spreads the manure onto the fields.

Manure tea : A liquid fertilizer made by mixing manures with water and filtering out. Pillow cases filled with cow or horse patooties and dunked in a pail of water.

Map : 1) verb: to determine the relative positions of loci (genes or DNA sequences) on a chromosome. Linkage maps are obtained from the frequency of recombination between loci. Physical maps are obtained commonly by the use of in situ hybridization of cloned DNA fragments to metaphase chromosomes, or by somatic-cell hybrids or radiation hybrids. 2) a diagram showing the relative position of, and distances between, loci on a chromosome.

Map distance : The standard measure of genetic distance between loci, expressed in centiMorgans (cM) or map units. Estimated from recombination fraction via a mapping function. For small recombination fractions, map distance in cM equals the recombination fraction in %.

Map projection : A mathematical formula that transforms feature locations between the earth's curved surface and a map's flat surface. A projected coordinate system includes the information needed to transform locations expressed as latitude and longitude values to x, y coordinates. Projections cause distortions in one or more of these spatial properties—distance, area, shape, and direction.

Marbling : The specks of fat (intramuscular fat) distributed in muscular tissue. Marbling is usually evaluated in the ribeye between the 12th and 13th rib.

Margin : The amount of money or collateral deposited by a customer with a broker, by a broker with a clearing member, or by a clearing member with the clearinghouse, for the purpose of insuring against loss on open futures contracts. The margin is not partial payment on a purchase. 1) Initial margin is the total amount of margin per contract required by the broker when a futures position is opened; 2) maintenance margin is a sum that must be maintained on deposit at all times. If the equity in a customer's account drops to, or under, the level because of adverse price movement, the broker must issue a margin call to restore the customer's equity. Sometimes called a performance bond.

Margin call : 1) A request from a brokerage firm to a customer to bring margin deposits up to initial levels; 2) a request by the clearinghouse to a clearing member to make a deposit of original margin, or a daily or intra-day variation payment, because of adverse price movement, based on positions carried by the clearing member.

Marginal plant : Plants that will grow on the edges of ponds or lakes and when cultivated will make nice plants around a water garden (i.e. iris).

Marginal values : The change in the value of a resource that is due to an incremental change in its quantity.

Marginally hardy : Close to the limit of hardiness that a plant can withstand. Planting plants that are marginally hardy is risky, because under the most severe conditions for that zone, the plant may not survive without extra protection.

Mariculture : cultivation of marine organisms, plant and animal, for purposes of human consumption. The growing of marine animals and plants under specialized culture conditions.

Marker : An identifiable DNA sequence that is inherited in Mendelian fashion, and which facilitates the study of inheritance of a trait or a linked gene.

Marker assisted selection : The use of molecular markers to follow the inheritance of genes, particularly those genes which cannot be readily identified. Selection of a marker flanking a gene of interest allows selection for the presence (or absence) of a gene in a new progeny.

Marker gene : A gene of known function or known location, used for marker-assisted selection or genetic studies.

Marker peptide : A portion of fusion protein that facilitates its identification or purification.

Market allocation : A quantity provision in a fruit or vegetable marketing order specifying the maximum amount of the regulated commodity that can be sold for a given use or market (such as the domestic fresh market).

Market failure : This occurs when market prices are not equal to the social opportunity cost of resources. External effects or externalities are evidence of market failure.

Market price : The price per bushel (or pound or hundredweight) of an agricultural commodity paid in the private sector. It can sometimes refer to the price paid at domestic seaports or large inland terminal markets and sometimes refers to the farm price.

Market structure : Characteristics of an industry that relate to its economic performance, such as the number of buyers and sellers, product differentiation among firms, barriers to entry, costs, degree of integration, and diversification.

Marl : A chalky clay soil.

MAS : Marker-Assisted Selection.

Mast fruiting : A period of massive fruit production.

Master gardener : County residents who volunteer and are trained to work with the extension service.

Mating system : The mode of transmission of genes from one generation to the next through sexual reproduction.

Matric potential : A water potential component, always of negative value, resulting from the presence of solid (often finely divided) surfaces; primarily responsible for water uptake by a dry seed prior to germination.

Matrix : 1) A two-dimensional array of numbers. The meaning of each number (or element) depends on its position in the matrix, that is, on the row and the column in which it occurs. 2. The generally rigid and connected material in which other matter is retained.

Matted-row : A system of planting where plants are placed off center or are centered on a diagonal.

Maximum Sustainable Yield (MSY) : The largest long-term average catch or yield that can be taken from a stock or stock complex under prevailing ecological and environmental conditions.

Maximum Tolerated Dose (MTD) : Loosely, the highest dose of a chemical that when administered to a group of test animals does not increase the death rate during a long-term study (other than deaths due to tumors caused by the chemical being tested, that is). The purpose of administering MTD is to determine whether long-term exposure to a chemical might lead to any adverse health effects in a population, when the level of exposure is not sufficient to cause premature mortality due to short- term toxic effects. The maximum dose is used, rather than a lower dose, to reduce the number of animals that need to be tested (and thus, the cost of animal testing), in order to detect an effect that occurs only rarely. This analysis is used in establishing chemical residue tolerances in foods.

Meadow : A tract of grassland where productivity of indigenous or introduced forage is modified due to characteristics of the landscape position or hydrology.

Mean : A measure of central tendency, for example, a 'sample mean'. The 'arithmetic mean' is obtained by dividing the sum of the observations by their number; the 'geometric mean' is the arithmetic mean of the logarithms.

Mean annual increment : In forestry, for a particular stand, the total increment of wood up to a given stand age (in years) divided by that age. The mean annual increment for a whole rotation is termed the final mean annual increment.

Meat : The flesh of animals that is used for food. Red meat includes beef, pork, goat and lamb. White meats are poultry and fish.

Mechanical thinning : Thinning in which a predetermined proportion of the trees is removed without regard to size or quality, such as, for example, every third tree.

Medfly : A shortened name for the Mediterranean fruit fly, a destructive pest of fruits and vegetables that is found throughout most of Central America. The Animal and Plant Health Inspection Service is involved in programs to keep the Medfly from spreading north into Mexico, where it could easily enter the United States on imported winter fruits and vegetables.

Median : In a set of measurements, the central value above and below which there are an equal number of measurements.

Medication Administration Record (MAR) : A flow sheet charting medications given to a patient over time.

Megabase (Mb) : A length of DNA consisting of 106 bases.

Megabase cloning : The cloning of large DNA fragments of the order of 1Mb.

MegaDalton (MDa) : One megaDalton is equal to 106 Dalton.

Megaesophagus : A pathologically dilated esophagus.

Meiosis : The process of division of sexual cells in which the number of chromosomes in each nucleus is reduced to half the normal number found in normal somatic cells. When two sexual cells fuse, each contributes its half of the chromosomes. The resulting embryo contains the full chromosome complement. Cells with half the chromosomes are called haploids : those with the normal chromosomal complement, diploids.

Meiotic analysis : The use of patterns of chromosome pairing at meiotic prophase and metaphase to detect relationships between chromosomes, from which can be deduced the relationship between the parents of the organism studied..

Meiotic drive : Any mechanism that causes a particular allele or chromosome to be over-represented in a population of gametes.

Melangestrol Acetate (MGA) : A hormone added to diets to suppress estrus cycling and improve feed efficiency and growth rate in feedlot heifers.

Membrane bioreactor : A vessel in which cells are cultured on or behind a permeable membrane, which allows the diffusion of nutrients to the cells, but retains the cells themselves. A variation is the hollow-fibre reactor.

Memorandum of Agreement (MOA) : An agreement between federal agencies, or divisions/units within an agency or department, which delineate tasks, jurisdiction, standard operating procedures or other matters which the agencies or units are duly authorized and directed to conduct. Sometimes referred to as a memorandum of understanding (MOU).

Memory cell : Long-lived B cells and T cells that mediate rapid secondary immune responses to a previously encountered antigen.

Memory stick : A memory stick is a small removable mass storage device about the size of a stick of gum. Used as non-volatile memory in digital cameras and other electronics made by Sony Corporation.

Menace reflex : Used to assess vision and the ability to close the eyelids.

Mendelian population : A natural, interbreeding unit of sexually reproducing plants or animals sharing a common gene pool.

Mendelian segregation : Occurs when alleles are inherited according to Mendel's Laws.

Mendel's laws : Two laws summarizing Gregor Mendel's theory of inheritance. The Law of Segregation states that each hereditary characteristic is controlled by two 'factors' (now called alleles), which segregate and pass into separate germ cells. The Law of Independent Assortment states that pairs of 'factors' segregate independently of each other when germ cells are formed.

Meningitis : Inflammation of the meninges.

Mentum : The chin-like protuberance occurring in certain orchid flowers, formed usually by the bases of the lateral sepals with the elongated column-foot

Mercado Commun del Sur (MERCOSUR) : A customs union between Argentina, Brazil, Paraguay, and Uruguay, which came into effect on January 1, 1995. Chile and Bolivia have become associate members.

Mericlinal : Refers to a chimera with tissue of one genotype partly surrounded by that of another genotype.

Mericloning : A propagation method using shoot tips in culture to proliferate multiple buds, which can then be separated, rooted and planted out.

Meristele : The branch of a stele supplying the leaf.

Meristem : 1) A plant tissue composed of dividing cells and giving rise to organs such as leaves, flowers, xylem, phloem, roots. 2) A region of a plant in which cells are not fully differentiated and are capable of repeated mitotic divisions.

Meristem culture : A laboratory technique that involves the taking of the growing meristem tip from within the new growth and culturing the nucleus of cells, in a similar way to germination of orchid seeds artificially.

Meristem tip : An explant comprising the meristem (meristematic dome) and usually one pair of leaf primordia. Also refers to explants originating from apical meristem tip or lateral or axillary meristem tip.

Meristem tip culture : Cultures derived from meristem tip explants. Used widely to achieve virus elimination and axillary shoot proliferation, less commonly for callus production.

Meristemoid : A localized group of callus cells, characterized by their accumulation of starch, RNA and protein, and giving rise to adventitious shoots or roots.

Merozygote : Partial zygote produced by a process of partial genetic exchange, such as transformation in bacteria.

Mesochile : The intermediate or middle part of the lip of orchids when this structure is separated into three distinct parts, as in Stanhopea

Mesoderm : The middle germ layer that forms in the early animal embryo and gives rise to parts such as bone and connective tissue.

Mesopelagic : Referring to depths between 200 to 1,000 meters in the ocean, seas and lakes.

Mesophile : A micro-organism able to grow in the temperature range 20-50 °C; optimal growth often occurs at about 37 °C.

Mesophyll : Leaf parenchyma tissue found between epidermal layers.

Mesophyllic bacteria : This group of bacteria species work to break down organic matter under "warm" conditions of 40 degrees up to 110 degrees. The ideal temperature of their environment is 70 to 90 degrees.

Mesophyte : A plant that requires a moderate amount of water for normal growth; includes most crop plants.

Metacentric chromosome : A chromosome in which the centromere is located in the middle and, consequently, the chromosome arms are of about equal length.

Metal affinity chromatography : A chromatographic technique, in which a compound interacting with a specific metal ion can be captured by immobilizing the relevant ion on the column's solid matrix.

Metalloenzyme : An enzyme which requires the presence of a metal in order to be catalytically active.

Metallothionein : A protective protein that binds heavy metals such as cadmium and lead.

Metamorphosis : The changes of form insects go through in their life cycle from egg to immature stages to adult.

Methylation : The addition of a methyl group ($-CH_3$) to a molecule, most commonly in the context of DNA where cytosine and, less often, adenine residues can be modified in this way, sometimes resulting in a change in transcription.

Metritis : Infection of the uterus. If the infection follows birthing, it is a postpartum metritis.

MFN : Most-Favored-Nation

MHC : Major Histocompatibility Complex.

MHz : In computers, is a measure of processor speed. Higher numbers reflect a faster computer processor.

Micro minerals : Minor mineral elements required in very small amounts in the ration of animals. Includes manganese (Mn), copper (Cu), zinc (Zn), selenium (Se) iron (Fe), cobalt (Co), iodine (I) and fluorine (Fl).

Micro organism : These are microscopic plants and animals. They exist in soil for the purpose of breaking down organic matter into basic mineral elements. They include bacteria, fungi, actinomycetes, algae, protozoa, yeast, germs, ground pearls, and nematodes.

Micro propagation : Also called propagating by tissue culture. Taking cell slices of plant material and starting growth on culture dishes.

Micro water catchment : A modification to the soil surface on a slope that traps and conveys runoff water to a small pit, adjacent to which a tree is planted. Part of water harvesting.

Microalgal culture : Culture in bioreactors of microalgae (including seaweeds).

Micro-carrier : Small particles used as a support material for (particularly mammalian) cells, which are too fragile to be pumped and stirred as bacterial cells are in a large-scale culture.

Microclimate : A physical area with a set of conditions different from those surrounding the area.

Microdroplet Array (MDA) : A technique used to simultaneously evaluate large numbers of media modifications, employing small quantities of medium into which are placed small numbers of cells or protoplasts. These form a monolayer at the droplet meniscus and can easily be examined.

Micro-element : A nutritional element required in very small quantities.

Microfibril : Microscopic fibres visible only at the high magnification of the electron microscope.

Microflora : The small plants that can be seen only with a microscope, such as algae, fungi.

Microinjection : A means to introduce a solution of DNA, protein, or other soluble material into a cell using a fine microcapillary pipet.

Micro-isolating system : Mechanical separation of single cells or protoplasts thus allowing them to proliferate individually.

Micronucleus : A nucleus, distinct from and smaller than the main nucleus, but lying within the same cell. They usually arise following abnormal meiotic or mitotic telophases, where individual chromosomes or chromosome fragments do not reach the pole.

Micropropagation : Various procedures by which small pieces of plant tissue are taken, surface sterilized and then grown on, or in, an appropriate medium under carefully controlled environmental conditions and provided with appropriate nutrients, growth hormones, and supplementary components, to allow cells to differentiate into small plantlets (explants). These are then transplanted (perhaps several times) and eventually hardened off before being planted out.

Micropyle : 1) A small opening in the surface of a plant ovule through which the pollen tube passes prior to fertilization. 2) A small pore in some animal cells or tissues.

Microsatellite : A segment of DNA characterized by a variable number of copies(typically 5-50) of a sequence of around 5 or fewer bases (called a repeat unit). At any one locus (genomic site), there are usually several different "alleles" in a population, each allele identifiable according to the number of repeat units. This existence of multiple alleles (high level of polymorphism) has enabled microsatellites to be developed as powerful markers in many different species. They are detected by the polymerase chain reaction..

Microspore : The immature male gametophyte in seed plants; the haploid male cell that ripens into a pollen grain.

Mid-parent value : The average of the phenotypic measure, with respect to a given trait, of the two parents used to generate the population being analysed.

Mid-water trawls : Work in mid-water rather than the sea bottom. Their front net sections are very often made with very large meshes, which herd the fish schools towards the back of the net. They may be towed by one or two boats.

MIF : Milk Industry Foundation

Mildew : Several different types of fungi. Two popular types are downy and powdery. It leaves a white coating on the leaves. Common to crepe myrtle, zinnias, grapes, and roses : even bee balms. It shows up in cool, wet weather. Drip irrigation can prevent some occurrence. Plant disease resistant varieties.

Miliary : Small', resembling a seed.

Milk fat test : The percentage of fat in the milk. To be legal, whole milk must contain at least 3.25% fat.

Milk marketing orders : Administered by the Agricultural Marketing Service, federal milk marketing orders were first instituted in the 1930s to promote orderly marketing conditions by, among other things, applying a uniform system of classified pricing throughout the farm milk market. Federal milk marketing orders regulate handlers that sell milk or milk products within an order region, by requiring them to pay not less than an established minimum price for the Grade A milk they purchase from dairy producers, depending on how the milk is used.

Milk replacer : A substitute for feeding whole milk to calves, generally consisting of milk by-products and/or plant products and is mixed with water. The higher quality replacers have more milk products.

Milk-feed price ratio : A measure of the value of 16% protein ration (feed) to one pound of whole milk. As with the hog-corn ratio, this relationship is an indicator of the profitability of milk production.

Milking machine : An electronic machine which uses air suction to bring milk out of the udder of an animal.

Milking parlor : A facility that functions to extract milk from a cow by means of vacuum.

Milo : A small drought-resistant grain sorghum with compact bearded heads of large yellow or whitish seeds.

Mimosine : An alkaloid toxic to animals, which is contained in some members of the legume family (mimosaceae) including leucaena leucocephala. Its toxicity minimizes the amounts of leafy material that can be fed, although ruminants can detoxify mimosine through bacterial action in the rumen provided they have the right microflora (either naturally or by inoculation).

Mineral soil : A soil containing lessthan 20% organic matter or having a surface organic layer less than 30 cm deep.

Mineral supplement : A rich source of one or more mineral elements.

Mineralization : Organic matter is broken down into humus, then acids, enzymes and compoinds, and finally into basic mineral elements.

Minerals : Supply food and nutrients for plants and microorganisms. Webster defines minerals as "any naturally occurring substance that is neither vegetable nor animal". In other words, these are the most basic form into which organic matter can be broken. At the mineral stage, the particles are inorganic.

Minimum inoculum size : The critical volume of inoculum required to initiate culture growth, due to the diffusive loss of cell materials into the medium. The subsequent culture growth cycle is dependent on the inoculum size, which is determined by the volume of medium and size of the culture vessel.

Minimum viable population : The smallest isolated population having a good chance of surviving for a given number of years despite the foreseeable effects of demographic, environmental, and genetic events and natural catastrophes.

Mini-prep : A small-scale preparation of plasmid or phage DNA. Used to purify cloned DNA from the DNA of the vector.

Minisatellite : A form of variable number tandem repeats in which the repeat unit size ranges from 10-100 bp. Used for DNA fingerprinting following Southern hybridization. Generally concentrated at the ends of chromosomes and in regions with a high frequency of recombination.

Miosis : Small pupil.

Mismatch : The occurrence of a non-complementary pairs of bases in a double helix of DNA, e.g. A:C, G:T.

Miticide : A pesticide that kills mites.

Mitochondrial DNA (mtDNA) : A circular DNA found in mitochondria. In mammals, mtDNA makes up less than 1% of the total DNA, but in plants the amount is variable. It encodes rRNA and tRNA and some mitochondrial proteins (up to 30 in animals).

Mitochondrion : Organelle possessing its own DNA which appear in all eukaryotic cells (and never in prokaryotic cells) and produce adenosine triphosphate as an energy source for the cell via oxidative phosphorylation. Mitochondria contain many enzymes of the respiratory cycle, although most of these proteins are nuclear encoded.

Mixed farming : Farming different types of crops and animals within one farm.

Mixed garden : A land-use form on private lands outside the village, dominated by planted perennial crops, mostly trees, under which annual (seasonal) crops are cultivated. When spices are grown they are called 'spice gardens'.

Mixed grazing : Grazing by two or more species of grazing animals on the same land unit, not necessarily at the same time but within the same grazing season.

Mixed stand : A stand in which less than 80% of the trees in the main canopy are of a single species.

Mobilization : 1) The transfer between bacteria of a non-conjugative plasmid by a conjugative plasmid. 2) The transfer between bacteria of chromosomal genes by a conjugative plasmid.

Mobilizing function : The genes on a plasmid that give it the ability to facilitate the transfer of either a non-conjugative or a conjugative plasmid from one bacterium to another.

Mode : In a frequency distribution, the class having the greatest frequency.

MOET : Multiple Ovulation And Embryo Transfer.

Moist but not wet : Plants that grow well in moist conditions but not entirely wet. Whether it be in the ground or in a container.

Molluscs : Soft-bodied, usually hard-shelled, animals of the phylum mollusca and divided into three categories : univalves (abalone, conch, and snails), bivalves (clams, oysters, and mussels), and cephalopods (squid and octopus).

Mollusk : Invertebrate animals with soft, unsegmented bodies, such as clams and snails, usually enclosed in a calcium shell.

Molt : To shed the exoskeleton to accommodate growth.

Monogenic : Trait controlled by a single gene.

Monohybrid : Heterozygous with respect to one gene.

Monohybrid cross : A cross between parents differing in only one trait or in which only one trait is being considered.

Monokine : Generic name for proteins that are released by monocytes to act on other cells involved in the immune response. A sub-class of cytokines.

Monolayer : A single layer of cells growing on a surface.

Monotypic : One type, such as one species in a genus

Moon gardening : A very romantic night garden created by using white night flowering plants or light variegated leaf varieties of plants.

Morbidity ; Rate of disease incidence; an important measure in epidemiological studies.

Morphogen : A substance that stimulates the development of form or structure in an organism.

Morphogenesis : The development, through growth and differentiation, of form and structure in an organism.

Most-Favored Nation (MFN) status : A commitment that a country will extend to another country the lowest tariff rates it applies to any third country. A country is under no obligation to extend MFN status to another country, unless they are both contracting parties to the GATT, or unless MFN status is specified in an agreement between them.

Motif : A conserved sequence of nucleotides or amino acids that can be associated with some function of, respectively, a length of DNA or a protein.

Motility : Progressive movement of sperm. A sign of health sperm.

MRU : Minimum Recognition Units.

Mt : Metric Ton - International Weigh Measure In Grain Trade.

MTD : Maximum Tolerated Dose

Mucosal immunity : A form of local immunity on the body surfaces of the respiratory, intestinal and genital tracts.

Müeller cells : Cells responsible for support and nutrition of the retina.

Mulch : A natural or artificial layer of plant residue or other material on the soil surface. Mulch reduces erosion, conserves soil moisture, inhibits weed growth, and can provide the soil with organic matter as it breaks down. Mulch till prepares the soil so as to leave plant residues (or other mulching materials) on or near the surface.

Muller's muscle : Smooth muscle in the eyelids which provides tone to the lids. Innervated by sympathetic fibers.

Multi-copy : Describing plasmids which replicate to produce many copies per host bacterial cell.

Multigene family : A set of genes (not necessarily mapping to the same genomic location) that are related in nucleotide sequence and/or that produce polypeptides with similar amino acid sequences. Sequence similarity does not always result in functional similarity.

Multigenic : Trait controlled by several genes, as opposed to monogenic.

Multilateral Trade Negotiations (MTN) : Negotiations between General Agreement on Tariffs and Trade (GATT) member nations that are conducted under the auspices of the GATT and that are aimed at reducing tariff and nontariff trade barriers. The World Trade Organization has now replaced the GATT as the administrative body.

Multi-Locus probe : A DNA sequence that hybridizes to a number of different genomic sites.

Multimedia card : A multimedia card is a small removable mass storage device. Used as non-volatile memory in digital cameras and PDA devices.

Multimer : A protein made up of more than one polypeptide chain.

Multi-modal : Using more than one method.

Multipath : Interference caused by reflected GPS signals arriving at the receiver, typically as a result of nearby structures or other reflective surfaces.

Multiple alleles : The existence of more than two alleles at a locus in a population.

Multiple arbitrary amplicon profiling : A collective term for a number of related polymerase chain reaction techniques, all of which use arbitrary primers, and which generate a number of distinct amplification products.

Multiple use : Multiple use of the national forests means the 'harmonious and coordinated management of the various resources, each with the other, without impairment of the productivity of the land, with consideration being given to the relative values of the various resources, and not necessarily the combination of uses that will give the greatest dollar return or the greatest unit output.' Multiple use implies a sustained yield of outdoor recreation, range, timber, watershed, and wildlife and fish values.

Multiplex : 1) The simultaneous amplification of a number of amplicons in a single polymerase chain reaction, achieved by including more than one set of primers in the reaction mix. 2) The inheritance pattern of alleles in autopolyploids.

Multivalent : A vaccine containing multiple antigens.

Mutagen : An agent that causes a permanent genetic change in a cell other than that which occurs during normal growth. Testing to determine mutagenicity is one component of assessing the potential chronic toxicity of pesticides and other chemicals.

Mutagenesis : Induction of heritable change(s) in the genetic constitution of a cell through alterations to its DNA.

Mutant : An organism or an allele bearing a mutation. Usually applied when a characteristic change in phenotype can be recognized.

Mutual self-help housing : A program to assist groups of low-income families in building their own homes. Each family is expected to contribute at least 700 hours of labor in building homes for each other. Participating families generally have low income and are unable to pay for homes built by the contract method.

Mutualistic : A relationship where both participants or parties benefit.

M-W price : Minnesota-Wisconsin price

Mycorrhiza : Fungi that form an association with, or have a symbiotic relationship with roots of more developed plants.

Mycotoxin : A substance produced by fungi and toxic to animals, e.g., vomitoxin, zearalenone and aflatoxin.

Mydriasis : Dilated pupil.

N

Nectar : A sugar and water substance secreted by flowers, this will attract pollinators like bees and hummingbirds searching for food.

Nectariferous : Having nectar

Neem : A botanical insecticide that is nontoxic. It is derived from the neem tree (azaderachta indica).

Negative autogenous regulation : Inhibition of the expression of a gene or set of co-ordinately regulated genes by the product of the gene or the product of one of the genes.

Negative control system : A mechanism by which a regulatory protein is required to turn off gene expression.

Neoplasia : Another term for cancer.

Neoplasm : Localized cell multiplication, forming a tumour. Generally the result of genetic transformation. Neoplasmic cells differ in structure and function from the original cell type.

Neoteny : The retention of juvenile body characters in the adult state, or the occurrence of adult characters in the juvenile state.

Nephrotoxic : A drug or chemical that causes damage to the cells of the kidneys.

Net Energy (NE) : The amount of feed energy actually available for animal maintenance and production. It represents the energy fraction in a feed left after fecal, urinary, gas and heat losses are deducted from the gross energy value of a feed.

Net farm income : The money and non-money income form operators realize from farming as a return for labor, investment, and management after production expenses have been paid. Net farm income is measure in two ways net farm income before inventory adjustment and net farm income after inventory adjustment. Net farm income doesn't include changes in the value of inventories such as crops and livestock at the end of the year.

Net pen culture : A type of aquaculture where fish remain captive throughout their lives in marine pens built from nets, used by the salmon industry.

Neurotransmitter : A substance released from a neuron of the central or peripheral nervous which excites or inhibit the target cell. Examples include : acetylcholine, norepinephrine, epinephrine, dopamine, substance P, enkephalins, endorphins and serotonin.

Neutral mutation : A mutation that changes the nucleotide sequence of a gene, but has no observable effect on the fitness of the organism.

Neutral theory : The theory that much of evolution has been primarily due to random drift of neutral mutations.

Nictitans : The third eyelid which is a fold of tissue covered by conjunctiva and containing a lacrimal gland on the inner (bulbar) surface.

Nif gene cluster : Group of bacterial genes responsible for the biological fixation of atmospheric nitrogen.

Nigropallidal encephalomalacia : A specific brain lesion seen in horses with yellow star thistle poisoning. The clinical sign is an inability to swallow.

Nikolsky sign : The epidermis may be rubbed off with slight trauma. Named after a Russian dermatologist.

Nitrification : The natural process in which nitrogen in plant and animal wastes is oxidized, first to nitrites and then to nitrates, through the action of soil-borne microbes.

Nitrocellulose : A derivative of cellulose, which has the property of binding to many biological macromolecules, in particular DNA, RNA and protein. Filters made from nitrocellulose are commonly used in Southern and northern blotting experiments.

Nitrogen : An element found in the air and in all plant and animal tissues. For many crops, nitrogen fertilizer is essential for economic yields. However, nitrogen can also be a pollutant when nitrogen compounds are mobilized in the environment (e.g., leach from fertilized or manured fields), are discharged from septic tanks or feedlots, volatilize to the air, or are emitted from combustion engines. As pollutants, nitrogen compounds can have adverse health effects and contribute to degradation of waters.

NMDA receptor : Glutamate dependent N-methyl-D-aspartate (NMDA)receptors. This type of receptor develops in the central nervous system in response to sustained pain and appears to be responsible for amplifying pain, and causing opioid tolerance.

NOAH : Network of Animal Health (on-line veterinary community through the AVMA).

Nociceptors : Peripheral receptors for pain which sense painful stimuli and transmit signals to the central nervous system where the sensation of pain is perceived.

Nodule : Swollen globular structures formed on the roots of legumes, containing the nitrogen-fixing bacteria.

Nomenclature : The system of naming

Non repetitive : DNA/RNA A nucleotide sequence which does not include a significant proportion of repetitive sequences of nucleotides.

Non Steroidal Anti Inflammatory Drug (NSAID) : A drug such as aspirin that has anti inflammatory properties but that is not a corticosteroid.

Nonadditive gene effects : Favorable effects or actions produced by specific gene pairs or combinations. Nonadditive gene action is the primary cause of heterosis. Nonadditive gene action occurs when the heterozygous genotype is not intermediate in phenotypic value to the two homozygous genotypes.

Non-additive genetic variation : The proportion of the total genetic variation in a population that does not respond to simple mass selection and that causes specific pairwise crosses to depart from performance values predicted by the breeding values of the parents.

Non-autonomous : A term referring to biological units that cannot function by themselves; such units require the assistance of another unit, or "helper".

Non-Protein Nitrogen (NPN) : Nitrogen not derived from true protein, but can be used by rumen microbes to build microbial protein.

Nonrenewable resources : Resources that do not naturally replenish themselves within the limits of human time, such as minerals, in contrast to renewable resources such as soil and water. An example of nonrenewable resource, also called a stock resource, important to agriculture is petroleum.

Non-resupinate : Orchid flowers normally position the lip at the bottom just above the column. Some genera, however, such as Cycnoches, Malaxis, and Nephelaphyllum position the lip uppermost with the column below making the flower appear to be up-side-down.

Non-road emissions : Pollutants emitted by non-road engines and non-road vehicles, e.g., farm and construction equipment, gasoline-powered lawn and garden equipment, and power boats and outboard motors.

Non-ruminant herbivore : Animals with simple stomachs able to digest roughages and other fibrous feeds because of the microbial population in their hindgut.

Nonselective pesticide : A poison that kills a wide variety of pest species.

Nonsense mutation : A mutation which converts an amino-acid-specifying codon into a stop codon, e.g. a single base change from UAU to UAG generates the premature termination of the polypeptide chain at the position where a tyrosine was incorporated in the wild type.

Non-Structural Carbohydrates (NSC) : Simple carbohydrates, such as starches and sugars, stored inside the cell which serve as a cellular energy source. Non-structural carbohydrates are rapidly and easily digested by the animal.

Non-terrestrial rabies : Rabies in mammals that do not walk on the ground : bats.

Normal crop acreage : The acreage on a farm normally devoted to a group of designated crops. When a set-aside programme is in effect, a participating farm's total planted acreage of such designated crops plus set-aside acreage cannot exceed the normal crop acreage.

Normal saline : 0.9% sodium chloride. It is isotonic. It contains only sodium and chloride. Sodium chloride is used when blood sodium is decreased; such as in Addison's disease because it has a higher concentration of sodium than does lactated Ringer's. It may be used in lieu of lactated Ringer's for rehydration in patients with lymphoma. It is used as a rehydration solution when a patient has an increased potassium or calcium, and the administration of additional calcium or potassium are contraindicated.

Normal yield : The average historic yield established for a particular farm or area. Can also describe average yields. Normal production would be the normal crop acreage planted multiplied by the normal yield.

No-till farming : A method of planting crops that involves no seed bed preparation other than opening the soil to place individual seeds in holes or small slits; usually no cultivation during crop production; chemical weed control is normally used. May also be referred to as slot tillage or zero cultivation.

Notobiotic environment : An environment with no germs whatsoever.

Novel food : GM food and other foods and food ingredients consisting of or isolated from micro-organisms, fungi, algae, plants or animals, or which have been obtained through new processes.

Novel protein : A diet that contain proteins to which an animal has not previously been exposed(fed).

Noxious stimulus : A stimulus that is potentially or actually damaging to tissue. A stimulus that is of adequate intensity to trigger a nociceptive reaction in an animal.

NPE : Nutrition Programme for the Elderly

Nuclease : A class of enzymes that degrades DNA and/or RNA molecules by cleaving the phosphodiester bonds that link adjacent nucleotides. In deoxyribonuclease (DNase), the substrate is DNA. In endonuclease, it cleaves at internal sites in the substrate molecule. Exonuclease progressively cleaves from the end of the substrate molecule. In ribonuclease (RNase), the substrate is RNA. In the S1 nuclease, the substrate is single-stranded DNA or RNA.

Nuclei (Nucleus) : A structure located within a cell. Contains amongst other substances the genetic information of the cell.

Nuclein : The term used by Friedrich Miescher to describe the nuclear material he discovered in 1869, which today is known as DNA.

Nucleo-cytoplasmic ratio : In a cell, the ratio of nuclear to cytoplasmic volume. This ratio is high in meristematic cells and low in differentiated cells.

Nucleolar organizer Region (NOR) : A chromosomal segment containing a large array of genes that encode ribosomal RNA; located at the secondary constriction of specific chromosomes.

Nucleolus : An RNA-rich nuclear organelle in the nucleus of eukaryotic cells, produced by a nucleolar organizer. It represents the storage place for ribosomes and ribosome precursors. The nucleolus consists primarily of ribosomal precursor RNA, ribosomal RNA, their associated proteins, and some, perhaps all, of the enzymatic equipment (RNA polymerase, RNA methylase, RNA cleavage enzymes) required for synthesis, conversion and assembly of ribosomes. Subsequently the ribosomes are transported to the cytoplasm.

Nucleoplasm : The non-staining or slightly chromophilic, liquid or semi-liquid, ground substance of the interphase nucleus and which fills the nuclear space around the chromosomes and the nucleoli. Little is known of the chemical composition of this ground substance, which is not easily defined. Sometimes called "karyoplasm" when it is gel-like, and "karyolymph" when it is a colloidal fluid.

Nucleus : A dense protoplasmic membrane-bound region of a eukaryotic cell that contains the chromosomes, separated from the cytoplasm by a membrane; present in all eukaryotic cells except mature sieve-tube elements and red blood cells.

Null allele : An allele which produces no functional gene product.

Nullisomy : An otherwise diploid cell or organism lacking both members of a homologous chromosome pair.

Number of contemporaries : The number of animals of similar breed, sex and age against which an animal was compared in performance tests. The greater the number of contemporaries, the greater the accuracy of comparisons.

Number-averaged molecular weight : The mean of the molecular weight of all the polymers in a solution. The number-averaged molecular weight tells you how quickly a fluid will exert an effect. The smaller the number-averaged molecular weight, the quicker the initial oncotic response.

Nurse culture : Culturing cells from a suspension culture on a raft of filter paper above a callus tissue piece (nurse tissue). The filter paper serves to prevent tissue union but allows the flow of essential substances from the nurse to the isolated cells.

Nurseryman : One who is state certified to practice growing techniques of plant material making the proper selection for specific needs.

Nutriceutical : A conventional food product that has been modified (potentially by genetic engineering) to have improved nutritional characteristics and/or pharmaceutical properties.

Nutrient gradient : A diffusion gradient of nutrients and gases that develops in tissues where only a portion of the tissue is in contact with the medium. Gradients are less likely to form in liquid media than in callus cultures.

Nutrient medium : A solid, semi-solid or liquid formulation for in vitro cell or tissue growth.

Nutrient pollution : Contamination by excessive inputs of nutrient : a primary cause of eutrophication of surface waters, in which excess nutrients, usually nitrogen or phosphorus, stimulate algal growth. Sources of nutrient pollution include runoff from fields and pastures, discharges from septic tanks and feedlots, and emissions from combustion.

Nutrient requirements : The minimal amounts of nutrients (energy, protein, minerals and vitamins) necessary to meet an animal's minimal needs for maintenance, growth, reproduction, lactation or work.

Nutrients : Feed components required for the maintenance, production and health of animals (water, carbohydrates, lipids, proteins, minerals and vitamins).

Nutrition assistance programmes : Federal programmes in Puerto Rico and American Samoa that provide food assistance through block grant funds in lieu of food stamps.

Nutrition Education and Training (NET) programme : Authorizes grants to states for a nutrition education programme targeting school children, teachers, parents, and food service workers.

O

Oestrogen : The generic term for a group of female sex hormones which control the development of sexual characteristics and control oestrus.

Oestrous cycle : The cycle of reproductive activity shown by most sexually mature non-pregnant female mammals. AlteRNAtive spelling: estrous.

Oestrus : In female mammals, the period of sexual excitement and acceptance of the male.

Offal : The less valuable byproduct material from the preparation of a specific product; primarily refers to the byproducts of meat and poultry plants, e.g., blood, bone, feathers, fat.

Offer versus serve : Refers to the option children may have to refuse one or more items offered as part of a federally subsidized school lunch or breakfast without losing eligibility for federal reimbursement.

Off-farm (Non-farm) income : That portion of farm household income obtained off the farm, including nonfarm wages and salaries, pensions, and interest income earned by farm families. On average for all farms in the United States, off-farm income accounts for about 90% of farm operator household income.

Offset : Liquidating a purchase of futures contracts through the sale of an equal number of contracts of the same delivery month, or liquidating a short sale of futures through the purchase of an equal number of contracts of the same delivery month. In other words, selling if one has bought, or buying if one has sold, a futures or option contract.

Offshoot : Short, usually horizontal, stem produced near the crown of a plant.

Offspring : New individuals resulting from sexual or asexual reproduction.

Oilseed crops : Primarily soybeans, sunflower seed, canola, rapeseed, safflower, flaxseed, mustard seed, peanuts and cottonseed, used for the production of cooking oils, protein meals for livestock, and industrial uses. These specific oilseeds are eligible for nonrecourse loans. Other oilseed crops include castor beans and sesame.

Okazaki fragment : Replicated DNA fragments formed on the lagging strand in DNA synthesis from a double-stranded template The fragments are subsequently joined together by DNA ligase.

OL : Operating Loans, Farm

Oligosaccharide : Carbohydrate consisting of several linked monosaccharide units.

Oliguria : A small volume of urine produced. In adult dogs and cats oliguria is defined as urine production of less than 0.5 ml/lb/hr (1 ml/kg/hr).

Omentum : A thin lace-like layer of tissue in the abdomen that partially covers the organs.

Omnistar : A subscription based differential GPS source. Omnistar is a satellite-based DGPS source that requires a special GPS antenna.

Oncogene : A gene that causes cells to grow in an uncontrolled (i.e. tumourous) manner. Oncogenes are mutant forms of normal functional genes (called proto-oncogenes) that have a role in regulating cell proliferation.

Oocyte : The egg mother cell; it undergoes two meiotic divisions (oogenesis) to form the egg cell. The primary oocyte refers to the state before completion of the first meiotic division; the secondary oocyte after completion of the first meiotic division.

Oogenesis : The formation and growth of the egg in an animal ovary.

Oogonium : 1) A germ cell of the female animal, that gives rise to oocytes by mitotic division. 2) The female sex organ of algae and fungi.

Oospore : A spore developing from a zygote of certain algae and fungi, following the fusion of heterogametes.

Open continuous culture : A continuous culture system, in which inflow of fresh medium is balanced by outflow of a corresponding volume of spent medium plus cells. In the steady state, the rate of cell wash-out equals the rate of formation of new cells in the system.

Open pollinated : Any plant that has been pollinated in the field. In direct contrast to hybrid varieties that will grow true to variety the plants produced will be true to the parents.

Open pollination : Pollination by wind, insects, or other natural mechanisms.

Operator : The region of DNA that is upstream from a gene or genes and to which one or more regulatory proteins (repressor or activator) bind to control the expression of the gene(s).

Operon : A functionally integrated genetic unit for the control of gene expression in bacteria. It consists of one or more genes that encode one or more polypeptide(s) and the adjacent site (promoter and operator) that controls their expression by regulating the transcription of the structural genes.

Opine : The condensation product of an amino acid with either a keto-acid or a sugar, produced by the plant host as a result of Agrobacterium infection, and used exclusively by the Agrobacterium as a carbon source for growth and reproduction within the plant.

Opiod : Synthetic compounds with effects like opium but which are not derived from opium.

Opportunist : A bacteria that causes clinical disease in animals that are some how weakened and can not fight off the infection.

Opportunistic pathogen : Parasites that are usually harmless commensals in their normal habitat, but can cause disease when they gain access to other body sites - e.g. Pasteurella haemolytica (pneumonia) and Staphylococcus aureus (mastitis). Impairment of animal's immune defense is the principle factor leading to opportunistic infections.

Opsinizing antibody : A type of antibody that coats particles, such as bacteria to promote phagocytosis.

Optic nerve : Formed by axons of the ganglion cells of the retina.

Optic neuritis : Inflammation of the optic nerve; can be unilateral or bilateral.

Optimum level of performance : The most profitable or favorable ranges in levels of performance for the economically important traits in a given environment and management system. For example, although many cows produce too little milk, in every management system there is a point beyond which higher levels of milk production may reduce fertility and decrease profit.

Option contract : An option contract gives the buyer the right, but not the obligation, to buy (call option) or sell (put option) a futures contract at a specific price within a specified period of time, regardless of the market price of that commodity.

Oral toxicity : Ability of a chemical to cause injury when ingested by mouth.

Oral transmission : Common route of animal-to-animal exposure due to contact with infected placenta, fetal fluids, milk.

Orbicularis oculi muscle : Muscle that encircles the eye and acts to closes the eye. It is innervated by cranial nerve 7, the facial nerve.

Orbital fascia : The connective tissue sheath that lines the orbit and envelopes all the structures within the orbit.

Orchidist : One who collects or is interested in orchids horticulturally

Orchidologist : A botanist who specializes in the technical sturdy of orchids

Orchitis : Inflammation of the testicles.

Orderly marketing : Coordination of the total supply of a commodity in order to achieve sellers' joint market objectives. This is an activity carried out by some marketing order programs.

ORF : Open Reading Frame.

Organic : Literally refers to something derived from plant or animal matter. Includes anything that is or was living, made from something living, excreted from something living. The term "organic" is used to describe a philosophy of working within the laws and systems existing in nature to achieve a healthy environment that is bountiful long-term. Healthy soil is the foundation of this philosophy, therefore, the term comes up frequently in discussions of home composting.

Organic complex : A chemically undefined compound added to nutrient media to stimulate growth, e.g. coconut milk; malt extract; yeast extract; casein hydrolysate.

Organic farming : Crop production systems that generally exclude the use of synthetic fertilizers, pesticides, and other chemicals. To the maximum extent feasible, organic farming systems rely on crop rotations, crop residues, animal manures, legumes, green manures, off-farm organic wastes, mechanical cultivation, and biological pest control to maintain soil productivity, to supply nutrients to plants, and to control weeds and pests.

Organism : An individual living system, such as animal, plant or micro-organism, that is capable of reproduction, growth and maintenance.

Organophosphates : Insecticides that contain phosphorus, carbon, and hydrogen. They are cholinesterase inhibitors; some are highly acutely toxic, but they usually are not persistent in the environment. Parathion is an example of an organophosphate.

Origin of replication : The nucleotide position on a DNA sequence from which DNA synthesis (replication) is initiated.

Ornamental : A plant that is grown strictly for its foliage or flower rather than for food or any other economic use.

Orphan gene : A gene or DNA sequence whose function is not known.

Orphan receptor : A receptor for which a cellular function or ligand has yet to be identified.

Ortet : The plant from which a clone is obtained.

Orthologous : Homologous genes/gene products that have evolved divergently between species; many rice genes have orthologues in other cereal genomes, because of the common ancestry of cereal species.

Osmotic potential : Change in the energy state of solvent brought about by dissolving a substance in the solvent - water in the biological sciences. The potential of aqueous solutions is always negative compared to pure water.

Solvent flows from higher to lower osmotic potential solutions by diffusion or osmosis.

Osmoticum : A chemical agent (e.g. polyethylene glycol, mannitol, glucose or sucrose) employed to maintain the osmotic potential of a nutrient medium equivalent to that of the cultured cells, i.e. the medium and the cells are isotonic. Because of this osmotic equilibrium, cells are not damaged in vitro.

Outbreeding : A mating system characterized by the interbreeding of genetically unrelated or dissimilar individuals. Since genetic diversity tends to be enhanced, and vigour or fitness of individuals increased by this process, it is often used to counter the detrimental effects of continuous inbreeding.

Outcrossing : Mating of individuals that are less closely related than the average of the breed. Commercial breeders and some purebred breeders should be outcrossing by periodically adding new sires that are unrelated to their cow herd. This outcrossing should reduce the possibility of loss of vigor due to inbreeding.

Outflow : The volume of growing cells that is removed from a bioreactor during a continuous fermentation process.

Ova : An egg.

Ovarian bursa : A structure that surrounds the ovaries and collects eggs released from the ovary and channels those eggs to the uterus.

Ovariohysterectomy (OHE OVH) : Surgical removal of the ovaries and uterus.

Ovary : 1) Enlarged basal portion of the pistil of a plant flower that contains the ovules. 2) The reproduction organ in female animals in which eggs are produced.

Over potting : Repotting a plant into a pot which is too large to allow successful establishment. The roots may die from too much moisture.

Over the Counter drugs (OTC) : Drugs that can be purchased with out a prescription.

Overdominance : Where heterozygote performance is superior to that of either parental genotype.

Overlapping reading frame : Start codons in different reading frames generate different polypeptides from the same DNA sequence.

Overseeding : Planting on top of an existing garden or lawn. Rye grass over lawns for winter. Wildflower seed in meadows.

Ovine Progressive Pneumonia (OPP) : A chronic inflammatory disease of the lung leading to eventual suffocation.

Ovulation : Release of the female germ cell, or egg, by the ovary. Cows usually ovulate several hours after the end of estrus or standing heat.

Oxygen-electrode-based sensor : Sensor in which an oxygen electrode, which measures the amount of oxygen in a solution, is coated with a biological material such as an enzyme which generates or absorbs oxygen when the appropriate substrate is present. When the biological reaction takes place, the amount of oxygen close to the electrode changes and the signal from the electrode changes, thus signalling the concentration of substrate.

Oxyglobin : A red blood cell substitute made from polymerized bovine hemoglobin.

Ozone (O_3) : A highly reactive molecule composed of three oxygen atoms. Environmentally, ozone is important in two completely separate contexts—one, as a naturally occurring screen of harmful radiation in the outer atmosphere (i.e., stratospheric ozone), and two, as a component of polluting smog formed from emissions resulting from human activities (i.e., urban smog). In the stratosphere 7 to 10 miles above the Earth, naturally occurring ozone acts to shield the Earth from harmful radiation.

P

Palatability : The appeal and acceptability of feedstuffs. Affected by the taste, odour, texture and temperature of the feed.

Paleontology : The study of the fossil record of past geo- logical periods and of the phylogenetic relationships between ancient and contemporary plant and animal species.

Palindrome : A segment of double-stranded DNA, in which the order of bases, read 5'?3' in one strand, is the same as that in the complementary antiparallel strand, also read 5'?3'. If the sequence is written in the normal convention, on two lines with paired bases shown one above the other, the base order on one strand runs in the opposite direction to that on the complementary strand. They are often found at the ends of transposable elements, and recognition sites for type II restriction endonucleases are also palindromes.

Palindromic sequence : A DNA locus whose 5'-to-3' sequence is identical on each DNA strand. The sequence is the same when one strand is read left to right and the other strand is read right to left. Recognition sites of many restriction enzymes are palindromic.

Palisade parenchyma : Elongated cells found just beneath the upper epidermis of leaves, typically rich in chloroplasts.

Palpebral fissure : The opening between the eyelids.

Palpebral or blink reflex : Used to assess sensation and the ability to close the eyelids.

Panmictic population : A population in which mating occurs at random.

Panmixis : Random mating in a population.

Panniculitis : Inflammation of subcutanious fat. Several proposed causes and is sterile in some breeds such as the Dachshund.

Pannus : Chronic superficial keratitis presumed to be immune-mediated.

Parabasal cell : Epithelial cells exfoloiated from the vagina during proestrus. The cells are small and round with large and distinct nuclei. The total area of the cytoplasm of the parabasal cell is smaller than the nucleus.

Paracentric inversion : A chromosomal rearrangement in which a segment of chromosome, excluding the centromere, is rotated.

Paradoxical CSF acidosis : Paradoxical CSF acidosis is a condition caused by the administration of a large amount of bicarbonate to an acidotic patient, which will result in neurologic dysfunction. When one gives bicarbonate, the equation is shifted towards the left of the screen, towards the generation of CO_2. CO_2 is very diffusible, and will diffuse across the blood brain barrier and then shift the equation in the cerebral spinal fluid towards the right with a generation of hydrogen ions. Even though additional bicarbonate is being generated in the CNS, the neurons perceive the increase in hydrogen ions and malfunction.

Paraffin (Wax) : A translucent, white, solid hydrocarbon with a low melting point. One use is as an embedding medium to support tissue for sectioning for light microscopy observation.

Paralysis : Abnormal function of nerves resulting in an inability to walk.

Parameter : A value or measurement that varies with circumstances, and is used as a reference to quantify a situation or a process.

Paraphimosis : Paraphimosis is when the penis is extruded from the prepuce and cannot be returned to its normal position. This may occur following breeding or sexual excitement such as being kenneled next to a bitch in heat, or by a traumatic fracture of the os penis.

Parasexual cycle : A sexual cycle involving changes in chromosome number but differing in time and place from the usual sexual cycle; occurring in those fungi in which the normal cycle is suppressed or apparently absent.

Parasite : Any plant that grows upon another. It steals its moisture and nourishment from its host. Mistletoe is a good example.

Parasitic : An organism that lives on or in another living organism (the host) and obtains nutrition from the host.

Parasiticide : A substance that kills parasites.

Parasitism : Denotes organisms which survive and persist on or within another living organism. The parasite usually does not harm the animal. The most successful parasites achieve a balance whereby both the parasite and host animal survive. Among the parasites found on or within animals are bacteria, protozoans, fungi, mycoplasmas, rickettsia, and viruses.

Paronychia : Inflammation of the nail fold.

Paroxysmal : The sudden onset of a symptom that reoccurs. For example paroxysmal seizures begin suddenly and occur more than once.

Parterre : Symmetry at its best. These are great ornamental garden beds that have been geometrically designed and separated by walkways. The gardens are most appreciated by an above view. One of the most famous being the gardens of Versailles.

Parthenocarpy : The development of fruit without fertilization.

Parthenogenesis : Production of an embryo from an unfertilized egg.

Parthenogenetic : Seed which develops without fertilization, but by stimulus only

Partial digest : Incomplete reaction of a restriction enzyme with DNA, such that only a proportion of the target sites are cleaved. Partial digests are often performed to give an overlapping collection of DNA fragments for use in the construction of a gene bank.

Partial parenteral Nutrition (PPN) : Providing energy and nutritional supplementation to a patient at 50 to 70% of the patient's nutritional needs.

Particle radiation : High energy nuclear emissions, used as physical agents of mutagenesis. Three major types typically used: alpha () (positively charged), beta () (negatively charged), or neutrons (uncharged).

Particle size : Measure of the diameter of granular feed materials and/or the length of roughage fragments. Particle size can affect mixing of feed ingredients and digestion rate.

Particulate matter : A category of air pollutants that refers to small, solid particles or liquid droplets suspended in the air, including soot, fumes, dust, pollen and spores, smoke, and spray. Particles vary in biological effect depending on their size and composition. Two National Ambient Air Quality Standards have been set for particulates : One, in effect since 1987, regulates particles smaller than 10 microns in diameter (PM10), a size range that includes fugitive dust from construction and tilling the soil. A 1997 change in how compliance with the PM10 standard is measured somewhat reduces the stringency of the standard, which will make it easer for areas not in compliance (41 in early 1997) to attain the standard. The second PM standard, promulgated in July 1997, regulates particles smaller than 2.5 microns (PM2.5), a size range dominated by combustion products, but which can include very fine fugitive dust and ammonia that can come from agricultural sources. Because of the need to develop monitoring and to assess ambient levels of PM2.5, it will be the mid- 2000s before pollution levels are established and any control programs might be instituted.

Partners for wildlife : A voluntary partnership program administered by the Fish and Wildlife Service to provide financial and technical assistance to private landowners who wish to protect or restore wetlands. This program has been widely used by rural landowners, including farmers.

Parturition : The act of giving birth; calving.

Passage : The transfer or transplantation of cells from one culture medium to another.

Passage number : The number of times cells in culture have been sub-cultured.

Passage time : Time interval between successive sub-cultures.

Passalong plants · Plants that are shared between friends and not easily found in catalogs. Usually some plant from an older garden.

Passive immunity : 1) Natural acquisition of antibodies by the foetus or neonate (newborn) from the mother. 2) The artificial introduction of specific antibodies by the injection of serum from an immune animal. In both cases, temporary protection is conferred on the recipient.

Passive transfer : The transfer of antibodies from colostrum into the cria's blood.

Pasteurization : The process of heating milk to kill pathogens that may be harmful to humans.

Pasture : A fenced area of forage, usually improved, on which animals are grazed.

Pastureland : Land used primarily for the production of domesticated forage plants for livestock (in contrast to rangeland, where vegetation is naturally-occurring and is dominated by grasses and perhaps shrubs). Rotation pasture or cropland under winter cover crops is not included in this definition. The 1992 national resources inventory recorded 126 million acres of pastureland, 9% of all nonfederal rural lands.

Pat gene : A gene obtained from Streptomyces sp. encoding resistance to glufosinate-ammonium containing herbicides. (These inhibit plant synthesis of glutamine). Used widely as a means of transgenically inducing herbicide resistance in crop plants.

Patent : A legal permission to hold exclusive right - for a defined period of time - to manufacture, use or sell an invention.

Patent period : The parasites are producing eggs with in the host.

Paternal : Pertaining to the father.

Pathogen : A disease-causing organism (generally microbial: bacteria, fungi, viruses; but can extend to other organisms: e.g. nematodes etc.).

Pathogenicity : Capacity of parasite to produce disease.

Pathogenesis related protein (PR protein) : One of a group of proteins that are characteristically highly expressed as part of a plant's response to pathogen attack. Many of these proteins are similarly expressed following infection with a broad range of pathogens, indicating their role in the hypersensitive response.

Pathogen-free : Uncontaminated with pathogen.

Pathotoxin : Substance secreted by certain pathogens, in order to attack the host tissue. Some pathotoxins are also toxic to non-hosts, especially animals or humans.

Pathovar : Strain of a plant-attacking bacterium or fungus that can be differentiated from others by their interaction with specific host cultivars.

Pavletic : A surgical technique used to repair lid defects using skin from the lip.

Payment rate : Generally, the amount paid per unit of production (i.e., bushel, pound, hundredweight) to each participating farmer for eligible production under commodity income and price support programs.

Payments In Lieu of Taxes (PILT) : A program administered by the Bureau of Land Management of the Department of Interior to compensate counties for the tax-exempt status of federal lands; the fixed payments per entitlement acre (on most but not all federal lands) are adjusted for low county populations and for other revenue-sharing payments (e.g., Forest Service county payments) in a complicated formula.

Pea gravel : Gravel about the size of a pea. Used a lot in driveways and walkways.

Peak milk : Maximum daily milk yield during lactation. Good peak yield is 100-120 lbs and occurs between 60-90 days in milk.

Peanut price support program : The federal program that supports the farm price of peanuts by offering price support loans to peanut growers and by placing limits on the amount of peanuts allowed to be sold for domestic food use. Farmers may sell peanuts produced in excess of marketing limits (referred to as the peanut poundage quota : one example of a marketing quota), primarily for export and crushing into peanut oil and meal.

Peat : The preserved and compressed remains of dead bog plants. Often known as peat moss because it is from sphagnum or sedge peat.

Peat pot : Compressed peat into a pot that can be used for starting seeds. When planting times comes this entire pot can be put in the ground and the roots will grow through the pot as it decomposes.

Pelleted seeds : Seeds that have been coated with an inert material just to make the handling of the seed easier.

Pelletized : The coating and forming into pellets of very small seed so they are easier to handle.

Pelodera dermatitis : Rhabditic dermatitis. Larvae of the free living nematode, Pelodera strongyloides which penetrate the skin of animals.

Peptide : A sequence of amino acids linked by peptide bonds; a breakdown or build-up unit in protein metabolism. Typically used to describe low molecular weight species.

Peptide bond : The chemical bond holding amino acid residues together in peptides and proteins. The (CO-NH) bond is formed by the condensation, with loss of a water molecule, between the carboxyl (-COOH) group of one amino acid and the amino ($-NH_2$) of the next amino acid.

Peptide expression library : A collection of peptide molecules, produced by recombinant cells, in which the amino acid sequences are varied.

Peptide Nucleic Acid (PNA) : A synthetic oligonucleotide analogue, in which the sugar backbone is replaced by a peptide chain, upon which the nucleoside residues are strung. Probes made from PNA appear to have greater specificity than those made from DNA.

Perennial : A plant which will live for three years or more under normal conditions.

Perennial ryegrass : A cool-season turfgrass with seeds that germinate quickly. The cultural requirements are similar to those of Kentucky bluegrass; however, it is not quite as hardy or disease resistant as bluegrasses.

Perennials : Plants that do not die after flowering, but live from year to year.

Perfoliate : Paired leaves which fuse around the stem.

Performance data : The record of the individual animal for reproduction, production and possibly carcass merit. Traits included would be birth, weaning and yearling weights, calving ease, calving interval, milk production, etc.

Performance pedigree : A pedigree that includes performance records of ancestors, half- and full-sibs and progeny in addition to the usual pedigree information. Also, the performance information is systematically combined to list estimated breeding values on the pedigrees by some breed associations.

Performance testing : The systematic collection of comparative production information for use in decision making to improve efficiency and profitability of beef production. Differences in performance among cattle must be utilized in decision making for performance testing to be beneficial. The most useful performance records for management, selection and promotion decisions will vary among purebred breeders and for purebred breeders compared with commercial cattle producers.

Pergola : Sometimes called an arbor, or walkway covered with trellis work. Usually climbing plants will cover the hardscape feature.

Perianal : The region around the anus.

Periclinal : The orientation of cell wall or plane of cell division parallel to the reference surface.

Periclinal chimera : 1) Genotypically or cytoplasmically different tissues arranged in concentric layers. 2) A chimera in which one or more layers of tissue derived from one graft member enclose the central tissue derived from the other member of the graft.

Pericycle : Region of the plant bounded externally by the endodermis and internally by the phloem. Most roots originate from the pericycle.

Perineal : The region around the anus.

Perlite : Granular volcanic rock, used to improve the aeration in potting soil. No nutrient value.

Permaculture : A very advanced system of trying to grow and provide food by using perennial plants instead of the annuals the agriculture world uses now for most of our food.

Permanent pasture : Pasture of perennial or self-seeding annual plants maintained through several years of grazing.

Permanent vegetative cover : Trees, or perennial grasses, legumes, or shrubs with an expected life span of at least 5 years. Permanent cover is required on cropland entered into the Conservation Reserve Program.

Permanent Wilting Point (PWP) : The moisture content of a soil below which plants wilt to such an extent that they fail to recover even when fully watered.

Permeable : Referring to a membrane, cell or cell system through which small molecules can diffuse.

Persistent : Chemicals with a long inactivation or degradation time, such as some pesticides. Persistent substances can become dangerously concentrated in the tissues of organisms at the top end of a food chain.

Persistent pesticides : Pesticides that do not readily break down in the environment. Becoming long-lived components of the ecosystem, these chemicals may have enduring effects at low concentrations or may bioaccumulate, posing hazards to higher predators.

Persistent Pupillary Membranes (PPMs) : Remnants of a blood vessels that once filled the anterior chamber and nourished the developing lens.

Petals : A whorl of structures that surround the inner reproductive organs of a flower. Together they are called the corolla. They often attract insects by color or nectar, facilitating pollination.

Petiole : Leafstock, slender stalk by which a leaf is attached to the stem.

Petri dish : Flat round glass or plastic dish with a matching lid, used for small-scale culturing of organisms, germinating seeds etc. Also referred to as plates, hence to plate a culture.

Phaeohyphomycoses : Subcutaneous nodules, granulomatous lesions and draining tracts caused by Pythium sp.(Hyphomyces sp.), Dreschlera sp and other species.

Phage : Abbreviation for bacteriophage.

Phagemids : Cloning vectors that contain components derived from both phage and plasmid DNA.

Phagocytes : Immune system cells that ingest and destroy viruses, bacteria, fungi and other foreign substances or cells.

Phagocytosis : The process by which foreign particles invading the body are engulfed and broken down by phagocytes.

Phalaenopsoid : Growing like a Phalaenopsis

Phenolic oxidation : Common aspect of the wound response in plants. Phenolic oxidation is often indicated by blackening of tissue and it may be a precursor to growth inhibition or, in severe cases, to tissue necrosis and death.

Phenolics : Compounds with hydroxyl group(s) attached to the benzene ring, forming esters, ethers and salts. Phenolic substances produced from newly explanted tissues are liable to oxidise, and as a result form coloured compounds visible in nutrient media.

Phenotype : The visible or measurable expression of a character; for example, weaning weight, postweaning gain, reproduction, etc. Phenotype is influenced by genotype and environment.

Phenotypic correlations : Correlations between two traits caused by both genetic and environmental factors influencing both traits.

Pheromone : A chemical substance that convey information to and produce specific responses in certain animals.

Phimosis : The penis cannot be extruded from the prepuce. Phimosis may be congenital due to a small preputial orifice or a persistent frenulum. Acquired inflammation or neoplasia can reduce the size of preputial orifice or increase the size of the penis causing phimosis.

Phloem : Specialized vascular plant tissue for the transport of assimilates (generally sugars) from the point of synthesis (in the leaf) to other parts of the plant. It consists of sieve tubes, companion cells, phloem parenchyma and fibres.

Phosphatase : An class of enzymes that catalyze the hydrolysis of esters of phosphoric acid, removing a phosphate group from an organic compound.

Phosphodiester (Phospho-diester) bond : A bond in which a phosphate group joins adjacent carbons through ester linkages. A condensation reaction between adjacent nucleotides results in a phosphodiester bond between 3' and 5' carbons in DNA and RNA.

Phospholipase A2 : An enzyme which degrades type A2 phospholipids.

Phospholipid : A class of lipid molecules in which glycerol is linked to a phosphate group and two fatty acyl groups. Contains both polar and non-polar regions. A major component of biological membranes.

Phosphorolysis : The cleavage of a bond by orthophosphate; analogous to hydrolysis referring to cleavage by water.

Phosphorus : An essential nutrient for plants and animals that is commonly applied to crops as a phosphate fertilizer. Phosphorus can contribute to the eutrophication of lakes and other water bodies. Sources of excess phosphorus include sewage and agricultural runoff.

Phosphorylation : The addition of a phosphate group to a compound.

Photoreceptor layer : Layer of the retina composed of the rods and cones.

Photosynthate : The carbohydrates and other compounds produced in photosynthesis.

Photosynthesis : A chemical process by which green plants synthesize organic compounds from carbon dioxide and water in the presence of sunlight.

Physical map : A map showing physical locations on a DNA molecule, such as restriction sites, and sequence-tagged sites.

Physiology : The science dealing with the functions of animals.

Phyto-(Prefix) : To do with plants.

Phytochemical : Molecules characteristically found in plants.

Phytohormone : A substance that stimulates growth or other processes in plants. Major species are auxins, abscisic acid, cytokinins, gibberellins and ethylene.

Phytoparasite : Parasite on plants.

Phytosterol : One of a group of biologically active phytochemicals present in the seeds of certain plants. Evidence suggests that human consumption of certain phytosterols, such as â-sitosterol, can help to lower total serum cholesterol and low-density lipoproteins levels, thereby reducing the risk of coronary heart disease.

Phytotoxic : Toxic to plants. Partially composted organic matter may have acids or alchohols present that will harm young or sensitive plants. Partially-decomposed compost is therefore referred to as phytotoxic.

Pigment : Compounds that are coloured by the light they absorb. Light absorption is exploited by plants both as a means of energy capture and as a signalling mechanism.

Pigmentary keratitis : The accumulation of pigment in the cornea in response to inflammation.

Pink bollworm : Cotton pest.

Pink root : Occurs in onions. Fungal disease that attacks roots, reducing bulb size and quality.

Pinking-up : A lay term used to indicate pink nipples in a queen which indicates increased blood flow to the nipples under the influence of progesterone.

Pinnae : The flap of the ear.

Pinna-femoral" reflex " : When the ear is rubbed, the dog scratches aggressively with the hind leg! Not a "real" reflex but is highly suggestive of scabies.

Pinnal dermatitis : Skin lesions on the ears.

Pinocytosis : The engulfing of a minute droplet of liquid by a living cell.

Pioneer plants : The very first species to grow of the soil has had a traumatic occurrence, like a fire, flood, earthquake. The first plants to take over when a farmstead has been abandoned.

Pip : Used in propagation. The side offshoot of a rootstock. A good example is lily of the valley.

Pizzle : Prepuce.

Placenta : After birth. An organ that allows for the mother to provide nutrition and remove wastes from the developing baby in the uterus.

Plans : In a problem oriented record there are diagnostic plans, therapeutic plans and plans to inform the client.

Plant Breeders' Rights (PBR) : Legal protection of a new plant variety granted to the breeder or his successor in title. The effect of PBR is that prior authorization is required before the material can be used for commercial purposes.

Plant breeding : Plant breeding is use of techniques involving crossing plants to produce varieties with particular characteristics (traits) which are carried in the genes of the plants and passed on to future generations. Conventional/traditional plant breeding refers to techniques others than modern biotechnology, in particular cross-breeding, back-crossing.

Plant cell culture : In vitro growth of plant cells.

Plant lice : This is a reference to aphids found in British publications.

Plant patent numbers : This generally is a catalog referral phrase. For the general gardener it may not be important but new plants, like inventions, can also be patented. This is a protection for the owner who created the "new" plant.

Plant regulator : A chemical that affects the physiological behavior of plants, for example through accelerating or retarding the rate of growth or maturation of produce. Typically the definition of plant regulator excludes nutrients. Plant regulators must be registered as pesticides under the Federal Insecticide, Fungicide, and Rodenticide Act.

Plantibody : An antibody expressed transgenically in an engineered plant.

Plantlet : A small plant off the original plant. A good example is the piggy back plant these will easily root. Used in propagation.

Plaque : A clear spot on a lawn of bacteria or cultured cells where cells have been lysed by viral infection.

Plasma : The clear part of blood that remains after blood is separated into cells and fluid before the blood clots. If the blood is allowed to clot then separated into cells and fluid, the fluid is then called serum.

Plasma cells : Antibody-producing white blood cells derived from B lymphocytes.

Plasma cell pododermatis : Swelling and ulceration of the foot pads. Seen most frequently in cats.

Plasmalemma : The lipid bilayer and associated proteins and other molecules that surrounding the protoplast, within the cell wall.

Plasmid (P) : A circular DNA molecule, capable of autonomous replication, which typically carries one or more genes encoding antibiotic resistance proteins. Plasmids can transfer genes between bacteria and are important tools of transformation for genetic engineers.

Plasmodesma : Fine protoplasmic thread that connects adjacent plant cells by passing through the plant cell wall. Exploited by viruses as a conduit for cell to cell movement.

Plasmolysis : Shrinkage of protoplasm caused by removal of water from a cell through osmosis when surrounded by a hypertonic solution.

Plastid : A general term for a number of plant cell organelles which carry non-nuclear DNA. Includes the pigment-carrying bodies: 1. chloroplasts in leaves, 2. chromoplasts in flowers, and 3. the starch-synthesizing amyloplasts in seeds.

Plastoquinone : One of a group of compounds involved in the transport of electrons as part of the process of photosynthesis.

Plate : 1) To distribute a thin film of micro-organisms or plant cells onto a solid medium. 2) refers to the two segments of a Petri dish or similar.

Platelets : Small pieces of cells in the blood stream that help an animal stop bleeding when it has been injured.

Plating efficiency : The percentage of inoculated cells which give rise to cell colonies when seeded into culture vessels.

Plumule : The first bud of an embryo, or that portion of the young shoot above the cotyledons.

Pluronic gel : Topical application of an analgesic.

Point : A measure of price change equal to 1/100 of one cent in most futures contracts traded in decimal units. In grains, it is one cent; in T-bonds, it is one percent of par.

Point mutation : A change in a single base pair of a DNA sequence in a gene.

Poison : Any substance that can cause an adverse effect when introduced into a biological system (not acting mechanically).

Polar bodies : In female animals, the products of a meiotic division that do not develop into a functional ovum. The first polar body comprises one of the two products of the first meiotic divisions, which may fail to divide at the second division. The second polar body comprises one of the products of the second division.

Polar mutation : A mutation that influences the functioning of genes that are downstream from the site of mutagenesis but are in the same transcription unit.

Polar nuclei : Two centrally located nuclei in the embryo sac that unite with a second sperm cell in a triple fusion. In some plant species (particularly the monocotyledons), the product of this fusion develops into the endosperm.

Pollakiuria : Frequent passage of small amounts of urine. Pollakiuria is indicative of diseases of the lower urinary tract and genital tract.

Pollard : A tree cut back to the trunk to make a dense cluster of branches and foliage.

Polled : Breed where there has been a genetic selection for no horns. Some sheep breeds are horned in both sexes, in others only the males are horned and in yet others (the majority of breeds) neither sex is horned.

Pollen : Spores or grains borne by the anther, containing the male element; in orchids, it is usually not granular, as in most other plants

Pollen culture : The in vitro culture and germination of pollen grains to generate haploid plants.

Pollen grain : The mature microspore, produced in the pollen sac of angiosperms or the microsporangium of gymnosperms. Unicellular, with variable shape and size, and an elaborately structured wall.

Pollination : Transfer of pollen from anther to stigma in the process of fertilization in angiosperms; transfer of pollen from male to female cone in the process of fertilization in gymnosperms.

Pollinator : An insect or other vehicle by which pollen is carried from one flower to another. A plant that provides pollen for a self-infertile plant.

Pollution : Alteration of the environment, as through the introduction of hazardous or detrimental substances, heat, or noise whose nature, location, or quantity produces adverse health or environmental effects.

Poly : Means several or too much such as polydactyly means having too many toes.

Poly(A) polymerase : Catalyzes the addition of adenine residues to the 3' end of pre-mRNAs to form the poly(A) tail.

Polyacrylamide gel : Inert electrophoresis matrix, formed by the polymerization of acrylamide monomer in the presence of the cross-linker N,N'-methylene-bis-acrylamide. Gels are usually supported between two glass plates, which need to be removed for post-electrophoresis manipulations. Sometimes referred to incorrectly as acrylamide gels.

Polyacrylamide gel electrophoresis : Electrophoresis through a matrix composed of a synthetic polymer, used to separate proteins, small DNA, or RNA molecules of up to 1000 nucleotides. Used in DNA sequencing.

Polyadenylation : Post-transcriptional addition of multiple adenine residues to the 3' end of eukaryotic mRNA. Also called poly-(A) tailing. The adenine-rich 3' terminal segment is called a poly (A) tail.

Polyembryony : The production of more than one embryo from a single egg cell (in animals) or from a range of embryogenic cell types (in plants). These embryos are genetically identical to one another.

Polygalacturonase (PG) : An enzyme which catalyses the breakdown of pectin. A tomato engineered to contain an antisense-PG gene succeeded in delaying the onset of softening, by inhibiting the expression of PG. This allowed the fruit to be picked at a riper stage than is conventionally possible, and represented the first commercialized genetically engineered crop plant.

Polygene : One of a number of genes, each of small effect, which together act to determine the phenotype of a quantitative trait. The result is continuous variation in the trait and a seemingly non-Mendelian mode of inheritance.

Polylinker : A synthetic segment of DNA, designed to include a number of different restriction endonuclease sites. When ligated to a DNA fragment that is to be cloned, this enables a wide choice of restriction endonucleases to be used for the cloning process.

Polymer : A macromolecule synthesized by the chemical joining of many identical or similar monomers. For example, amino acids, monosaccharides and nucleotides give rise to proteins, polysaccharides and nucleic acids respectively. Water is eliminated between the monomers as they link to form chains. The individual monomer units condensed within a chain are often referred to as residues, a term which is also employed for the bases incorporated in polynucleotides.

Polymerase : An enzyme that catalyses the formation of polymers from monomers. A DNA polymerase synthesizes DNA from deoxynucleoside triphosphates using a complementary DNA strand and a primer. An RNA polymerase synthesizes RNA from ribonucleoside triphosphates and a complementary DNA strand.

Polymyositis : Inflammation of several muscles at one time.

Polynucleotide : A linear polymer composed of covalently linked nucleotides. Each link is formed by a single phosphodiester bond. The term is used to describe DNA and RNA.

Polypeptide : A linear polymer composed of covalently linked amino acids. Each link is formed by a single peptide bond. Sometimes used as a synonym for protein, but also describes non-natural and low-molecular-weight polymers.

Polyunsaturates : Oils in which some of the carbon-carbon bonds are not fully hydrogenated - i.e. of the form -CH=CH-, rather than -CH2-CH2-.

Polyurethane : A type of plastic used to make, among other things, IV catheters.

Polyuria (PU) : Increased volume of urine.

Polyvalent : A vaccine containing several antigens (multivalent).

Polyvalent vaccine : A recombinant organism into which antigenic determinants have been cloned from a number of pathogens, for use as a vaccine.

Pork bellies : One of the major cuts of the hog carcass that, when cured, becomes bacon. Futures contracts for pork bellies are traded in the futures market.

Posilac : Trade name for rBST marketed by Protiva, a unit of Monsanto.

Position effect : The influence of the location of a gene (particularly a transgene) on its expression and hence its effect on phenotype.

Positional candidate gene : A gene known to be located in the same region as a DNA marker that has been shown to be linked to a single-locus trait or to a QTL, and whose deduced function suggests that it could be the source of genetic variation in the trait in question.

Post renal azotemia : An increase in nitrogen containing wastes in the blood due to an inability to excrete urine as a consequence of an obstruction to urine passage or to a ruptured bladder.

Posted county Price (PCP) : This price is calculated for wheat and feed grains for each county by the Farm Service Agency. The PCP reflects changes in prices in major terminal grain markets (of which there are 18 in the country), corrected for the cost of transporting grain from the county to the terminal. It is utilized under the marketing loan repayment provisions and loan deficiency payment provisions of the wheat and feed grains commodity programs.

Postmortem inspection : As used in the meat and poultry inspection program, the phrase refers to the inspection that Food Safety Inspection Service inspectors are required to conduct of all animal carcasses immediately after they are killed.

Post-partum : After parturition. After giving birth.

Postprandial : The period of time immediately after eating.

Potpourri : A mixture of sweet smelling leaves, petals, blooms to create a perfume in a room. Tussie - massies in the Victorian era were popular nosegay potpourri creations.

Potting medium : Material used for growing plants in containers. Mixes may include vermiculite, perlite, sand, peat, charcoal, loam and fertilizer.

Potting up : Taking the young seedlings or transplants into a specific container for mature growth.

Poundage quota : A quantitative limit on the amount of a commodity that can be marketed (also called a marketing quota) under the provisions of a permanent law. Once a common feature of price support programs, this supply control mechanism now only restricts the production and/ or sale of tobacco and peanuts.

Pounds of retail cuts per day of age : A measure of cutability and growth combined, it is calculated as follows: cutability times carcass weight divided by age in days. Also, it is reported as lean weight per day of age (LWDA) by some associations.

Prairie potholes : A type of wetland characteristic of glaciated areas in the Upper Midwest (North Dakota especially) that is at the center of a shallow depression. Many potholes are wet during only a portion of the year, usually early spring. They provide important nesting habitat for migratory waterfowl, and were designated as a national priority area by the Secretary of Agriculture under the Conservation Reserve Program.

Pre-anesthetic : A drug given before general anesthesia; usually a sedative or tranquilizer which is given to reduce apprehension and to allow the use of lower doses of the more potent anesthetic agents.

Pre-breeding evaluation : Examination of potential breeding animals to assess their capability to produce offspring.

Precautionary principle : The approach whereby any possible risk associated with the introduction of a new technology is avoided, until a full understanding of its impact on health, environment etc. is available. Particularly applied to the release of genetically modified organisms, since unlike many technologies, these cannot be recalled if problems arise.

Precision farming : Farmers use global positioning (GPS) technology involving satellites and sensors on the ground and intensive information management tools to understand variations in resource conditions within fields. They use this information to more precisely apply fertilizers and other inputs and to more accurately predict crop yields.

Precocious germination : Early germination of a seed or embryo, prior to the full maturation of the embryo.

Predicted transmitting ability (PTA) : Genetic merit of parent transmitted to its progeny.

Premature : Born too early.

Premix : A uniform mixture of one or more microingredients and a carrier, used to facilitate uniform dispersion of micronutrients into a larger mixture.

Prepotent : The ability of a parent to transmit its characteristics on its offspring so that they resemble that parent, or each other, more than usual. Homozygous dominant individuals are prepotent. Also, inbred cattle tend to be more prepotent than outbred cattle.

Preproduction expenses : Expenses incurred prior to the period when a farm activity begins producing, primarily raising orchard trees or breeding animals.

Prepuce : The tissue that covers the penis. Sometimes called the sheath.

Prerenal azotemia : An increase in nitrogen containing waste products in the blood caused by reduced renal blood flow as a consequence of hypovolemia or dehydration. Untreated prerenal azotemia can progress to intrinsic renal disease.

Pressure potential : The pressure generated within a cell, being the net difference between the cell's osmotic potential and the water potential of the external environment.

Pressure treated lumber : Lumber that has been treated with chemicals to prevent rotting.

Pre-transplant : A stage in micropropagation - the rooting and hardening process prior to transfer to soil.

Prevalence : The proportion of sampled animals that display a condition of interest at a given point in time. It is a single measurement of each animal in a group. It is usually a static measure in which the time is short (1-7 days).

Prevented planting acreage : Land on which a farmer intended to plant a program crop or insurable crop, but was unable to because of drought, flood, or other natural disaster. Used in the calculation of disaster payments and crop insurance indemnity payments.

Prickle : Small sharp spine or thorn

Primary : First in order of time or development.

Primary abnormality : Morphologic abnormalities of sperm that occur while the sperm are being produced in the testes.

Primary antibody : In an ELISA or other immunological assay, the antibody that binds to the target molecule.

Primary culture : A culture started from cells, tissues or organs taken directly from organisms. A primary culture may be regarded as such until it is sub-cultured for the first time. It then becomes a cell line.

Primary growth : 1) Apical meristem-derived growth; the tissues of a young plant. 2) Explant growth during the initial culture period.

Primary immune response : The immune response that occurs during the first encounter of a mammal with a given antigen.

Primary meristem : Meristem of the shoot or root tip giving rise to the primary plant body.

Primary uterine inertia : Ineffective or absent uterine contractions during parturition. Primary uterine inertia should be considered when a bitch is not able to start uterine contractions. This condition occurs most often in older bitches and/or bitches with hypocalemia and/or hypoglycemia.

Prime farmland : Land that is best suited to and available for the production of food, feed, forage, fiber, and oilseed crops. It can be cropland, pastureland, rangeland, forestland, or other land. It has the soil quality, growing season, and moisture needed to produce high yields of crops each year economically, if managed according to acceptable farm practices. Prime farmland produces the highest yields with minimal expenditure of energy and economic resources and does so with the least damage to the environment.

Primer : A short oligonucleotide annealed to a template of single-stranded DNA, providing a doubled stranded structure from which DNA polymerase will synthesize a new DNA strand to produce a duplex molecule.

Primer walking : A method for sequencing long (>1 kbp) cloned pieces of DNA. The initial sequencing reaction reveals the sequence of the first few hundred nucleotides of the cloned DNA. Using this, a new primer of about 20 nucleotides is synthesized, which is complementary to a sequence near the end of sequenced DNA, and used to sequence the next few hundred nucleotides of the cloned DNA. This procedure is repeated until the complete nucleotide sequence of the cloned DNA is determined.

Prior converted wetland : Under the swampbuster program, these are wetlands that were converted to cropland before swampbuster was enacted on December 23, 1985, and meet wetland criteria for saturated soils or water-loving plants. Under swampbuster, there are no restrictions on either drainage maintenance or additional drainage on prior converted wetlands, which are estimated to total more than 50 million acres.

Probiotics : A live microbial feed supplement which beneficially affects the host animal. Claims include reduced early mortality, increased growth rate, improved feed conversion, egg quality and animal health.

Problem : A problem is anything that interferes with the patient's well being and requires further management or evaluation.

Problem list : A list of what is wrong with a patient based on the information that is gathered from history, physical examination and the results of disgnostic tests.

Problem oriented Medical Records (POMR) : The POMR system is a logical system centered around the identification and resolution of the patient's problems. The problem oriented approach differs from other approaches in which a list of differential diagnoses are generated in the exam room, without giving much consideration to the possibility that not all the patient's problems are due to the same cause. Although the problem based approach is also intended to lead to a diagnosis, the problem based approach prevents the clinician from "jumping to a diagnosis" with tunnel vision and potentially overlooking important aspects of the patients disease(s).

Problem specific data base : The minimum amount of information that is planned to be collected for patients with specific types of problems. For example, a chest radiograph may be recommened to be preformed on all patients that were hit by a car.

Processor : A silicon chip that contains a CPU. In the world of personal computers, the terms microprocessor and CPU are used interchangeably. At the heart of all personal computers is a microprocessor. Microprocessors also control the logic of almost all digital devices, from clock radios to fuel-injection systems for automobiles.

Procumbent : Having stems that trail along the surface.

Producer Subsidy Equivalent (PSE) : A measure of the value of monetary transfers to agricultural producers resulting from agricultural policies in a given year. It includes both transfers from consumers of agricultural products (through domestic market price supports) and transfers from taxpayers (through budgetary or tax expenditures).

Production Credit Association (PCA) : Farm Credit System institutions that have direct lending authority to make short and intermediate term loans to eligible retail customers.

Production environment : All input-output relationships, over time, at a particular location. The relationships include biological, climatic, economic, social, cultural and political factors, which combine to determine the productive potential of a particular enterprise. Production environments are classified as high-, medium- and low-input

Production expenses : Measures the aggregate business cost of farming. The two main components are current farm operating expenses and overhead costs. Farm production expenses are accounted for differently in the farm income measures. Only production expenses paid in cash are included in net cash farm income. Gross farm income and net farm income include both cash and noncash production expenses. Non-cash expenses include such overhead costs as charges for depreciation and other capital consumption associated with farm buildings and other structures, motor vehicles, farm machinery and equipment, and expenses associated with farm operator dwellings.

Production traits : Characteristics of animals, such as the quantity or quality of the milk, meat, fibre, eggs, work, etc., they (or their progeny) produce, which contribute directly to the value of the animals for the farmer, and that are identifiable or measurable at the individual level.

Prokaryote : A member of the large group of organisms, including bacteria and blue-green algae, in which the chromosome is not enclosed within a nucleus, but instead exists as a linear or circular strand. Prokaryotes do not undergo meiosis and do not have functional organelles such as mitochondria and chloroplasts.

Prolactin : A hormone, produced by the anterior pituitary gland, that stimulates and controls lactation in mammals.

Prolapse : The abnormal position of an organ in which the organ pouches through an opening from which it does not normally protrude.

Proliferation : Increase by frequent and repeated reproduction; growth by cell division.

Pro-meristem : The embryonic meristem that is the source of organ initials or foundation cells.

Promoter : 1) A short DNA sequence, usually upstream of (5' to) the relevant coding sequence, to which RNA polymerase binds before initiating transcription. This binding aligns the RNA polymerase so that transcription will initiate at a specific site. The nucleotide sequence of the promoter determines the nature of the enzyme that attaches to it and the rate of RNA synthesis. 2) A chemical substance that enhances the transformation of benign cells into cancerous cells.

Promotion program : Any program by an approved commodity promotion board or marketing order, including paid advertising, to present a favorable image of an agricultural commodity to the public to stimulate sales and improve the competitive position of the commodity in the marketplace. Funds are collected through a mandatory check-off on marketings to finance the promotion activities.

Pro-nuclear micro-injection : An early, low success-rate method to achieve transgenesis in animals, involving the micro-injection of many gene copies into one of the two pro-nuclei of a fertilized egg. Now being replaced by micro-injection into a culture of cloned embryos produced by nuclear transfer, which can be tested for expression of the transgene before transfer to recipient females.

Proprioception : Maintenance of posture and movement through stimuli originating in the receptors in the joints, tendons, muscles, and labyrinth.

Proptosis : Bulging of the eye out of the socket.

Prorate : A quantity provision in a fruit or vegetable marketing order that is intended to even out weekly shipments (or shipments for some other specified periods of time); it aims to prevent too much of the regulated commodity from entering the commercial market at the same time and depressing prices.

Prostaglandin (PGF2alpha) : A drug that among other actions, causes contraction of the uterus and is used in treatment of pyometra.

Prostaglandin analogs : DRugs used in the treatment of glaucoma. They cause extreme miosis and may have an influence on the unconventional outflow of aqueous. Lantoprost (trade name Xalatan) is available as a 0.005% topical solution.

Protected fat : A fat that has been treated or combined with another substance to prevent breakdown in the rumen.

Protein : Naturally-occurring compounds containing nitrogen, carbon, hydrogen and oxygen, and sometimes sulfur or phosphorus. Proteins are made up of complex combinations of amino acids and are essential for animal growth, production and reproduction.

Protein crystallization : The production of a pure preparation of a protein. In this form, the three-dimensional structure of the molecule can be determined.

Protein engineering : Generating proteins with modified structures that confer novel properties such as higher catalytic specificity or thermal stability.

Protein kinase : An enzyme that adds phosphate groups to a protein molecule at serine, threonine, or tyrosine residues.

Protein supplement : A feed containing protein, vitamins, and minerals which is fed to livestock to provide a complete diet.

Protein synthesis : The creation of proteins from their constituent amino acids, in accordance with the encoding gene DNA sequence.

Protocol : The step-by-step experiments proposed to describe or solve a scientific problem, or the defined steps of a specific procedure.

Protocorm : A tuberous structure, formed following the germination of orchid seeds, from which develops a complete plant. It develops from an unorganized embryo in the seed, comprising only a few hundred cells. In culture, vegetative explants of several orchid species form round, smooth protocorms which can be multiplied indefinitely or induced to regenerate into a whole plant.

Protoderm : A primary meristem tissue that gives rise to epidermis.

Protozoa : Single-celled organisms.

Protozoans : Eukaryotic (true nucleus) organisms without chlorophyll and cell walls.

Proud flesh : Excessive granulation tissue, seen especially on wounds on horse's lower legs that are allowed to heal themselves.

Provenance : The geographical and/or genetic origin of an individual.

Provirus : A double stranded DNA copy of the single RNA strand of a retrovirus, which has been integrated into a host genome.

Pseudohyperparathyroidism : Pseudohyperparathyroidism causes hypercalcemia and most commonly occurs in patients with lymphoma or tumors of the apocrine anal sac. Pseudohyperparathyroidism has been reported associated with other tumor types.

Pseudomonas spp. : A widely distributed Gram-negative bacterial genus. Many of the soil forms produce a pigment that fluoresces under ultraviolet light, hence the descriptive term fluorescent Pseudomonas.

Pseudomycetomas : Deep dermal or subcutaneous infections by dermatophytes. They present as nodules and draining lesions, that histologically are pyogranulomatous to granulomatous panniculitis. M. canis is the causative organism in the cat.

Puddling : destruction of soil structure, reducing porosity and permeability. A dense soil of massive structure, almost impervious to air and water, occurs when wet, plastic soil is worked too much or is trampled by animals.

Punctuated equilibrium : The occurrence of speciation events in bursts, separated by long intervals of species stability.

Punctum : Holes in the edges of the eyelids through which tears enter the nasolacrimal ducts.

Puncture vine (Goat heads) : Annual plant notorious for its seed pods that can puncture automobile tires and lower the quality of hay and forage crops. Move by attaching to anything that comes by. Difficult to manage.

Pupa : A stage in complete metamorphosis when an insect transforms from the larval to adult stage of development.

Pupillary Light Response (PLR) : The ability of the pupil to constrict in response to light.

Pure live seed : purity and germination of seed expressed in percent; calculated as pls = % germination x % purity/100.

Put option : An option contract to sell a futures contract at an agreed price and time at any time until the expiration of the option. A put option is purchased to protect against a fall in price. The buyer pays a premium to the seller of this option. The buyer has the right to sell the futures contract or enter into a short position in the futures market if the option is exercised.

Pyoderma : Skin infection with bacteria. Pyodermas involve coagulase positive bacteria, most commonly Staphylococcus intermedius.

Pyrogen : Bacterial substance that causes fever in mammals.

Pyuria : White blood cells in the urine.

Q

Quantitative genetics : The area of genetics concerned with the inheritance of quantitative traits that show continuous variation, as opposed to qualitative traits. Since many of the critical targets in both plant and animal breeding are of this type, most practical improvement programs involve the application of quantitative genetics.

Quantitative inheritance : Inheritance of measurable traits that depend on the cumulative action of many genes and/or involve a significant proportion of non-genetic determination.

Quantitative restrictions, trade : Quantitative restrictions are limitations on the quantity or value of a product that may be permitted to enter a country. They are probably the most familiar of the nontariff barriers and include quotas, embargoes, restrictive licensing, and other means of limiting imports. The Uruguay Round Agreement on Agriculture requires the conversion of quantitative restrictions to bound tariffs and tariff rate quotas.

Quantitative Structure-Activity Relationship (QSAR) : A computer modelling technique that enables the prediction of the likely activity of a molecule before it is synthesized. QSAR analysis relies on recognizing associations of molecular structures and activity from historical data.

Quantitative trait : A measurable trait that shows continuous variation (e.g. height, weight, colour intensity, etc.) - i.e.

the population cannot be classified into a few discrete classes.

Quantitative trait Locus (QTL) : A locus where allelic variation is associated with variation in a quantitative trait. The presence of a QTL is inferred from genetic mapping, where the total variation is partitioned into components linked to a number of discrete chromosome regions.

Quantitative traits : Those traits in which there is no sharp distinction between phenotypes, with a gradual variation from one phenotype to another, such as weaning weight. Usually, many gene pairs and environmental influences are involved.

Quotas, import : A quantitative limit placed on the importation of specific commodities. The protection afforded by quotas is more certain than can be obtained by raising import duties as the effect of the latter will depend on the price elasticities of the imported commodities. Quotas, like tariffs, can also be used to favor preferred sources of foreign supply. Quotas may be specified as an absolute limit or changed from year to year in response to changes in domestic supply and demand.

R

Radical : Belonging or pertaining to the root or base

Radicle : The portion of the plant embryo which develops into the primary root.

Radicums : These plants are special in that their stems have roots that will cling as they grow vertically or grow over the ground. Ivy is a good example.

Radio-Allergosorbent test (RAST) : Test to measure specific serum IgE levels.

Radiograph : The image generated by an x-ray. Often the term x-ray is used incorrectly to refer to a radiograph.

Radioimmunoassay (RIA) : An assay based on the use of a radioactively labelled antibody, where the amount of radiation detected indicates the amount of target substance present in the sample.

Radioisotope : An unstable isotope that emits ionizing radiation.

Raised bed : Any ornamental or vegetable bed that has soil higher than the surrounding immediate area. Sometimes it is bordered by boards, stone, brick or any material to hold in the soil. Created to make a supreme growing area.

RAM : Acronym for random access memory, a type of computer memory that can be accessed randomly; that is, any byte of memory can be accessed without touching the preceding bytes. RAM is used as temporary memory used to quickly access commonly used files.

Ramet : An individual member of a clone, descended from the ortet.

Ramification : The mode or style of branching of a plant

Ramp-up : A period of time during which effective blood levels of a drug are building up.

Random Amplified Polymorphic DNA (RAPD) : A PCR-based genotyping technique in which genomic template is amplified with single, short (usually 10-mer) randomly chosen primers. Typical patterns consist of a small number of amplified products of up to 2 kbp in length, which are separated by electrophoresis.

Random mating : A system of mating where every female (cow and/or heifer) has an equal or random chance of being assigned to any bull used for breeding in a particular breeding season. Random mating is required for accurate progeny tests.

Random mutagenesis : A non-directed change of one or more nucleotide pairs in a DNA molecule.

Random primer method : A method for labelling DNA probes, mainly for Southern hybridization experiments. A mixture of short oligonucleotides is hybridized to a single-stranded DNA probe. In the presence of DNA polymerase and deoxyribonucleotides - one of which is labelled - DNA synthesis then generates labelled copies of probe DNA.

Range betterment fund : Money collected from livestock grazing on federal lands and used for rangeland improvements. The Bureau of Land Management calls these funds Range Improvement Funds and uses them solely for labor, materials, and final survey and design of projects to improve rangelands. The Forest Service calls these funds Range Betterment Funds and uses them for planning and building rangeland improvements.

Rangeland : Land on which the natural potential (climax) plant cover is principally native grasses, grasslike plants, and shrubs. It includes natural grasslands, savannahs, certain shrubs and grasslike lands, most deserts, tundra, alpine communities, coastal marshlands, and wet meadows. It also includes lands that are revegetated naturally or artificially and are managed like native vegetation.

Rate-limiting enzyme : The enzyme whose activity controls the output of final product from a multi-enzyme metabolic pathway.

Ration : The 24-hour feed allowance for an individual animal.

Rational drug design : A systematic method of creating compounds by analysing their structure, function and stereochemical interactions.

Reading frame : A series of triplet codons beginning from a specific nucleotide. Depending on where one begins, each DNA strand contains three different reading frames.

Read-through : Transcription or translation that proceeds beyond the normal stopping point because of the absence of the usual transcription or translation termination signal of a gene.

Reaginic antibody : IgE.

Receptor : A trans-membrane protein located in the plasma membrane that can bind with a ligand on the extracellular surface, as a result of which it induces a change in activity on the cytoplasmic surface. More generally, a site in a molecule that allows the binding of a ligand.

Receptor-binding screening : A biotechnology-based method for drug discovery, which relies on the fact that many drugs act by binding to specific receptors on or in cells. Since receptors in vivo bind to hormones or to other cells, and thereby control the cell's behaviour, a receptor bound with a drug will likely affect the normal activity of the cell.

Recessive : Describing an allele whose effect with respect to a particular trait is not evident in heterozygotes.

Recessive allele : Allelic state of a gene, where homozygosity is required for the expression of the relevant phenotype.

Recessive gene : Recessive genes affect the phenotype only when present in a homozygous condition. Recessive genes must be received from both parents before the phenotype caused by the recessive genes can be observed.

Recessive oncogene : A single copy of this gene is sufficient to suppress cell proliferation; the loss of both copies of the gene contributes to cancer formation.

Reciprocating shaker : A platform shaker used for agitating culture flasks, with a back and forth action at variable speeds.

Reclamation : The process of rehabilitating disturbed lands, or converting unproductive lands to productive uses. The term is also used for the process of recycling or reusing water. In the context of the Reclamation Act and reclamation law, it means putting arid lands to use through irrigation.

Recognition sequence (Site) : A nucleotide sequence--composed typically of 4, 6, or 8 nucleotides--that is recognized by a restriction endonuclease. Type II enzyrnes cut (and their corresponding modification enzymes methylate) within or very near the recognition sequence.

Recognition site : A nucleotide sequence, typically 4-8bp long and often palindromic, that is recognized by, and at which a restriction endonuclease binds to the DNA. For some restriction endonucleases, the presence of a methylated residue within the recognition site abolishes recognition.

Recombinant : A term used in both classical and molecular genetics. 1) In classical genetics: An organism or cell that is the result of meiotic recombination. 2) In molecular genetics: A hybrid molecule made up of DNA obtained from different organisms. Typically used as an adjective, e.g. recombinant DNA.

Recombinant dNA (rDNA) : The technique of isolating DNA molecules and inserting them into the DNA of a cell ('recombining DNA'). Also known as genetic engineering.

Recombinant DNA technology : A set of techniques for manipulating DNA, including: the identification and cloning of genes; the study of the expression of cloned genes; and the production of large quantities of gene product.

Recombinant human (RH) : A prefix denoting molecules made through the use of recombinant DNA technology.

Recombination : The production of a DNA molecule with segments derived from more than one parent DNA molecule. In eukaryotes, this is achieved by the reciprocal exchange of DNA between non-sister chromatids within an homologous pair of chromosomes during prophase of the first meiotic division.

Recombination fraction : The proportion of recombinant (with respect to two loci) gametes arising from meiosis. Linkage maps are based on estimates of recombination fraction between all pair-wise combinations of loci.

Recombination frequency : The frequency at which crossing over occurs between two chromosomal loci--the probability that two loci will become unlinked during meiosis.

Recombinational hot spot : A chromosomal region where recombination appears to occur more frequently than expected.

Redefined : A problem is redefined if a more specific lable can be applied. For example vomiting is redefined or updated to acute pancreatitis as laboratory results become available that support the diagnosis of pancreatitis.

Redefined problem : A patient's problem is redefined if it is updated to a higher level...for example, vomiting may be updated to uremia as the results of diagnostic tests become available and show an elevated BUN.

Regulatory gene : A gene with the primary function of controlling the rate of synthesis of the products of one or several other genes or pathways.

Regulatory sequence : A DNA sequence involved in regulating the expression of a gene, e.g. a promoter or operator region (in the DNA molecule).

Regurgitation : Backward movement of food from the esophagus out the mouth.

Rehydration solution : A solution administered to a dehydrated animal to return it's hydration state to normal. Most dehydrated dogs and cats have isotonic dehydration and are rehydrated with iostonic, iso-ionic solutions such as LRS or RS.

Reinsurance companies : Private companies that sell federal crop insurance policy. The private company conducts all activities to serve the client and is reinsured by the Federal Crop Insurance Corporation against most operational and actuarial losses.

Rejuvenation : 1) Reversion from adult to juvenile stage. 2) The process of regular reproduction of seed stocks or collections in gene banks, in order to ensure continued viability.

Renature : The reannealing (hydrogen bonding) of single-stranded DNA and/or RNA to form a duplex molecule.

Renewable resources : Natural resources, such as soil and water, that replenish themselves within the limits of human time. Sometimes defined as flow resources. Alternatively, the surface resources from forests and rangelands, including timber, livestock forage, recreation, water, and wildlife and fish. Mineral and petroleum resources are nonrenewable, or stock resources.

Renewal spur : On grapevines, the cane pruned to one or two nodes on the cordon; becomes the fruiting cane the following year.

Rennin : An enzyme, secreted by cells lining the stomach in mammals, responsible for the clotting of milk. Used in the manufacture of certain dairy products.

Renovation : Removing an old planting and putting in a new one or removing and replacing only part of a planting. In strawberry culture, this process involves removing the leaves of the plants and cultivating the aisle to reduce the width of the row of plants to no more than 15 inches.

Repayment contract : A contract between a water user's organization and the Bureau of Reclamation by which the organization obligates itself to repay a share of the reimbursable construction and other costs (not all construction costs are reimbursed by water users) of a Bureau project in installments determined in accordance with reclamation law in exchange for delivery of water.

Repeat unit : A sequence of nucleotides that occurs repeatedly, often in a head-to-tail arrangement (tandemly).

Repent : Creeping, and typically rooting at the joints

Reporter gene : A gene that encodes a product that can be readily assayed. Used as a marker to confirm the incorporation of a transgene into a cell, organ or tissue, and as a means of testing the efficiency of specific promoters.

Repressible enzyme : An enzyme whose activity can be diminished by the presence of a regulatory molecule.

Repressible gene : A gene whose expression can be diminished or extinguished by the presence of a regulatory molecule.

Repression : Inhibition of transcription by preventing RNA polymerase from binding to the transcription initiation site.

Repressor : A protein which binds to a specific DNA sequence upstream from the transcription initiation site of a gene and prevents RNA polymerase from commencing mRNA synthesis.

Reproduction : 1) Sexual reproduction: the regular alteRNAtion of meiosis and fertilization which provides for the production of offspring. The main biological significance of sexual reproduction lies in the phenomenon of recombination. 2) Asexual or agamic reproduction: the development of a new individual from a single cell or group of cells in the absence of meiosis.

Reproductive cycle : Events that happen in the female such as ovulation, hormone production, receptivity, etc. In camelids the cycle does not follow regular time periods as it does in horses or cattle.

Re-project : Is the process of converting a map from one map projection to a different map projection. For example, Lat/Long to UTM coordinates.

Resolved problem : A patient's problem is resolved if it no longer exists either due to the intervention of the veterinarian or Mother Nature's.

Resource Management Plan (RMP) : A BLM planning document, prepared in accordance with Section 202 of the Federal Land Policy and Management Act. The plan contains guidelines for making resource management decisions for specific areas managed by BLM, known as resource areas.

Respiration : The process where food is oxidized (burned) to release energy.

Respiratory transmission : The most common route of human exposure in countries where infection is controlled in animals and where there is pasteurization of milk.

Rest period : A physiological condition of viable seeds, buds or bulbs that prevents growth even in the presence of otherwise favourable environmental conditions.

Restriction-fragment-Length Polymorphism (RFLP) : Differences in nucleotide sequence between alleles at a chromosomal locus result in restriction fragments of varying lengths detected by Southern analysis.

Resuscitative fluid : A fluid used in cardiopulmonary resuscitation (CPR) in an attempt to restore circulation.

Retaining wall : A wall that has been built on a slope to keep the soil from sliding or eroding. It would stabilize the area.

Reticular activating formation : A collection of neurons in the brain that mediates many aspects of consciousness.

Reticulocyte : A slightly immature red blood cell.

Retinal dysplasia : A congenital anomalous development of the retina.

Retinoids : Synthetic derivatives of vitamin A.

Retractor bulbi muscle : The muscle that pulls the eyeball back into the orbit.

Retrobulbar : Located behind the globe.

Reversal transfer : Transfer of a culture from a callus-supporting medium to a shoot-inducing medium.

Reverse genetics : Using linkage analysis and polymorphic markers to isolate a disease gene in the absence of a known metabolic defect, then using the DNA sequence of the cloned gene to predict the amino acid sequence of its encoded protein.

Reverse osmosis : A process used to purify water by forcing contaminated water through a semipermeable membrane. The membrane allows the water molecules to pass through but not the other substances contaminating the water. Reverse Osmosis is used to commercially purify sea water as well as by hikers to remove impurities from water found along the trail.

Reverse transcriptase (RNA-dependent DNA polymerase) : An enzyme isolated from retrovirus-infected cells that synthesizes a complementary (c)DNA strand from an RNA template.

Rhizobacterium : A micro-organism whose natural habitat is near, on, or in, plant roots.

Rhizobia : Bacteria in a symbiotic relationship with leguminous plants that results in nitrogen fixation.

Rhizobium : Prokaryotic species which are able to establish a symbiotic relationship with leguminous plants, as a result of which elemental nitrogen is fixed or converted to ammonia.

Rhizome : The woody parts of the rootstock at the base of the orchid which grows along or just under the surface of the ground or along host. New growth of sympodial orchids always begins at the end of the rhizome.

Rhizosphere : The soil region in the immediate vicinity of growing plant roots.

Ribose : A monosaccharide found in all ribonucleosides, ribonucleotides and RNA. Its close analogue, 2-deoxyribose, is similarly found in all deoxyribonucleosides, deoxyribonucleotides and DNA.

Ribosomal binding site : A sequence of nucleotides near the 5' end of a bacterial mRNA molecule that facilitates the binding of the mRNA to the small ribosomal sub-unit. Also called the Shine-Delgarno sequence.

Ribulose Biphosphate (RuBP) : A five-carbon sugar combined with carbon dioxide to form a six-carbon intermediate in the first stage of the dark reaction of photosynthesis.

Rill erosion : An erosion process in which numerous small channels, typically a few inches deep, are formed. It occurs mainly on recently cultivated soils or on recent cuts and fills.

Rinderpest : Cattle plague; a viral infection of cattle, sheep and goats.

Ringent : Gaping; said of lipped flowers with an open throat or mouth

Ringer's solution : Ringer's solution does not contain lactate. It contains a higher concentration of chloride compared to lactated Ringer's solution. Ringer's solution is considered an acidifying solution. This does not mean that it can cause metabolic acidosis, but it can assist a patient who has a metabolic alkalosis correct their own acid base abnormality.

Risk communication : The interactive exchange of information and opinions throughout the risk analysis process concerning hazards and risks, risk-related factors and risk perceptions, among risk assessors, risk managers, consumers, industry, the academic community and other interested parties, including the explanation of risk assessment findings and the basis of risk management decisions.

Risk-benefit analysis : Comparison of the short- and long-term risks to the overall societal benefits of an activity, chemical use, or technology. When risks and benefits are expressed in monetary terms, this is effectively cost-benefit analysis.

R-loops : Single-stranded DNA regions in RNA-DNA hybrids formed in vitro under conditions where RNA-DNA duplexes are more stable than DNA-DNA duplexes.

Rol genes : A family of genes, present on the Ri plasmid of Agrobacterium rhizogenes, that when transferred to a plant upon infection by the bacterium, induce the formation of roots. Used as a means of root induction on different species and cultivars of micropropagated fruit trees.

Rolling herd : The most recent 12 month herd mild production average.

ROM : Acronym for read-only memory, computer memory on which data has been prerecorded. Unlike RAM, ROM retains its contents even when the computer is turned off.

ROM is referred to as being nonvolatile, whereas RAM is volatile.

Root : The descending axis of a plant, normally below ground, which serves to anchor the plant and to absorb and conduct water and mineral nutrients.

Root cutting : The root is used for propagation. Plants that grow away from the mother plant and root, can be dub up and transplanted.

Root girdling : Encircling roots at or below the surface of the ground that tend to strangle the plant.

Root hairs : Outgrowths from epidermal cell walls of the root, specialized for water and nutrient absorption.

Root nodule : A small round mass of cells attached to the roots of leguminous plants, containing symbiotic nitrogen-fixing bacteroids, particularly Rhizobium spp.

Root-bound : Often, when plants are left too long in their container, the roots become entangled and begin to grow in circles. There is hope by separating the roots the plants will survive when planted.

Rooting hormone : A chemical in powder or liquid form which promotes the formation of roots at the base of a cutting. Contains hormones and anti-fungus growth prohibitors.

Rootstock : The trunk or root material to which buds or scions are inserted in grafting.

Rosarian : Those hobbyists or professionals who specialize in the cultivation of roses.

Rotational crossbreeding : Systems of crossing two or more breeds where the crossbred females are bred to bulls of the breed contributing the least genes to that female's genotype. Rotation systems maintain relatively high levels of heterosis and produce replacement heifers from within the system. Opportunity to select replacement heifers is greater in rotation systems than in other crossbreeding systems.

Rotenone : Material used a lot by organic gardeners. It is derived from the roots of tropical legumes. It does break down in sunlight and the side effect is that it is toxic to good and bad insects.

Roughage : A term used to describe a feed high in fibre (greater than 18% crude fibre). Roughage tends to be bulky, coarse, and low in energy. Examples : hay, silage, straw.

Roundup-readyä : Describing transgenic crop varieties that carry the bacterial gene which detoxifies the herbicide glyphosate, thereby making them resistant to its application.

Row crops : The rows or planting beds are far enough apart to permit the operation of machinery between them for cultural operations.

Rule-Outs (R/O) : Rule-outs are also known as differential diagnoses and are possible causes for the problems displayed by a patient. For example, kidney failure is one rule out (or possible cause) for polyuria in a dog or cat.

Ruminant : An animal with a stomach that has four compartments, and a more complex digestive system than other mammals. Ruminants include cattle, sheep, goats, deer, bison, elk, and camels. Swine, dogs, and humans are examples of nonruminants.

Rupicolous : Dwelling in or on rocks or stones

Rural : The Bureau of the Census defines the rural population (in contrast to urban) as all persons living in the open country, plus those in places of less than 2,500 inhabitants that are beyond the densely settled (1,000 or more persons per square mile) suburban fringes of metropolitan cities.

Rust : A generic descriptor for various serious fungal plant pathogens, which infect the leaves and stems of crops. The appearance of spores is reminiscent of metallic rust, although the colour varies, according to species, from yellow to reddish-brown.

S

Salami : Any of a family of boldly seasoned sausages similar to "cervelats," except that they tend to contain more garlic and are coarser and drier than cervelats. Salamis are rarely smoked. "Pepperoni" is a popular type of salami.

Saline soil : 1) A soil containing enough soluble salt (sodium chloride) to reduce its fertility. 2) A non-alkali soil that contains enough salts to interfere with the growth of most crop plants. Conductivity of the saturated extract is greater than 4 mmhos cm -1, exchangeable sodium percentage is > 15, and the ph is usually > 8. 5. 3. Soil containing high amounts of the sulphates and chlorides of sodium and calcium. Saline soils occur in hot climates, have a typically uneven surface, show little change down the profile and are low in humus. If the sodium salt is carbonate then the reaction can be around ph 9. 0.

Salinity : Concentration of dissolved salts in water (g kg-1) when the organic matter has been oxidized, the carbonate converted into oxides, and the bromine and iodine converted into chlorine.

Salisbury steak : A ground beef patty seasoned with onions and seasonings before it is broiled or fried and served with gravy. Named after Dr. J. H. Salisbury who recommended eating a lot of beef for a wide variety of ailments.

Salmon : Perhaps the best-known of all fish, pictures of salmon from 12,000 B.C. have been found. Salmon migrate from the seas into freshwater to spawn. Over the years, some varieties have become landlocked in lakes.

Salmon : Several species of anadromous fish found in both the atlantic and pacific.

Salmonella : A bacterium found in water, soil, insects, factory and kitchen surfaces, animal fecal matter, and raw meats, poultry (including eggs) and seafood. Acute symptoms of the illness caused by the salmonella species include nausea, vomiting, diarrhea, abdominal cramps, headache and fever. Salmonella bacteria are destroyed by proper cooking.

Salmonid : Belonging to the family salmonidae, which includes the salmon, trout, char, and whitefish.

Sample : A proportion or a segment of a fish stock which is removed for study, and is assumed to be representative of the whole. The greater the effort, in terms of both numbers and magnitude of the samples, the greater the confidence that the information obtained is a true reflection of the status of a stock.

Sample grade : In commodities, usually the lowest quality of a commodity, too low to be acceptable for delivery in satisfaction of futures contracts.

Sampling unit : An individual plot or quadrat. A collection of many such units, each of which is a different small fragment of the community under study, constitutes a sample.

Sand : 1) Particles between 2. 00 and 0. 05 mm diameter, or one of several separates such as coarse or medium sand; a soil textural class. 2) Mineral or rock fragments that range in diameter from 2. 00 to 0. 02 mm in the international system, or 2. 00 to 0. 05 mm in the usda system.

Sand separator : A mechanical device or series of course ways used to settle sand from sand-laden manure.

Saphrophyte : Plants often lacking chlorophyll; receiving nourishment from dead or decaying organic matter; needing the services of certain fungi to be able to absorb food.

Sapling : 1) Begins with the end of the seedling stage and ends when trees reach 10 cm diameter at breast height, the crowns are well elevated, and usually many of the lower branches have died. 2) A loose term for a young tree no longer a seedling but not yet a pole, that is, a few metres high and 2-3 cm in diameter at breast height, growing vigorously and without dead bark or more than an occasional dead branch. 3) A young tree, large enough to be above goat height, but still immature and not producing fruit.

Saprophytism : Organisms survive and persist in non-living or decaying organic matter. They are not usually parasitic, although may cause disease under certain circumstances - e. g. Aspergillus fumigatus and bovine abortion.

Sapwood : The outer part of the wood of a trunk, in which the sap flows.

Sarcoid : A tumor that occasionally occurs on the eyelids of horses.

Sarcoma : Cancer originating from fibrous tissues.

Sardine : The name describing several varieties of weak-boned fish including the Alewife, French Sardine, Herring, and Sprat. Named after the French island of Sardina. Often salted, smoked, or canned and packed in oil, tomato, or mustard sauce.

SARE : Sustainable Agriculture Research and Extension Program

Sashimi : A japanese dish of raw fish, shellfish, and mollusks served with soy sauce, wasabi, and pickled vegetables. Sushi is similar but it is served with vinegared rice, and may also include nori seaweed, vegetables, and strips of cooked eggs similar to omelets.

Satellite : DNA Highly repetitive DNA in plant and animal genomes, consisting of millions of copies of sequences typically in the range 5-500 bp long. Thousands of copies occur tandemly (head-to-tail) at each of many sites. It can be isolated from the rest of the genomic DNA by density gradient centrifugation.

Satellite RNA (Viroids) : A small, self-splicing RNA molecule that accompanies several plant viruses, including tobacco ringspot virus.

Savannah or savanna : Grassland with scattered trees, fairly common in the central plains of the U.S. before development. Bret Rappaport writes, "...it is theorized that humans are genetically predisposed to favor open grass-type landscapes as an artifact of our species' development on the savannas and grasslands of East Africa."

Saw timber : 1) Trees of a size and quality suitable for sawing into timber. 2) Begins at end of the 'pole' stage when height growth falls off and the period of maximum diameter growth begins. Terminates when trees become overmature and die or are cut.

Scale operator : Weighs product prior to packing.

Scale up : Conversion of a process, such as fermentation of a micro-organism, from a small laboratory scale to a larger industrial scale.

Scaling : A method for Forest Service personnel, or an independent third-party, to measure the volume of timber actually removed as a result of a timber sale. Scaled sales are a timber sales that use scaling for billing purchasers at the stumpage price for the timber cut.

Scallop : A bivalve mollusk with a ribbed, fan-shaped shell. In U.S. markets, only the adductor muscle, which opens and closes the shell is available. The Bay scallop is smaller, sweeter and a bit more succulent that their deep sea counterparts.

Scampi : The Italian name for the tail portion of any of several varieties of miniature lobsters. In the U.S., the term refers to large shrimp that are split and brushed in a garlic oil or butter, then broiled. "Scampo" is the singular form.

Scan : Ultrasonic detection of unborn animals (foetus)to establish if mother is pregnant

Scandent : Climbing, usually without tendrils.

Scanning Electron Microscope (SEM) : An electron-beam-based microscope used to examine, in a three dimensional screen image, the surface structure of prepared specimens.

Scientific assessment panel : A group of biologists, economists, and sociologists put together by a federal fishery management council to review scientific data on the condition of a stock of fish and the interests of the fishermen and seafood processors who use the stock. Panel members generally come from universities and state and federal fisheries agencies.

Sclera : The white part of the eye beneath the upper eyelid. The sclera normally has small blood vessels running across the surface.

Sclerenchyma : A strengthening tissue in plants, composed of cells with heavily lignified cell walls.

Screen : Preliminary characterization of a sample collection on the basis of a set of simple established criteria (biochemical, anatomical, physiological, etc.). Often applied to the process of selection for specific purposes, such as for disease resistance or for improved agronomic performance in crop plants.

Screenings : Small, imperfect kernels, broken grains, hulls, weed seeds and other foreign material obtained from the cleaning of grain.

Scrod : Scrod is the name for young cod (and haddock) that weight less that 2.5 pounds. It is a popular fish from the Pacific and the North Atlantic with a lean, firm, white flesh. "Haddock," "hake," and "pollock" are close relatives of the cod.

Scup : Also know as "porgie" or "sea bream." These fish are generally lean, and coarse-grained. Scup is often grilled, poached, and pan-fried.

Scurfy : Describes a surface covered with bran-like particles.

Scurs : Incomplete horn growth resulting from inadequately removing the horns. Usually these are just short pieces, but sometimes have to be removed if they begin to grow into the goat's skull.

Sea trout : An anadromous (spawns in fresh water) brown trout that spends part to its life cycle in the sea. Sea trout have meat that is pink to red in color and is very comparable to salmon. May be prepared any way appropriate for salmon.

Secondary antibody : In an ELISA or other immunological assay system, the antibody designed to bind to the primary antibody, and to which a label is generally attached.

Secondary cell wall : The innermost layer of cell wall, giving rigidity to the cells. Characterized by its highly organized microfibrillar structure, and only formed in certain cells after cell elongation has ceased.

Secondary closure : Do not suture the wound and let the tissue granulate in.

Secondary forest : Natural forest growth after some major disturbance (e. g. Logging, serious fire, or insect attack).

Secondary oocyte : An ovum that has released its polar body and is ready to be penetrated by sperm.

Secondary pests : Those species within an ecosystem that are normally kept in check by natural enemies.

Secondary phloem : Phloem tissue formed by the vascular cambium during secondary growth in a vascular plant.

Secondary thickening : Deposition of secondary cell wall materials which result in an increase in thickness in stems and roots.

Secondary uterine inertia : Ineffective or absent uterine contractions during parturition. Secondary uterine inertia may occur when a bitch is tired or exhausted from pushing to deliver and "gives-up" on delivering puppies.

Secondary value : The value of ecosystem functions.

Secondary vascular tissue : Vascular tissue (xylem and phloem) formed by the vascular cambium during secondary growth in a vascular plant.

Secund : To one side, as flowers on an inflorescence.

Sedentarization : Permanent settlement of once-nomadic people.

Sedges : Plants of the genus Carex, which includes over 1,500 species; sedges look similar to grasses.

Sedimentation : Includes the seftling of disturbed soil and sand particles. As a result, sub-aquatic vegetation and marine life (including fish) can be smothered.

Seed drill : This is used to plant cereal and grass seeds. Works like a planter.

Seedstock breeders : Producers of breeding stock for purebred and commercial breeders. Progressive seedstock breeders have comprehensive programs designed to produce an optimum, or desirable, combination of economical traits (genetic package) that will ultimately increase the profitability of commercial beef production.

Segment-polarity gene : A gene that functions to define the anterior and posterior components of body segments in Drosophila.

Selection culture : A selection based on difference(s) in environmental conditions or in culture medium composition, such that preferred variant cells or cell lines (presumptive or putative mutants) are favoured over other variants or the wild type.

Selection differential (Reach) : The difference between the average for a trait in selected cattle and the average of the group from which they came. The expected response from selection for a trait is equal to selection differential times the heritability of the trait.

Selection harvest : Harvesting individual trees or small groups or trees at periodic intervals (usually 8 to 15 years) based primarily on their vigor and age. Selection harvesting perpetuates and uneven-aged stand.

Selection index : A formula that combines performance records from several traits or different measurements of the same trait into a single value for each animal. Selection indexes weigh the traits for their relative net economic importance and their heritabilities plus the genetic associations among the traits.

Selection pressure : The strength of the tendency to eliminate undesirable genotypes or phenotypes, usually expressed in terms of a selection differential or as the portion of total trees that are selected.

Selection response : The difference between the mean of the individuals selected to be parents and the mean of their offspring. Predicted response is calculated as the product of narrow-sense heritability and selection differential.

Selective breeding : Making deliberate crosses or matings of organisms so that the offspring will have a desired characteristic derived from one of the parents.

Selective cutting : A system of cutting in which single trees, usually the largest, or small groups of such trees, are removed.

Selective herbicide : 1) A herbicide that, if used appropriately, will result in control of some plant species without injury to others. 2) A herbicide that kills only certain groups of plants, for example, 2, 4-d, which kills broadleaf plants but not grasses.

Selective thinning : Removing chosen trees, usually so as to give the maximum benefit to those remaining.

Selectivity : The ability of a type of gear to catch a certain size or kind of fish, compared with its ability to catch other sizes or kinds.

Selemectin : Trade name is Revolution, marketed by Pfizer. A neurotoxin recommended as a monthly topical "pour'on" insecticide. This product is also labeled for use as against scabies, ear mites, internal parasites, and for tick control.

Self : To place pollen from a male flower on a female flower on the same plant; a plant resulting from such pollination. Self-pollination, hence 'selfing'.

Self-mulching soil : 1) A soil with a high swelling potential in the surface layers so that it cracks into a granular mulch on drying. 2) A soil with a naturally formed, well-aggregated surface, which does not crust and seal under the impact of raindrops.

Self-pollination : Pollen of one plant is transferred to the female part of the same plant or another plant with the same genetic makeup.

Semen : The composite fluid ejaculated which includes sperm and supporting fluids.

Semen extender : A substance added to semen to provide an appropriate environment and energy for the sperm to survive in vitro.

Semen liquid : That carries sperm collected from a bull for artificial insemination

Semi-conservative replication : During DNA duplication, each strand of a parent DNA molecule acts as a template for the synthesis of a new complementary strand. Thus, one half of a pre-existing DNA molecule is conserved during each round of replication.

Semi-evergreen : Those shrubs that will keep some of their green foliage usually in mild climates.

Sense RNA : The RNA transcript of the coding strand DNA (often represented as the (+)-strand). Opposite: antisense RNA. When both sense and antisense transcripts of a gene are present simultaneously, gene silencing is often the result.

Sensible fluid losses : Sensible fluid losses are those that can be easily detected and measured. Sensible losses can occur through the urinary and gastrointestinal tracts. The loss of fluid through the GI tract is negligible in healthy dogs and cats but can be substantial through vomiting or diarrhea.

Sensitivity : In diagnostic tests, the smallest amount of the target molecule that the assay can detect.

Sensitivity analysis : A method of discovering by how much the estimates used in a model can vary without changing the result.

Sensitivity tests : Tests used to determine the most effective method of treatment of disease by testing the resistance of the microorganism to classes of antibiotics.

Sensitizing soup : Chemical mediators released by cells following tissue damage and inflammation that individually or collectively results in pain sensitivity.

Sensory-discriminative dimension of pain : This dimension of pain gives the individual information about the location, onset, intensity, type and duration of pain.

Sepals : Structures that usually form the outermost whorl of a flower. Together, they are called the calyx.

Separator : 1) Formerly a centrifuge device used to remove the fat from milk on the farm, but now used primarily at processing plants. 2) A device used to separate manure into solids and effluent and accomplished by trickling manure over a sloped screen or mechanically forcing through a screen.

Sepsis : Destruction of tissue by pathogenic micro-organisms or their toxins, especially through infection of a wound.

Septic arthritis : A bacterial infection in a joint causing inflammation.

Sequence : The linear order of nucleotides along a DNA or RNA molecule, and the process of obtaining this. Genome sequencing aims to generate the linear order of all nucleotides present in the nuclear DNA of an organism.

Sequence Characterized Amplified Region (SCAR) : A molecular marker obtained by the conversion to a sequence-tagged site of a single random amplified polymorphic DNA product.

Sequence divergence : The percent difference in the nucleotide sequence between related nucleic acid sequences, or in the amino acid sequence in a comparison between related proteins.

Sequence grazing : The grazing of two or more land units in succession that differ in forage species composition. Sequence grazing takes advantage of differences among forage species and species combinations, grown in separate areas for management purposes, to extend grazing seasons enhance forage quality and/or quantity, or achieve some other management objective.

Seral (Successional) community : One of a series of biotic communities that follow one another in time on any given ecological site.

Seroconversion : A change in immune status from having no measurable antibodies against an infectious agent to development of measurable antibodies in the blood.

Serology : The study of serum reactions between an antigen and its antibody. Mainly used to identify and distinguish between antigens, such as those specific to particular micro-organisms or viruses.

Seroprevalence : The frequency of occurance of exposure to an infectious agent based on measuring antibodies to the agent in the blood.

Sessile : Of a leaf, without a petiole (leaf stalk), that is, borne directly on the stem.

Set : In reference to shallot bulbs and small onions, as in sets of onions.

Set aside : Land that arable farmers must take out of production for one or more years. In exchange for setting aside the land from production the farmer receives compensation for the crop he would otherwise have grown

Set net (Gillnet) : Most have a series of floats at the top, and a series of weights at the bottom that keep the net upright in the water. Fish are caught as they swim into the net. The size of the mesh in the set net determines the size and species of fish caught. Used properly, this method is a selective fishing method.

Setaceous : Bristle-like, very narrow.

Settling pond : A manure pit where the flow rate of liquid manure is slowed to allow suspended materials to collect at the bottomed, where they can later be removed.

Sex duction : The incorporation of bacterial genes into F factors and their subsequent transfer, by conjugation, to a recipient cell.

Sex factor : A bacterial episome (e. g. the F plasmid in E. coli) that enables the cell to be a donor of genetic material. The sex factor may be propagated in the cytoplasm, or it may be integrated into the bacterial chromosome.

Sex hormones : Steroid hormones that control sexual development in animals.

Shanks' pony : To walk. Shank is the lower leg. On one's own legs, often the only mean of transportation for a swagger.

Shapefile : A vector data format for storing the location, shape, and attributes of geographic features. A shapefile is stored in a set of related files and contains one feature class, point, line or polygon.

Share (Plough) : That part of the plough which operates horizontally and cuts the furrow bottom.

Shares : The wearing edges on a plough that cut into the soil

Shark : A flavorful, low-fat fish that includes varieties such as Leopard, Mako, Spiny Dogfish, Soupfin and Thresher. Shark meat tends to have an ammonia-like smell that can be eliminated by soaking the flesh in milk or acidulated water.

Sharp sand : Builders sand. This sand is rough. Great for drainage, and propagation, not to mention starting of seeds.

Shatter : The falling off and consequent loss of potentially harvestable foliage or fruits. Also called 'shattering'.

Sheath : Any elongated, more or less tubular sructure enveloping an organ or plant part.

Sheep : A small, ruminant animal (4 stomachs), raised for wool and meat (mutton).

Sheep ked : Wingless fly that is a problem in sheep. Moves about through contact.

Sheepshead : A saltwater fish belonging to the wrasse family. Also called "California Sheephead," "Fathead," and "Redhead." Its meat is white, tender, and lean.

Shelter expense deductions : For the purpose of the food stamp program, shelter expense deductions are calculated as any shelter expense (including items such as utilities and insurance) in excess of 50% of a household's monthly income after all other potential deductions have been taken out. In effect, this means that all shelter expenses above roughly 35% of a typical household's total cash income are themselves deductible.

Shelterbelt : An extended windbreak of living trees and shrubs established and maintained for the protection of farmlands over an area larger than a single farm.

Shipping : Transfers finished, packages product onto trucks for delivery.

Shipping fever : A complex seen in cattle, especially feedlot cattle, where the stress of shipping weakens their immune system and they develop viral and then oportunistic bacterial infections.

Short Interspersed Nuclear Element (SINE) : Families of short (150-300 bp), moderately repetitive DNA elements of eukaryotic genomes. They appear to be DNA copies of certain tRNA molecules, created presumably by the unintended action of reverse transcriptase during retroviral infection.

Short selling : Selling a futures contract with the idea of delivering on it or offsetting it at a later date.

Short shoot : Where there is shoot dimorphism (two kinds of shoots), these are often specialized shoots with greatly compressed internodes, often bearing leaves and usually flowers; not contributing to the overall architecture of the tree. sometimes called a 'spur'.

Short-day plant : A plant which will not flower until triggered to do so by exposure to one or a number of dark periods equal to or longer than its critical period. Other plant species are long-day and some are daylength neutral. Genetic variation for daylength sensitivity is present in many crop species.

Shrubby : Applied to woody plants which at maturity are less than 20 ft. high, have more than one stem, and no definite crown shape (a purely arbitrary definition).

Shrubland : An open or closed stand of shrubs up to about 2 m tall.

Shuttle : A device on a tractor or handler which allows direction to be reversed at the flick of a lever with no requirement to use the clutch.

Shuttle vector : A plasmid capable of replicating in two different host organisms because it carries two different origins of replication and can therefore be used to transfer genes from one to the other.

Sib : A term meaning brother or sister, that is, an individual belonging to the same family. 'Half-sibs' have one parent (usually the seed parent) in common. 'Full-sibs' have seed and pollen parents in common. Hence, sibs are progeny of the same parents derived from different gametes.

Sieve cell : A long and slender sieve element in vascular plants, characterized by relatively unspecialized sieve areas and tapering end walls that lack sieve plates.

Sieve element : The phloem cell concerned with longitudinal conduction of food materials.

Sieve plate : Perforated wall area in a sieve tube element, through which strands connecting sieve tube protoplasts can pass.

Sieve tube : A tube within the phloem tissue of a plant, composed of joined sieve elements.

Sigma factor : The sub-unit of prokaryotic RNA polymerases responsible for the initiation of transcription at specific initiation sequences.

Silage : Grass or other crops that have been cut, allowed to wilt but not completely dry out, and are then preserved in plastic wrapping or in a large mound or pit (called a clamp) from which all air is excluded. Silage is fed to livestock through the winter when fresh grass is not available.

Silage additives : Substances added during the ensiling process to enhance the correct and rapid fermentation of the feed.

Silage bags : Large plastic tubes in which forages are fermented. Plastic is removed and discarded as the ensiled feed is fed.

Silencing : Loss of gene expression either through an alteration in the DNA sequence of a structural gene, or its regulatory region; or because of interactions between its transcript and other mRNAs present in the cell.

Silicone : A polymer of alternating oxygen and silicon atoms combined with other organic groups. Catheters made of silicone are relatively inert and have less stimulation of clot formation compared to other materials.

Silk : A filament secreted by a silkworm to spin a cocoon as part of its metamorphosis to a moth. The term also refers to the fabric woven from this fiber.

Silver salmon : This high-fat variety of salmon provides a firm-textured, pink to orange-red flesh. Also called the "coho salmon."

Silverbright : Chum salmon that have been harvested at sea rather than in freshwater.

Silvopastoral system : Any agroforestry system that include trees or shrubs and pastures and animals.

Silvopisciculture : Growing trees as part of a fish-farming enterprise.

Simple : Said of a leaf when not compound, or of an inflorescence when unbranched.

Simple bud : Bud containing either leaf or flower primordia but not both.

Simple random sample : Sample selected in such a way that every individual in the population stands an equal chance of being selected.

Single Nucleotide Polymorphism (SNP) : A genetic marker resulting from variation in sequence at a particular position within a DNA sequence. SNPs are commonly the result of transition changes (A for G, T for C), but also transversions (G or A for T or C) and single base deletions. Such variation is extensive throughout all genomes, and offers the particular advantage of being detectable without the need for gel electrophoresis.

Single-Cell Protein (SCP) : Protein produced by micro-organisms, particularly yeast. Used as either a feed or a food additive.

Single-seed descentbreeding method : A means of advancing populations while preserving genetic variance for later selection. The method uses less labour and space than the backcross and the bulk breeding methods. A single seed is taken from each plant and used to propagate the population. Eventually, pure lines can be generated from existing lines.

Slit-lamp biomicroscopy : Provides magnification and depth for examination of the eyelids, puncta, conjunctiva, sclera, cornea, anterior chamber, iris, lens, and anterior vitreous.

Slope : The degree of deviation of a surface from horizontal, measured in a numeric ratio, percentage or degrees.

Slot limit : A limit on the size of fish that may be kept. Allows a harvester to keep fish under a minimum size and over a maximum size, but not those in between the minimum and maximum.

Slotted floor : A concrete floor design in which slats are positioned in the floor so that cow traffic may work manure through the slats and into a pit beneath the floor of the barn.

Slow release fertilizer : Generally a natural fertilizer that over a period of time will release its nutrients. Always a good practice to use.

Slurry : The semi-liquid animal waste (faeces and urine) that accumulates where animals are confined with little or no bedding. It can be diluted and spread on grassland or crop fields, but there is a risk of spreading salmonella infection.

SNE : Society for Nutrition Education

SNF (Solids-Non-Fat): These are the proteins, minerals and other ingredients in milk when water and fat are removed.

Snow blower : This machine blows snow off of things, like driveways.

SNP : Single Nucleotide Polymorphism.

Soaker hose : A porous tube that allows water to seep from it; used to irrigate plants. It is used to conserve water and to avoid wetting plant foliage.

Social forestry : The planting and tending of trees or shrubs for the well-being and betterment of local communities.

Social impacts : The changes in people, families, and communities resulting from a fishery management decision.

Social opportunity cost : The opportunities forgone by society, including externalities, in using a resource in some way. For biological resources this may be different than the market price of that resource.

Socioeconomicdeterminants : Factors such as marketing facilities, the land tenure system and credit, which influence the cropping systems of a given area.

Socioeconomics : A word used to identify the importance of factors other than biology in fishery management decisions. For example, if management results in more fishing income, it is important to know how the income is distributed between small and large boats or part-time and full-time fishermen.

Sockeye salmon : Prized for canning, the sockeye salmon has a firm, red flesh. Also known as the "redeye salmon."

Sodium : A chemical found in common salt. Salt is essential for animal heath and which can also boost yields of root crops.

Sodium Dodecyl Sulphate (SDS) : A detergent used to solubilize protein and DNA from biological materials. Specific use in sodium dodecyl sulphate polyacrylamide gel electrophoresis.

Sodium dodecyl Sulphate Polyacrylamide Gel Electrophoresis (SDS-PAGE) : A widely employed electrophoretic method for the separation of proteins from biological samples. The sodium dodecyl sulphate gives a uniform charge density to the surface of proteins or nucleic acids, so that their rate of migration through the gel is determined largely by their molecular weight.

Softshell crab : The "soft-shell crab" is actually the blue crab caught just after molting (discarding its shell). This crab is found along the Gulf and Atlantic coasts. It is sold in both its soft and hard-shell stages.

Software : The programs, procedures, algorithms (set of rules), and their associated documentation, for a computer system.

Softwood : A term used in the timber trade to describe the wood of most conifers (gymnosperms), as distinct from the hardwood, broadleaved species (angiosperms).

Softwood cutting : A nonwoody piece of a woody plant that is cut from the stock plant to asexually propagate a new individual plant.

Soil : 1) The superficial part of the earth's crust resulting from weathering of rocks under the combined effect of living beings and climate. 2) A dynamic natural body composed of mineral and organic materials and living forms in which plants grow. The collection of natural bodies occupying parts of the earth's surface that support plants and that have properties caused by the integrated effect of climate and living matter acting upon parent material, as conditioned by relief, over periods of time.

Soil aeration : The process by which air in the soil is replenished by air from the atmosphere. In a well-aerated soil, the soil air is similar in composition to the atmosphere above the soil. Poorly aerated soils contain more carbon dioxide and less oxygen. The degree of aeration depends on the soil porosity.

Soil conservation : A combination of all management and land-use methods that safeguard the soil against depletion or deterioration (loss of fertility) caused by nature or humans.

Soil dry weight : Weight of solid soil particles when all water has been vapourized after heating the particles to 105°c.

Soil fertility : The quality that enables a soil to provide adequate nutrients in a proper balance for specified plant growth, other factors such as light, moisture, temperature and the physical condition of the soil being favourable.

Soil frodibility : A measure of the inherent susceptibility of a soil to erosion, without regard to topography, vegetation cover, management, or weather conditions.

Soil permeability : The quality of a soil enabling it to pass air or water.

Soil pH : Basically, pH is a measure of the amount of lime (calcium) contained in your soil. A soil with a pH lower than 7.0 is an acid soil, a soil pH higher than 7.0 is alkaline soil. Soil pH can be tested with an inexpensive test kit.

Soil polymers : Super absorbent polymers that have been around for a while, that can be added to retain moisture containers. It will absorb many times over its weight in water.

Soil porosity : The percentage of the soil (or rock) volume that is not occupied by solid particles, including all pore space filled with air and water. The total porosity includes both 'capillary' and 'non-capillary' porosity (capillary refers to the very small pores).

Soil profile : 1) A section of two dimensions extending vertically from the earth's surface so as to expose all the soil horizons and a part of the relatively unaltered underlying material. 2) A vertical section of the soil from the surface through all its horizons into the parent material.

Soil quality (Health) : Soil quality includes consideration of measures related to both productivity for crops and environmental factors.

Solarization : The process by which one can sterilize the soil by the sun. Cultivate the area to be isolated, water well, and then cover with 2 - 4 mil of clear plastic.

Soldier settlements : The Government had acreage subdivided to resettle returned servicemen from World War I and World War II. The owners of the land did receive compensation and some properties had fallen back into the Government hands when previous farmers could not make ends meet. The land court had to approve sales.

Sole : A popular flatfish with a delicate flesh with a firm, fine texture. The best-known variety is "Dover sole" (also called "channel sole)." Much of what is sold as "sole" is actually a variety of flounder, which isn't a true sole.

Source dNA : The DNA from an organism that contains a target gene, and used as the starting material in a cloning experiment.

Source organism : A bacterium, plant or animal from which DNA is purified and used in a cloning experiment.

Source separation : In homes or commercial operations, waste is separated into categories for recycling, composting, or landfilling. This is a fancy name for separating your newspapers, glass, yard wastes, plastic bottles, etc. into separate containers or piles for waste processing.

Spa : The special programme for africa (full name : The special programme for sub-saharan african countries affected by drought and desertification).

Spacer sequence : A DNA sequence separating neighbouring genes; spacer sequences are not usually transcribed.

Sparger : A device that introduces, into a bioreactor, air in the form of fine bubbles.

Spawning Potential Ration (SPR) : SThe number of eggs that could be produced by an average recruit in a fished stock divided by the number of eggs that could be produced by an average recruit in an unfished stock. SPR can also be expressed at the spawning stock biomass per recruit (SSBR) of a fished stock divided by the SSBR of the stock before it was fished.

Spawning stock Biomass (SSB) : The total weight of all sexually mature fish in the population. This quantity depends on year class abundance, the exploitation pattern, the rate of growth, fishing and natural mortality rates, the onset of sexual maturity and environmental conditions.

Speaning : Weaning, especially of lambs.

Specific epithet : The second name of the binomial given to a species; for instance, "rubrum" is the species epithet of Acer rubrum.

Specimen plant : A plant that is high lighted to show off its special qualities. Sometimes used as a focal point.

Speculator : In commodity trading, an individual who does not hedge, but who trades in futures contracts with the objective of achieving profits through the successful anticipation of price movements.

Spent : Bulbs and flowers of a plant that have finished blooming. It's time to deadhead them.

Spent medium : After sub-culture, medium which is discarded because it has been depleted of nutrients, dehydrated, or accumulated toxic metabolic products.

Sperm : Spermatozoa. The male structure that fertilizes an egg.

Spheroplast : A microbial or plant cell from which most of the cell wall has been removed, usually by enzymatic treatment. Strictly, in a spheroplast, some of the cell wall remains, while in a protoplast the cell wall has been completely removed. In practice, the two words are often used interchangeably.

Sphincter : A ring-shaped muscle that allows an opening to close tightly, such as the sphincter muscle in the lower end of a cow's teat.

Sphincter : A structure that closes and opens.

Spicate : With spikes.

Spices : Seeds, fruits, or roots (rhizomes) used to flavor cooking.

Spinose : Beset with spines.

Spinothalamic : A tract in the spinal cord which conveys impulses associated with pain and temperature sensation, and tactile sensation. Somatic pain pathway.

Spiral feeder : Feeds product into a spiral feeder.

Spitting off : When the female is no longer receptive to the male indicating she has ovulated.

Splay-legged : A condition in newborn pigs that involves a muscle weakness so they are unable to stand and bear their weight.

Spleen : An organ in the abdomen that stores cells. The spleen can be removed if it is diseased.

Spliceosome : A complex of small nuclearribonucleo proteins and other proteins that assemble on an immature mRNA and catalyse the excision of an intron.

Splicing : 1) During the maturation of eukaryotic mRNA, the process that removes intron sequences and covalently joins exon sequences.

Splicing junction : The DNA sequence immediately surrounding the boundary between an exon and an intron. There is a degree of sequence conservation in these regions, allowing the identification of introns in newly sequenced genes.

Spore : 1) A reproductive cell that develops into an individual without union with other cells; some spores such as meiospores are the product of the germ line, but others are asexual in nature. 2) A small, protected resting body, often synthesized by micro-organisms when nutrient levels are low.

Spot market : A public or open marketplace (such as open exchanges or auction houses) where products (including agricultural products such as livestock, grain, cotton, etc.) are bought and sold. The Minneapolis Grain Exchange and the National Cheese Exchange are examples. Spot also refers to a maturing delivery month of a futures contract.

Spot price : The price at which a physical commodity for immediate delivery is selling at a given time and place.

Spreading : Growing outward or horizontally.

Spreading grass : Grass that spreads by creating new plants from existing plants by running roots across or under the ground (stolons or rhizomes, respectively), creating a dense turf. Also called sod-forming grass.

Spring barley : Cereal planted in spring to produce grain for beer, whiskey or animal feed

Springer or fresh : Cow/heifer that has recently calved.

Square-foot gardening : A system of gardening developed by Mel Bartholomew that uses 4 foot by 4 foot plots subdivided into 1-foot squares for growing a specific number of a particular type of vegetable to maximize space and facilitate ease of maintenance.

Squash bug : Problem in pumpkin and other vegetables.

Squid : This ten-armed cephalopod is related to the octopus and the cuttlefish. Squid varies in size from 1 inch to 80 feet in length. The meat is firm and chewy, with a somewhat sweet flavor. Over-cooking can lead to a rubbery texture.

Squirrel : An abundant, largely arboreal rodent. Red and gray squirrels are commonly eaten in the U.S. The gray squirrel is fatter and has a flavor considered by many as superior to the red squirrel. Squirrels do not have a strong "gamey" taste.

Staggered cuts : Symmetrically cleaved phosphodiester bonds that lie on both strands of double-stranded DNA, but are not opposite one another.

Staggers : Medical condition caused by a lack of magnesium in lactating stock.

Stag-head : A tree dead at the top as a result of injury, disease, or deficient moisture or nutrients.

Stake : A piece of pointed wood or metal that is driven into the ground to support a plant.

Staking : The practice of driving a stake into the ground next to, and as a support for a plant. When attaching the plant to the stake, be sure that it is tied loosely so it doesn't strangle the stem. When staking a potted plant, the stake should be set into the planter before the plant is added.

Stalk : A supporting structure of a leaf, flower or fruit.

Stalked : Said of buds with scales elongated perceptibly below the lowest scales (alder).

Standard : 1) A small tree commonly produced by grafting a weeping or dwarf form on a trunk of the desired height. 2) The erect petals of an iris flower, as opposed to the broader and often drooping falls petals. 3. The upper, more or less erect petals of a pea-like flower which consists of three types of petals: standard, wings and keel.

Starter culture : Micro-organisms that are deliberately added to foods to alter flavour, colour, texture, smell, or taste.

State variable : In simulation modelling, a variable that characterizes the state of the system and directly determines the processes that bring about changes in the endogenous variables.

Station : When selling a property a station includes the sheep and a run is without the sheep.

Stationary phase : The plateau of the growth curve after log growth, during which cell number remains constant. New cells are produced at the same rate as older cells die.

Statistic : 1) Any quantity calculated from data. 2) The characteristics of a sample in some respect.

Status of exploitation : An appraisal of exploitation is given for each stock discussed in the Species Synopsis section using the terms unknown, protected, not exploited, underexploited, moderately exploited, fully exploited, and over-exploited. These terms describe the effect of current fishing effort on each stock, and is based on current data and the knowledge of the stocks over time.

Stelidia : Column teeth

Stellate : Star-like; with several arms radiating from a center. Often said of hairs that are once or twice forked.

Stipel : A stipule of a leaflet.

Stipellate : Having stipules at the base of the leaflets.

Stipular : Having stipules at the base of the leaves.

Stipule scars : A pair of marks left after the stipules fall off, to either side of the leaf scar.

Stipules : Small leaf-like organs occurring in pairs on either side of the leaves; occasionally each one extends half way around the twig, respectively.

Stock : A part of a fish population usually with a particular migration pattern, specific spawning grounds, and subject to a distinct fishery. A fish stock may be treated as a total or a spawning stock. Total stock refers to both juveniles and adults, either in numbers or by weight, while spawning stock refers to the numbers or weight of individuals which are old enough to reproduce.

Stock agent: Attached to a firm and based in the community town. Arranges the buying and selling of farmers' livestock. Can give advice on farming supplies and livestock.

Stress : Environmental stress. The effects on plants of a lack or excess of environmental resources (light, water, nutrients), either singly or combined. 'Water stress' includes soil water and the effects of high saturation water vapour pressure deficits. Unsuitable temperatures (high or low) and frost, as well as the effect of wind, either from direct mechanical damage or as the combined effect of exposure, are also factors.

Stressed area : An area in which there is special concern regarding harvest, perhaps because the fish are small or because harvesters are in conflict.

Sub-aquatic vegetation : Is any type of underwater plant life. This can include plants that are partially submerged, such as mangroves, or totally submerged such as kelp and seagrass.

Submerged bud : A bud hidden by the petiole or embedded in the callus of the leaf scar.

Subopposite : Said of paired leaf scars that are close, but not at exactly the same height on the twig (staggered).

Subpopulation : A subset of a natural or artificial breeding population. Artificial subsets may be developed for different sites or characters.

Subsoil : That layer of soil normally below cultivation depth but which has a great effect on the performance of the topsoil. Subsoiling is an operation where a deep cultivator runs through the subsoil at a depth of around 450 mm when the soil is dry to shatter it.

Subspecies : A geographically localized subdivision of a species, genetically and morphologically distinguishable from other subspecies, described according to taxonomic rules, and given a latin name. A subspecies tends to be larger than a taxonomic variety but there is no clear distinction between the two.

Succulent : Succulent plants have leaves and/or stems which are thick and fleshy. They often have waxy outer layers that allow the plants to retain water well.

Sucker : A name popularly applied to various types of freshwater fish closely related to carp. Suckers live and feed near the bottoms of streams. They may be cooked in any way appropriate for other fish.

Suckering : Type of vegetative propagation where lateral buds grow out to produce an individual that is a clone of the parent.

Suckler cow : The mother of a calf raised for beef production.

Sugar beet pulp : The remains of the sugar beet root after sugar has been extracted. A tasty food for cattle and sheep, high in energy, may be wet or dried. Dried SBP must not be fed to horses as it will swell up inside their stomach.

Suitable timberland : Timberland from which timber cutting is proposed in forest planning.

Sulfites : Additives used to delay melanosis, or black spot, on raw shrimp.

Sulphur : A non metallic trace element which is essential in plant growth. Atmospheric deposition has been adquate to replenish soil reserves until recently when fossil fuel emmissions have been 'cleaned up'. Sulphur (sulfur) must now be applied to crops in fertilisers.

Summer country: Country that can only be used in the summer for grazing sheep. "The back hill blocks and and mountain slopes are good summer tussock country".

Summer fallow : Cropland in semi-arid regions that is purposely kept out of production during a cropping season mainly to conserve moisture for the next season. It is common for wheat producers in semi-arid regions to rotate half their cropland to summer fallow each year.

Sun scorch : Spots on leaves that are caused by exposure to strong sunlight. Often not acclimating plants for the season creates sun spots. Just trim off and let new growth develop.

Sunfish : Any of a number of North American freshwater fish closely related to the perch. Known for their bright, sunny colors and interesting shapes, popular varieties include "Bluegill," "Crappie," and "Calico Bass," commonly called "Sunnies."

Sunken garden : A landscape design where some of the garden is at a lower point than the rest of the garden. Created for interest.

Sunscald : Plant injury caused by exposure to bright sunlight, excessive heat and/or wind.

Superbug : Jargon for a particular engineered strain of Pseudomonas, in which various hydrocarbon-degrading genes, derived from different plasmids, were combined into one genotype. This provided the basis for the precedent-setting legal decision that declared that genetically engineered organisms were patentable.

Supercoil : The conformation of a double-stranded DNA molecule placed under torsional stress as a result of interactions with proteins. The stress is accommodated by a twist imposed on the duplex. A left-handed supercoil favours unwinding of the double helix; a right-handed supercoil favours tighter winding.

Supercoiled plasmid : The predominant in vivo form of most plasmids, in which the DNA is coiled around histone-like proteins. When supporting proteins are stripped away during DNA extraction from the bacterial cell, the plasmid molecule also tends to supercoil around itself in vitro.

Superficial : On the surface, not connected to inner tissues.

Supernatant : The liquid phase remaining after insoluble materials are pelleted by centrifugation or precipitation.

Superposed : Said of extra buds that appear above the true axillary buds; usually flower buds.

Superspecies : A taxonomic category comprising two or more species deemed to be sufficiently closely related and of such recent evolutionary divergences to comprise a taxonomic category not far above that of species.

Supine : Lying flat, face upwards.

Supplement : Feed or feed mixtures rich in one or more of protein, energy, vitamins, minerals or antibiotics. Combined with other feeds to produce a more complete feed.

Supply control programs : Any of several government programs to influence the supply of farm products on the market. Some, such as acreage allotments and marketing quotas, are considered mandatory, in that farmers who produce or market in excess of assigned levels can be legally penalized. Others, such as cropland set-asides, acreage reductions and diversions, and farmer-held grain reserves, are considered voluntary, in that farmers are usually encouraged to participate through financial incentives.

Supportive treatment : supportive treatment corrects or modifies abnormalities that occur secondary to a disease process. For example fluid and electrolyte therapy for a patient with hypoadrenocorticism.

Suppressor mutation : A mutation that reverses the effect of an earlier mutation, e. g. a mutation in a gene for a tRNA that permits it to read and override an amber mutation.

Surimi : A fish paste made from minced fish meat (usually pollock) which has been washed to remove fat, blood, pigments and odorous substances and mixed with cryoprotectants (such as sugar and/or sorbitol) for a good frozen shelf life.

Surimi seafood : Analog shellfish products made from surimi that is thawed, blended with flavorings, stabilizers and colorings and then heat-processed to make fibrous, flake, chunk and composite molded products, most commonly imitating crab meat, lobster tails and shrimp.

Swedish meatballs : A combination of ground meat (often a combination of beef, pork, or veal), sautéed onions, milk-soaked breadcrumbs, beaten eggs, and seasonings. The mixture is formed into small balls, then sautéed until brown.

Sweet feed : A commercial feed sweetened with molasses to improve palatability.

Sweet potato whitefly : An insect pest of cotton, fruit and vegetable, and greenhouse crops. The Animal and Plant Health Inspection Service works cooperatively with producers to implement pest management strategies based on integrated pest management and biological control techniques.

Swing parlor : Parlor characterized by having the milking units positioned in the middle of the parlor for use by cows on both sides.

Swiss steak : Round or chuck steak that has been tenderized by pounding, coated with flour, and browned on both sides. The meat is then smothered in chopped tomatoes, onions, carrots, celery, broth, and seasonings, then baked for about two hours.

Syncytium : A group of cells in which cytoplasmic continuity is maintained; the effect is of a multinucleate cell.

Syndrome : A group of specific characters that occur together, and are characteristic of a particular disease or genetic condition.

Synecology : The study of groups of organisms that are associated as a unit. The emphasis may be on the fit of one organism into the system, on the relationships between organisms, or on the whole system as a unit.

Synergid : One of the two haploid nuclei at the micropylar end of the embryo sac of higher plants. The third nucleus is the egg.

Systems analysis : The orderly and logical organization of data and information into models, followed by the rigorous testing and exploration of the models necessary for their validation and improvement.

T

Target : In diagnostic tests, the molecule or nucleic acid sequence assayed in a sample. In mutagenesis, the gene sequence that needs to be altered to generate the desired change in phenotype.

Target area : Large priority development area in a country for which improved cropping system technologies are developed through on-farm cropping systems research conducted at sites in the area.

Target catch : That portion of the catch which is retained on board and which was the focus of a directed fishery.

Target prices : The minimum level of prices determined by law to provide an economic safety net. Sometimes call the guaranteed price level. The target price, based on cost of production, becomes the price support level at which the government will bolster farm income by making price support payments to qualifying farmers when national average market prices fall below the target.

TATA box : A widely conserved adenine- and thymine-rich DNA sequence found 25-30 bp upstream of the transcription initiation point of many eukaryotic genes. The TATA box is implicated in the promotion of gene transcription as it acts as a binding site for RNA polymerase. Analogous to the Pribnow box in prokaryotic promoters.

TEA : Targeted Export Assistance Program

Team nutrition : Coordinated effort by the FCS to implement the school meals initiative for healthy children.

Teat orifice : The opening at the bottom of the teat where milk exits. This opening serves as a potential route for bacteria to enter the teat.

Teat sealant : A product that forms a mechanical barrier on the teat end to protect the teat. Generally used at dry-off after antibiotic infusion.

Technology transfer : The transfer of knowledge or equipment to enable the manufacture of a product, the application of a process, or the rendering of a service.

Tekapo sale : The annual Tekapo Fine Wool Sheep Sale is held at Lake Tekapo. The two-tooth and adult sale was held on 27 February 1998 with 14,569 sheep offered and the lamb sale drew a yarding of about 15,800 head made up of mainly wether and ewe lambs. Neat to see all the sheep, farmers and their hats, flat bed trucks, the big three decker sheep trucks, dust, the cool cool lake, lupines and picnic.

Telescopic : Telescopic handlers are a development of the traditional forklift. They have a boom which can be raised or lowered within which is another section which can be extended to give greater height or reach. Most can have a variety of attachments fitted such as grain buckets manure forks bale grabs or pallet forks.

Tendril : A slender, coiling, modified leaf or stem of climbing plants, such as peas, that supports the plant by attaching it to surrounding surfaces.

Tepal : A segment of perianth not differentiated into calyx or corolla. E.g.- tulip, magnolia.

Terminal market : A central site, often in a metropolitan area, that serves as an assembly and trading place for agricultural commodities. Terminal markets are usually at or near major transportation hubs.

Terminal sire : Sires used in a crossbreeding system where all their progeny, both male and female, are marketed. For example, F1 crossbred dams could be bred to sires of a third breed and all calves marketed. Although this system allows maximum heterosis and complementary breeds, replacement females must come from other herds.

Terminal transferase : An enzyme that catalyses the addition of nucleotides to the 3' end of a DNA molecule.

Terminalization : Repelling movement of the centromeres of bivalents in the diplotene stage of the meiotic prophase, that appears to move visible chiasmata toward the ends of the bivalents.

Termination signal : In transcription, a nucleotide sequence that specifies RNA chain termination.

Territorial sea : The area from average low-water mark on the shore out to three miles for the states of Louisiana, Alabama, and Mississippi, and out to nine miles for Texas and the west coast of Florida. The shore is not always the baseline from which the three miles are measured. In such cases, the outer limit can extend further than three miles from the shore.

Tertiary hyperparathyroidism : Tertiary hyperparathy- roidism is a relatively uncommon event occurring in some chronic renal failure patients, which may result in a moderate increase in calcium.

Tertiary period : The first period of the cenozoic era, beginning 65 million years ago and closing with the start of the pleistocene, 2.5 million years ago.

Tertiary structure : The three-dimensional conformation taken up by complete macromolecules as a result of intramolecular interactions, such as hydrogen-bonding.

Test fishing : Fishing activity designed to provide data from which an estimate of run size can be generated.

Teteur : A French word meaning "trainer". Any structure that is in the shape of an obelisk or pointed tower. This trellis will support vines of color.

Tethering : To tie an animal with a rope or chain to allow grazing but prevent straying.

Tetracycline : An antibiotic that interferes with protein synthesis in prokaryotes. A gene encoding resistance to tetracycline has been widely used as a marker to distinguish between transformed and non-transformed cells in the production of transgenic plants.

Tetrad : The four haploid cells formed after the second meiotic division in plants (pollen tetrads) or fungi (ascospores).

Thermal time : 1) The time-temperature integral above a specified 'base temperature'; usually for a set of processes if individual processes have the same base temperature.2) The integral of time and temperature in degree-days needed for the completion of a particular development process.

Thermograph : A self-recording thermometer.

Thermolabile : Not resistant to heat, often in the context of a molecule which is unstable upon heating.

Thermophilic bacteria : This group of bacteria species work to break down organic matter under "hot" conditions of 104 degrees up to 170 degrees. This type of bacteria can perform the greatest decomposition in the shortest amount of time.

Thermosensitivity : Loss of biological activity of a molecule at high temperature.

Thigh cutter : Scores and cuts the thigh bone joint.

Thigh deboner : Removes the bones from thigh meat.

Thigh inspector : Inspects boneless thigh meat for bone fragments, blood clots, etc..

Thinning : 1) Removal of older stems to promote new growth. 2) Removal of excess fruits to improve the size and quality of the remaining fruits. 3) Removal of seedlings spaced too closely for optimum growth.

Thinning out : A type of pruning operation in which entire shoots are removed. An extension of, or complement to, heading back.

Three-point linkage : Ferguson's invention of a connection that permitted a tractor to lift as well as drag a plough or other implement. This made it possible to cultivate a much wider range of soils then before.

Three-way cross : This hybrid is produced over two generations. A single cross hybrid is produced in the first season and crossed with an inbred line in the following. This additional production step requires resources in terms of time, land and money, but it normally guarantees for more reliable yields than inbred lines.

Thymidine triphosphate : TTP; dTTP is strictly correct but rarely used.

Ti plasmid : Tumour-inducing plasmid. A large plasmid present in pathogenic Agrobacterium tumefaciens, responsible for the induction of tumours in plant with crown gall disease. Engineered forms of this plasmid are central to the production of transgenics in many crop species.

Tick : A type of mite which is suited only to one host animal per species. They feed on the blood of the host.

Tickler : A chain that is dragged along the bottom of the ocean in front of a net to scare fish up from the bottom and into the net.

Timber : The wood product of a tree obtained by sawing and milling. Timber is a major product of forests. It differs from poles or roundwood only in that it is cut.

Timber height : The height of a tree to the point at which the stem breaks into branches (the 'crown spring') or to the point at which the diameter of the stem is 7 cm over bark, whichever is reached first. On a felled tree this point is called the 'timber point'.

Timber sale : A contract for the sale of federal timber to a private purchaser with the right to cut and remove trees for an agreed-upon stumpage price; the contract includes an estimated volume of wood and an appraised stumpage price, which is the basis for competitive bidding by purchasers.

Topiary : The horticultural art of clipping and training woody plants to form geometric shapes or interesting patterns.

Total Digestible Nutrients (TDN) : A term describing the energy value of feedstuffs, comparable to DE in accuracy. TDN over- estimates the energy value of roughages in comparison to grains.

Total economic value : The sum of use and non-use values with due consideration of any trade-offs or mutually exclusive uses or functions of the resource/habitat in question.

Total environmental value : It is a function of primary value and total economic value.

Total extracts : Contain the whole spectrum of ingredients present in the original herb, plus any new active compounds formed during processing.

Total length : The length of a fish as measured from the tip of the snout to the tip of the tail.

TPR : A common medical abbreviation for temperature, pulse, and respiration.

TPRG : Trade Policy Review Group

Tracer : A substance (typically a radioactive isotope or a fluorescent dye) that can be detected by physical means, and which is used to analyse the progress of a chemical reaction or a biological process.

Tracheid : An elongated, tapering xylem cell, with lignified pitted walls, adapted for solute conduction and physical support. Found in conifers, ferns and related plants.

Tract : A unit of contiguous land under one ownership which is operated as a farm or part of a farm.

Traditional resource rights : The term trr encompasses intellectual property rights, but denotes broader 'bundles of rights' including for example, human rights, land rights, religious rights, and cultural property.

Trailing : Any plant that grows long stems and will grow along the ground and will root as it goes along.

Trait : A characteristic of a plant, a group of plants, or part of a plant. Traits may be attributes (quantitative values such as alive/dead or diseased/healthy) or variables (quantitative values such as 'diameter at breast height' or 'basal area').

Transboundary stock : Any fish stock that crosses a jurisdictional boundary, either between two coastal nations, or between a coastal nation's exclusive economic zone and the high seas.

Transcapsidation : The partial of full coating of the nucleic acid of one virus with a coat protein of a differing virus.

Transformant : A cell or organism that has been genetically altered through the integration of a transgene(s). Primary: the first generation following the transformation event. Secondary: progeny of the primary transformant.

Transgenic animal : Genetically enginnered animal or offspring of genetically engineered animals. The transgenic animal usually contains material from at lease one unrelated organism, such as from a virus, plant, or other animal.

Transgenic plant : Genetically engineered plant or offspring of genetically engineered plants. The transgenic plant usually contains material from at least one unrelated organisms, such as from a virus, animal, or other plant.

Transgressive variation : The appearance, in a segregating generation, of individuals showing expression of a trait outside the extremes defined by the parent of the cross that was used to generate the population.

Transhumance : A situation in which farmers with a permanent place of residence send their herds, tended by herdsmen, for long periods of time to distant grazing areas.

Transient expression : Short-term activity of a transgene following its introduction into target tissue. Transient expression usually implies non-integration of the transgene into the host genome.

Translation : The process of converting the genetic information of an mRNA on ribosomes into a polypeptide. Transfer RNA molecules carry the appropriate amino acids to the ribosome, where they are joined by peptide bonds.

Translocated herbicide : A herbicide that, after uptake, is moved within the plant and can affect parts of the plant remote from the point of application.

Translocation : 1) The movement of nutrients or products of metabolism from one location to another. 2) Change in position of a segment of a chromosome to another, non-homologous chromosome.

Transmissibility/Contagiousness : Capacity of parasite to spread between animals - e.g. Salmonella dublin is regard as highly contagious between heifers and calves via feces.

Transmissible Spongiform Encephalopathies (TSEs) : The name of a number of degenerative brain diseases that infect humans and animals. For example, bovine spongiform encephalopathy (BSE) infects cattle; Creutzfeldt-Jacob disease (CJD) infects humans.

Transperation : Evaporation of water from plant tissue to the atmosphere. Transpiration occurs mainly through the stomates in the leaves.

Transplant lines : Juvenile shrubs and trees planted in nurseries from seedlings or rooted cuttings, to reach acceptable size for planting elsewhere.

Transplanting : Digging up a growing plant from one location to plant it in another location.Transplanting happens in many forms—seedlings in pots, with open-rooted seedlings, balled-root seedlings and with stumps.

Transposable (Genetic) element : A DNA element that can move from one location in the genome to another.

Transposase : An enzyme encoded by a transposon gene that catalyses the movement of a DNA sequence to a different site in a DNA molecule.

Trauma : A wound or injury.

Travasol : An amino acid solution used in TPN and PPN.

Trawls : Towed nets consisting of a cone-shaped body, closed by a bag or codend and extended at the opening by wings. Strong steel cables (called warps) connect the net to the trawler. They can be towed by one or two vessels and may be used on the bottom (bottom trawls) or in mid-water (mid-water or pelagic trawls). In some fisheries, vessels may tow two (or even four) trawls at the same time.

Tubulin : The major protein component of the microtubules of eukaryotic cells.

Tull jethro : Invented a seed drill. The sowing of seed in rows made it possible to use a horsedrawn hoe and thereby increase efficiency.

Tumble tube : A glass tube mainly used in vitro to agitate and consequently aerate suspension cultures. The tube, which is commonly attached to a slowly revolving platform, is closed at both ends, with a side-neck opening.

Tumbleweed (Russian thistle) : Annual plant that breaks away from its roots in the fall and is driven by the wind, releasing seeds. Approximately 200,000 seeds per plant.

Tumid : Swollen

Tumor : A swelling of any structure but not always neoplastic.

Tumor virus : A virus capable of transforming a cell to a malignant phenotype.

Turtle excluder devices : Panels of mesh webbing or metal grids inserted into funnel-shaped shrimp trawl nets. As the nets are towed, shrimp and other small animals pass through the ted and into the codend of the net, the narrow bag at the end of the funnel where the catch is collected. Sea turtles, sharks, and fish too large to get through the panel are deflected out an escape hatch.

Tusk : A large saltwater fish related to the cod. It has a firm, lean flesh. Also called "cusk."

Tussah (or tasar, tussore) : A wild silk of the Antherea mylitta caterpillar which eats the leaves of the Arjun tree (terminalia arjun), Asan (terminalia tomentosa) or Oak (querus). This caterpillar is raised in the forested regions of China, Korea and India. The silk is honey beige colour.

T-value (or t-level) : For a specific soil, the maximum average annual soil loss expressed as tons per acre per year that will permit current production levels to be maintained economically and indefinitely, the soil loss tolerance level. T values range from 2 to 5 tons per acre per year. According to the 1992 national resources inventory, about 63 million acres of highly erodible cropland are still eroding at more than their 'T' value, including 21 million acres that are still eroding at three times 'T'.

U

Ultraviolet radiation : Radiation beyond the violet (high energy) end of the visible light spectrum. Uv-b is the middle range wave-length of the three uv bands, and is largely absorbed in the earth's atmospheric ozone layer; prolonged exposure to uv-b can be biologically damaging.

Umbel : An indeterminate, convex or flat-topped i' in which the pedicels of the cluster arise from a common point

Umbilical cord : The tubular structure that connects the fetus to the placenta and carries nutrients to the fetus and removes its wastes.

Umbrella species : Species whose occupancy area (plants) or home range (animals) are large enough and whose habitat requirements are wide enough that, if they are given a sufficiently large area for their protection, will bring other species under that protection.

Undegradable Intake Protein (UIP) : Portion of ingested protein that escapes rumen degradation and is digested directly in the other stomachs or small intestine; generally a more expensive source of protein. Commonly referred to as 'bypass' protein.

Under bark : Measurement of the diameter or circumference of a trunk or branch made with the bark removed.

Under glass : A term in older books referring to "growing under glass", essentially growing in a greenhouse.

Undercut seedling : a nursery-grown seedling that has had its tap root cut by passing a blade or wire through the seedbed a few centimetres below ground level. This process encourages the growth of lateral roots and is an alternative to transplanting as a means of obtaining sturdy planting stock with a well-branched root system. Often moved as balled roots.

Underplanting : Growing short plants such as a ground cover under taller plants. Under taller trees, some shrubs would be used as an underplanting.

Understory trees : Small trees that grow well under larger ones. Common understory trees in a birch-poplar-spruce forest include ironwood, mountain maple, and serviceberry. Other common understory trees in a mixed maple-hardwood forest are witch hazel and black cherry.

Underutilized species : A species of fish that has potential for large additional harvest.

Underwood : A tree crop growing beneath the main canopy and forming a distinct lower storey. It is usually of coppice but can be of planted or naturally seeded trees.

Undifferentiated : Undifferentiated cells are those which have not been committed to become part of a specialized tissue.

Undulate : Wavy, as a leaf margin.

Unencapsidated : A virus not enclosed by a coat protein or capsid.

Unequal crossing over : Abnormal meiotic event, in which one chromatid contains a duplication and the other a deletion. Often arises in a region containing repeated DNA sequences, which can pair out of register.

Uneven-aged : The presence of at least three distinct age classes, usually a range of size classes ('seedling', 'sapling', 'pole' and 'sawtimber').

Unfinished lambs : Butchers will only buy lambs that have reached a certain weight and level of fatness. How long it takes a lamb to grow to this size varies according to breed, birth weight and food available. Some lambs finish sooner than others. On hill farms where there is not enough outdoor feed for lambs, any remaining at the end of the year may be sold as stores, to be finished on lowland farms during the winter and spring.

Ungrazed : The status of grazing land that is not grazed by animals. Also, the status of plants or plant parts that are not grazed by animals.

Unicellular : Tissues, organs or organisms consisting of a single cell.

Unidirectional externality : These are externalities in which the external costs or benefits of the resource use are "one way".

Uniformity trial : Planting a test crop at a carefully controlled planting density and under a consistent level of good management over an area on which a field experiment is to be carried out, so as to use the data when it is harvested from small, equal-sized plots over the whole area, to assess how 'uniform' this area is. It can be used to define blocks where non-uniformity occurs and locational control is part of the experimental design (for example, in a 'randomized block layout', or for covariance analysis).

Unintended release : Any release of gmos which is not a deliberate release.

Uniparental inheritance : The inheritance of genes exclusively from one parent, e.g. chloroplast DNA is inherited either maternally (many angiosperms) or paternally (most gymnosperms).

Unique farmland : Land, other than prime farmland, that has combined conditions to produce sustained high quality and high yields of specialty crops, such as citrus, nuts, fruits, and vegetables when properly managed.

Unisexual : Higher organisms (animals or plants) possessing either male or female reproductive organs, but not both.

Unisexual flowers : Flowers having either pistils or anthers, but not both.

Universal soil loss equation : A formula used to estimate erosion rates by considering climate, soils, and topographic conditions at a site, as well as any degree to which the use and management of the soil reduce erosion. It is being replaced by a revised universal soil loss equation.

Universality : Referring to the genetic code, the triplet codons are translated to the same amino acid, with minor exceptions, in virtually all species.

Unloading vehicle : Unloads product and/or materials for use in the processing plant.

Unorganized growth : In vitro formation of tissues with few differentiated cell types and no recognizable structure; typical structure of calli formed in tissue culture.

Unprojected map : A map that is not projected to a coordinate system. Refers to data containing latitude and longitude coordinates.

Upstream : 1) The stretch of DNA lying in the 5' direction from the site being considered. Where the reference point is the initiation of transcription, the first transcribed base is designated +1 and upstream nucleotides are marked with minus signs, e.g. -1, -10; 2. In chemical engineering. those phases of a manufacturing process that precede the biotransformation step.

Upwelling : A process by which water rises from lower depths into the shallows, usually the result of divergence or offshore currents.

Upwelling zones : Areas of the oceans where deep-ocean waters rich in nutrients rise to the surface. Although these natural upwelling zones amount to only about 0.1% of the surface of the oceans, the are very fertile, producing 44% of all the fish humans use for food.

Uro-vagina : Presence of urine in the vagina.

Urticaria : An allergic reaction of the skin characterised by reddened irregular, elevated patches and severe itching. Also called hives.

Usable stock : The number or weight of all fish in a stock that lie within the range of sizes customarily considered usable (or designated so by law).

Use : The proportion of current years forage production that is consumed or destroyed by grazing animals.

Use value : Values obtained through the use of a resource. This includes direct and indirect use values and instrumental values. Preservation in this sense is as much a use as development.

Uterine tubes : Tubes that connect the ovarian bursa to the uterus. Eggs are transported through these tubes to the uterus.

Uteroverdin : A green pigment present in the placenta attached to the endometrium of a bitch. As placental separation occurs during whelping the pigment is discharged.

Uterus : The female organ in which the fetus develops. Composed of a body and 2 horns.

Utility : Utility breeds are the traditional "barnyard" birds, bred for a combination of egg laying abilities and meat production capabilities. These are all-purpose breeds.

Utility function : A description of the way in which the well-being of individuals depends on different combinations of goods and services consumed.

V

Vandaceous : From the genus name Vanda, alluding to any orchid having the characteristics of a Vanda species; large monopodial orchids such as genera Aerides, Arachnis Rhynchostylis, and Renanthera.

Variability : absence of uniformity. Quality of differing from the average value. This term is usually used in a general sense and qualified by such words as 'low', 'moderate', and 'high'. For quantitative comparisons, the concept of a variance is used.

Variable : 1) A quantity able to assume different numerical values. When considering two variables at the same time, one can sometimes be considered the dependent variable and the other the independent variable, for example crop growth (dry matter) and intercepted solar radiation (mj m-2) respectively. 2. Any quantity or quality likely to show variation from one individual to the next in the same population.

Variable costs : These are costs which vary directly with the scale of the enterprise. For example to grow one hectare of wheat requires £100 spent on seed, fertilizer and sprays. One hundred hectares will cost 100 times as much.

Variable stocking : The practice of allowing a variable number of animals on a fixed area of land during the time when grazing is allowed.

Variable Surface Glycoprotein (VSG) : One of a battery of antigenic determinants expressed by a micro-organism to elude immune detection.

Variable-rate technology : Instrumentation such as a variable-rate controller for varying the rates of application of fertilizer, pesticides and seed as one travels across a field.

Variance : 1) In statistics, of a set of observations, the mean of the squared deviations from their mean value. 2) A statistical measure of variability defined in an exact manner. Many types of variances can be calculated, for example within-block variance and within-plot variance among individual plants. Examining the ratios between two calculated variances provides a way of determining if observed differences, or relationships, are large enough to be caused by factors other than chance.

Variance : A statistical term representing a measure of the dispersion of data from the overall mean. Used to quantify the variability of a population.

Variety name : This is the scientific name or botanical name of a specific plant. It is in italic print.

Variety release : The official approval of a variety for multiplication and distribution.

Vascular : Plant tissue specialized for the conduction of water or nutrients

Vascular bundle scar : minute spot within the leaf scar where the vessels were positioned.

Vascular cambium : In biennials and perennials, cambium giving rise to secondary phloem and secondary xylem.

Vascular plant : Plant species possessing organized vascular tissues.

VEG : Value-enhanced grain. VEG is defined as grain with particular quality characteristics that add end-user value.

Vegetation : An all encompassing word for the plants of an area or territory.

Vegetative : Part of a plant not directly concerned with repoduction as the stem and leaves.

Vegetative controls : Nonpoint source pollution control practices that involve planting cover crops to reduce erosion and minimize loss of pollutants.

Vegetative propagation : An asexual reproduction process of trimming growing stems from aplant and allowing them to root.

Vein : A blood vessel that carries blood back to the heart. The pressure in veins is lower than in arteries. Veins contain less oxygen and nutrients than arteries and contain waste products that they carry to the lungs or other organs for disposal.

Veneer : a product made from round logs of certain trees by turning a log and slicing a continuous sheet from it. This sheet is then cut into lengths and glued to lower quality wood for making panelling, table tops, doors and other products with improved appearance.

Venereal : Sexually transmitted. Transmissible venereal tumors occur on the genital organs; penis or vagina, and are transmitted from dog to dog by sexual contact.

Venison : This term covers the meat from antelope, caribou, elk, deer, moose, and reindeer. Venison is probably the most popular large game meat eaten today.

Venous : Referring to the system of veins.

Vent cutter : Opens the back end of bird to remove evisceration.

Vermicast : A single worm casting or a quantity of worm castings. Worms "work" material by ingesting, excreting, and re-ingesting it. Vermicast is extensively worm-worked and re-worked. It may be overworked and has probably lost plant nutrients as compared vermicompost. Vermicast has a fine, smooth texture, which may dry with a crust on the surface.

Vermicompost : Mixture of partially decomposed organic waste, bedding, and worm castings (excretions). Contains recognizable fragments of plant, food, or worm bedding material, as well as cocoons, worms, and associated organisms. As a verb "to carry out composting with worms."

Vermicomposting : The process of using worms and associated organisms to break down organic waste into material containing nutrients for plant growth.

Vermiculite : A light-weight, mineral called mica that is added to potting mixtures to improve root growth via aeration and has moisture retaining abilities. There is no nutritive value in the mineral.

Vernation : The arrangement of leaves within a bud.

Verrucose : Covered with or furnished with wart-like projections

Vertebrae : The segments of the backbone. Each vertebrae is separated from adjacent vertebrae by a spongy structure called a disk.

Vertical integration : The integrating of successive stages of the production and marketing functions under the ownership or control of a single management organization. For example, much of the broiler industry is highly vertically integrated in that processing companies own or control the activities from production and hatching of eggs, through the growth and feeding of the chickens, to slaughter, processing, and wholesale marketing.

Vfn : Indicate whether or not a plant is resistant to verticillium wilt, fusarium wilt, or certain nematodes. Many times all three.

Viability : 1) A measure of the potential for seeds to germinate and grow. A seed of short viability will germinate well only within a short time after harvest. Some tree seeds have long viability and will germinate readily, possibly with pretreatment, long after collection.

Viability test : Assay of the number or percent of living cells or plants in a population following a specific treatment. Often used to describe quality of seed following long-term storage.

Viable : Capable of growing or developing.

Vienna sausage : A small frankfurter, often served as an hors d'oeuvre.

Village forest garden : Larger than the homegarden, less densely planted and not so well tended. Planted with higher trees and often containing spontaneous species of herbs or lianas.

Villous : Having long, soft, shaggy hairs that are not matted.

Viral coat protein : A protein present in the layer surrounding the nucleic acid core of a virus.

Viral oncogene : A viral gene that contributes to malig- nancies in vertebrate hosts.

Viral pathogen : A disease-causing virus.

Viral vaccine : Vaccine consisting of live viruses, genetically engineered to avoid causing the disease itself.

Virgin : Never been bred.

Virgin stock : A stock of fish with no commercial or recreational harvest. A virgin stock changes only in relation to environmental factors and its own growth, recruitment, and natural mortality.

Virion : A complete infectious virus particle.

Viroid : A plant pathogen that consists of a naked RNA molecule of approximately 250-350 nucleotides, whose extensive base pairing results in a nearly correct double helix.

Virtual population Analysis (VPA) : A type of analysis that uses the number of fish caught at various ages or lengths and an estimate of natural mortality to estimate fishing mortality in a cohort. It also provides an estimate of the number of fish in a cohort at various ages.

Virucide : A substance that kills viruses.

Virulence : The degree of ability of an organism to cause disease. The relative infectiousness of a bacterium or virus, or its ability to overcome the resistance of the host metabolism.

Virulent phage : A phage that destroys its host bacterium.

Viruliferous : A vector (usually insect) organism that carries virions and spreads the virus from host to host by mechanical means.

Virus : An infectious particle composed of a protein capsule and a nucleic acid core, which is dependent on a host organism for replication. A double-stranded DNA copy of an RNA virus genome that is integrated into the host chromosome during lysogenic infection.

Vivonex : by Norwich Eaton. A hypoallergenic elemental diet.

Vmax : The maximal rate of an enzyme-catalysed reaction. Vmax is the product of Eo (the total amount of enzyme) and Kcat (the catalytic rate constant).

Vogt-koyanagi-harada syndrome : Uveodermatologic syndrome or "uveitis with poliosis and vitiligo". Syndrome of uveitis, alopecia, depigmentation and whitening of the hairs.

Volatile Fatty Acids (VFA) : By products of digestion in the rumen that make an acidic environment and keep pathogenic bacterial populations down.

W

Warble fly : The larva of the warble fly cause much discomfort to cattle as it moves from the hoof to the animal's back under the skin.

Wardian case : In the 19th century a plant explorer and collector by the name of Dr. Nathaniel Ward designed a glass case to transport his findings. He traveled between Australia and England. During the Victorian era often Wardian Cases were highlighted in the home.

Warehouse receipt : A document certifying possession of a commodity in a licensed warehouse. Some warehouse receipts are recognized for delivery purposes by a commodity futures exchange.

Warm season grass : Grass that grows and "greens up" in summer, sets seed in fall, and goes dormant (loses its green color and stops growing) during winter and spring. According to Easy Lawns, most warm-season grasses are bunchgrasses and will not tolerate any shade.

Warm-season crops : Crops that are harmed by frost and do not grow well until the temperatures are in the 70s.

Warp : The vertical threads of a textile that are stretched on the loom.

Wash out : Uses an offline antimicrobial treatment to clean product before placing product on line.

Waste treatment pond : A shallow lagoon or similar storage facility, often man-made, used to treat liquid agricultural wastes, particularly liquid manure from livestock production farms, through the interaction of sunlight, wind, algae, and oxygen. Through natural biological processes, microscopic organisms consume wastes present in the water.

Water balance : 1) The distribution of water in space, and over time, within a system. Where plants are growing on land this means considering rainfall (and also interception loss, stemflow and throughfall), drainage, evapotranspiration, runoff and soil water storage. 2) Balance of input and output of water within a given defined hydrological area such as a basin or a lake, taking into account net changes of storage. Also used for smaller areas, for example, a field or a plot.

Water race : Dug in the early days with a shovel and barrow or a horse and plough. A creek is dammed, partially, to redirect water down a channel which runs for miles through many farmers paddocks often along fences and across a corner of a adjoining paddock so stock will have water and to assist with irrigation. The farmers keep the race cleaned out on their own properties. When a flood washes out the intake the farmer whose property it is on repairs the intake again with stones.

Water service contract : A type of contract, authorized by the Reclamation Project Act of 1939, whereby water is furnished for irrigation or municipal or miscellaneous purposes at rates to produce revenue sufficient to cover charges reimbursable to the federal government.

Water soluble vitamins : Includes B complex vitamins and vitamin C. Not normally supplemented for ruminants after two months of age because rumen microbes are able to manufacture enough to meet the animal's requirements.

Water spreading : 1) The application of water to lands to increase the growth of natural vegetation or to store it in the ground for subsequent withdrawal by pumps for irrigation. Part of water harvesting. 2) Methods of controlling the flow of water locally so as to distribute it better over a farmer's fields. A way of avoiding damage ('gullying') where there is a likelihood of large inflows from any land above a farm or plot.

Water stress : Occurs when plants are unable to absorb enough water to replace that lost by transpiration. Short-term water stress leads to turgor loss (wilting). Prolonged stress leads to cessation of growth, and eventually plant death.

Water table : 1) The upper edge of free water in the soil. When a hole is dug, water will fill the hole to the level of the water table. 2) The level below gound at which free water persists.

Water-based allotment : an allotment whose permit is based on the ownership of livestock water sources instead of land, with grazing use dependent upon each source.

Waterfowl production areas : A small component of the National Wildlife Refuge System. There are over 2,000,000 acres of this prime duck-producing land, mostly prairie potholes in the Dakotas, Minnesota, and Montana. The Fish and Wildlife Service owns, leases, or holds easements on the lands.

Water-holding capacity : Of a soil, the amount of water that it is capable of holding, between field capacity and permanent wilting point.

Waterlogged : 1) A condition of land where the groundwater stands at a level that is detrimental to plants. It may result from over irrigation, seepage or inadequate drainage. 2) Saturated with water. A soil condition with a high or a perched water table; detrimental to plant growth.

Watershed : 1) A physiographic unit in the landscape defined by the drainage dividers around the area drained by a particular body of water. If a lake, there is often one watershed with subunits for contributing streams. If a river, it may be defined for any point or all. 2) The whole surface drainage area that contributes water to a lake. The total area above a given point on a stream that contributes water to the flow at that point. 3) The total area, regardless of size, above a given point on a waterway that contributes runoff water to the flow at that point. A major drain-area subdivision of a drainage basin on the basis of this concept.

Water-stable aggregate : a soil aggregate stable to the action of water such as falling drops or agitation as in wet-sieving analysis.

Water-use efficiency : The above-ground dry matter or harvested portion of a crop produced per unit of rainfall received on the same area of ground i.e. Including water lost from the soil surface or by runoff and drainage as well as that used in transpiration.

Water-use ratio : The ratio of the weight of water actually transpired by a crop during its growing season to the weight of dry matter produced (usually exclusive of roots). Also called the 'transpiration ratio'.

Wattles : Hair-covered appendages of flesh hanging from the throat area. Sometimes there are "misplaced" wattles on other parts of the body. They serve no real function.

Waveband : A remote sensing term used to describe a contiguous range of wavelengths of electromagnetic energy. Visible wavelengths (seen by the human eye) which range from 400 to 700 nanometers. Near infrared (NIR) wavelengths are at 700 to 2600 nanometers.

Wax : Water-insoluble esters of long-chain acids with long-chain alcohols. Waxes form protective waterproof layers on leaves, stems, fruits, animal fur and integuments of insects.

Wean : To take the young animal away from their mother so they are not able to get milk. This is done so the animal will learn to eat on its own.

Weaner : Lamb after weaning to 12 months. No exact age but approx from to 12 months.

Weaner pellets : Small or juvenile animal pellets are usually smaller in size with adjusted ingredients.

Weave : Two systems of threads interlacing with one another at right angles.

Web blotch : Occurs in peanuts. Leaf disease that reduces yield and quality. Predictive computer models can help producers time fungicide applications to control the disease.

Web of life : The concept that all organisms are interrelated. If one part of the "web" is broken, the entire web is affected.

Weed : 'A plant growing in the wrong place.' End users have demanded fewer weed seeds in grain etc. over the years requiring fields to become weed free. Field margins however maintain the diversity necsessary to support various 'weeds'.

Weediness : The ability of a plant to colonize a disturbed habitat and compete with cultivated species.

Weeding : The elimination of competing vegetation around young trees, for example, by cultivation, by the use of herbicides, or by cutting or slashing. When the trees are big enough to overcome weed competition, a tree plantation is said to be 'established'.

Weighted silk : The practice formerly used to compensate for the loss of the sericin weight during silk processing. Usually done with tin salts. This caused the fabric to be brittle and wear badly.

Welfare : an index of well-being.

Wellhead protection area : A surface and subsurface land area regulated to prevent contamination of a well or wellfield supplying a public water system. This program, established under the Safe Drinking Water Act, is implemented through state governments.

WEQ : Wind Erosion Equation

Western blot : A technique whereby a complex mixture of size-separated proteins is fixed to a solid support, and then probed with a labelled antibody. Useful, for example, for the measurement of levels of production of a specific protein in a particular tissue or at particular developmental stage.

Wet cow average : Average milk production by lactating cows. Goal is 70 to 80 lbs/day, 21,000-24,000 per year.

Wet feet : A condition when the roots of plants are in standing water. They will eventually rot if they don't normally grow in wet conditions like aquatic plants.

Wetable powder : A material that will not dissolve in water, but remains suspended in it. Most often referred to pesticides when used as sprays.

Wether : A castrated male sheep. A two-tooth wether is sometimes killed for mutton for a homestead.

Wettable powder : a type of formulation for pesticides or herbicides for spray application in which the active materials are mixed with an inert carrier, finely ground, and with a surface-acting agent added, so that it will form a suspension when agitated with water.

Wetting agent : A substance (usually a detergent) that improves the contact of a liquid to a solid surface by reducing its surface tension.

Wheal : A circumscribed raised lesion of edemma of the dermas. A large number of wheals is urticaria.

Wheat : The major cereal crop. Wheat falls into two categories; hard generally suitable for milling (flour) and soft usually used for distilling animal feed and biscuit making.

Wheatfeed : A byproduct of flour milling. It contains fragments of bran, seedcoat and some flour. Rather dusty but a useful animal food.

Wheel : The cross-sectional center cut from large fish like sharks and swordfish.

Whelk : A large marine snail that belongs to the mollusk family. The flavorful foot-like muscle is rather tough and must be tenderized by pounding. Look for whelk in Chinese or Italian markets or specialty food stores.

Whip : A very thin shoot with no lateral branches of a woody plant. Sometimes the first year of a grafted tree.

White grubs : The larval stage of May and June bugs. An annual problem in lawns and turf.

White muscle disease : Another name for a selenium deficiency.

Whitefish : A high-fat, mild-flavored member of the salmon family with a firm white flesh. The whitefish can be poached, baked, broiled, grilled, pan fried, or stuffed. Its roe (eggs) can be cooked or made into caviar by adding salt.

Whiting : A small gray and white saltwater fish sometimes called the "silver hake." This low-fat fish, which is related to both the "cod" and the "hake," has a tender white fine-textured flesh and a flaky, delicate flavor.

WHO : World Health Organization

Whole fish : Fish as harvested, also called landed or round weight.

Whole herd buyout program : Another term for the dairy termination program.

Wholesale price index : A composite index of prices of commodities sold in primary U.S. markets. 'Wholesale' refers to sale in large quantities by producers, not to prices received by wholesalers, jobbers, or distributors. In agriculture, it is the average price received by farmers for their farm commodities at the first point of sale when the commodity leaves the farm.

Whorl : An arrangement of three or more leaves or other organs in a circle about an axis

Whorled : An arrangement of three or more structures arising from a single node.

WIC : Special Supplemental Nutrition Program for Women, Infants and Children

Wide cross : a sexual cross between distantly related species that normally would not breed.

Wide crossing : In plant breeding this refers to the process of undertaking a cross where one parent is from outside the immediate genepool of the other, i.e. Landrace or primitive line crossed with a modern cultivar.

Wide row gardening : A method in which vegetables and cutting gardens are laid out usually two to three feet wide instead of a single file row of plants. This is to be efficient in spacing the plants. Many plants grow together.

Wide-row planting : Growing the smaller vegetable crops in a space up to 3 feet across to better utilize space while reducing weeding.

Wild crop : Any plant or portion of a plant that is collected or harvested from a site that is not maintained under cultivation or other agricultural management.

Wild oat : A grass weed which has incredible survival traits. It can be a major problem in cereal crops where it reduces yield and grain quality.

Wild relative : Plant or animal species that are taxonomically related to crop or livestock species and serve as potential sources for genes in breeding of new varieties of those crops or livestock.

Wild silkworms : There are more than 500 kinds of silk-producing caterpillars. We can harvest silk from only a few, tussah being the most common. The silk made by the rest is not strong enough or is impossible to unravel.

Wild type : An organism as found in nature; the organism before it is genetically engineered.

Wilderness : An area of federal land, usually 5,000 acres or more, where the impact of man is largely unnoticeable, and which has been designated as wilderness by Congress.

Wildflower : Plants that can be native or exotic when growing out in a non-cultivated area. They flower and are enjoyed by all. Many wildflowers of course can be cultivated in backyard gardens.

Wilding : a young seedling that develops in the wild without the help of humans. This type of seedling is the best source of stock for some species.

Wildlife habitat incentives program : A program established by the FAIR Act of 1996 to promote voluntary implementation of on-farm management practices to improve wildlife habitat. Landowner activities under this program implement a state plan. Cost-sharing will be available with funding authorized at $50 million for fiscal years 1996-2002 from Conservation Reserve Program funds.

Wildlife refuges units of the National wildlife refuge system : They may be designated under general authorities of the Migratory Bird Treaty Act, the Endangered Species Act, or (rarely) by specific acts of Congress. There are over 500 refuges, with over 89,000,000 acres.

Willingness to accept : Is the amount of compensation an individual is willing to take in exchange for giving up some good or service. This may be elicited from stated or revealed preference approaches.

Willingness to pay : Is the amount an individual is willing to pay to acquire some good or service. This may be elicited from stated or revealed preference approaches.

Wind up : Sensitization of the central nervous system in response to sustained pain. With sustained pain, new receptors (NMDA receptors)are formed in the central nervous system. These receptors use a very fast neurotransmitter and cause a marked increase in the amount of pain transmitted to the brain. They also prevent opioids from working to their full effectiveness.

Windbreak : a group of trees or shrubs in any arrangement that will afford protection from high winds to animals or crops or both. When the arrangement is in a long line the group is called a shelterbelt. If an associated reason is also to harvest timber at some future date it is sometimes called a 'timberbelt'.

Window box : A container placed under a window, very cottage-like in gardening decor.

Windrow : Similar to a swath. The crop is laid in rows to be dried by the wind and sun.

Winter baby syndrome : Crias born in the winter months that are deficient in vitamin D.

Winter barley : Cereal planted in autumn to produce grain for beer, whiskey or animal feed

Winter kill : A condition that happens when plants have not hardened enough to withstand sever winter conditions. The plants may not be hardy for the zone. Die back needs to be pruned in the spring clean up.

Withdrawal time : Time required after the last drug treatment to lower drug residues to acceptable levels. These times are established using healthy animals according to label directions. An amount of time required following use of a medication in an animal before milk or meat can be entered into the human food supply.

Withholding period : The time after a drug is administered, before the animal can be marketed.

Withholding time : Time milk must be withheld from sale following treatment to avoid appearance of residues in milk.

Wobble hypothesis : An explanation of how one tRNA may recognize more than one codon. The first two bases of the mRNA codon and anticodon pair properly, but the third base in the anticodon has some flexibility that permits it to pair with either the expected base or an alternative.

Wolf fish : A firm, white-fleshed saltwater fish with a large head, strong jaws, and sharp canine teeth and molars that can grind clams, whelks, and other mollusks. Sometimes sold under the confusing name of "ocean catfish."

Wood : 1) Lignified secondarily thickened plant tissue. The structural parts of woody perennials. 2) A small grove of trees of mixed species complete with undergrowth. The size is variable but it does not cover a large area.

Wood pigeons : Or kererus are often seen and heard around the farms with native bush in the gullies. They are the only birds big enough to swallow karaka and tawa berries and disperse them. They also help move miro seeds into clearings where they can germinate. Kereru are a keystone species vital to the health of mixed podocarp-broadleaf forests.

Wood's light : An ultraviolet light filtered through nickel oxide. Of the common dermatophytes, only M. canis fluoresces, 25 to 50% of the time.

Wooded grassland : Land covered with grasses and other herbaceous species, and with woody species that cover between approximately 10 to 40% of the ground.

Woodland : an open stand of trees > 8 metres high and with a canopy cover of 40% or more, usually among grasses. Woodland is often described by its dominant species, for example, 'acacia woodland','acacia-themeda woodland', 'combretum woodland'.

Woodland garden : This garden is usually established beneath deciduous trees. It may vary from partial to deep shade and usually with plant material where roots need to remain undisturbed.

Woodlot : a small plot of trees grown for fuelwood, which can also provide small timber and poles.

World Agricultural Outlook Board (WAOB) : As part of the Office of the Chief Economist, the WAOB coordinates the USDA's commodity forecasting program; monitors global weather and analyzes its impact on agriculture; and coordinates USDA's weather, climate and remote sensing work.

World food Program (WFP) : A UN agency that contributes commodities, services, and cash to developing countries to meet emergency food needs or to carry out economic and social development projects using food or local currencies generated from the sale of food aid commodities.

World Trade Organization (WTO) : The international organization established by the Uruguay Round of multilateral trade negotiations to oversee implementation of the General Agreement on Tariffs and Trade and the agreements arising from the Uruguay Round, including the Uruguay Round Agreement on Agriculture.

Worm (Eisenia foetida) : As opposed to earthworm worms are generally intestinal worms of livestock which are normally contracted by infected pasture. Animals may be treated with anthelmintics to control worms.

Worm castings : Undigested material, soil, bacteria deposited through the anus of a worm. Worm manure.

X

Xerophilous : able to withstand drought.

Xerophyte : A plant very resistant to drought, typically adapted to extremely dry environments.

X-linked : The presence of a gene on the X-chromosome.

X-linked disease : A genetic disease caused by a mutation on the X chromosome. In X-linked recessive conditions, a normal female "carrier" passes on the mutated X chromosome to an affected son.

X-ray : The x-ray is the high energy beam that produces a "picture" of a body part which is called the radiograph. Radiographs are commonly, but incorrectly, referred to as x-rays

X-ray crystallography : The diffraction pattern of X-rays passing through a pure crystal of a substance.

Y

Year-long grazing : Continuous grazing for a calendar year.

Yeast : A single cell fungi which improves feed digestion by stimulating microbial activity and stabilizing digestive tract pH. Products packaged as "yeast" consist of cells only; "yeast culture" includes live yeast cells plus growth media.

Yeast artificial chromosome : A vector which can be propagated in budding yeast (Saccharamyces pombe), consisting of the minimal elements required for a chromosome to replicate, and allowing for the cloning of large DNA fragments (hundreds of kilobase pairs).

Yeast episomal vector : A cloning plasmid vector for the yeast Saccharomyces cerevisiae maintained as an extrachromosomal nuclear DNA molecule.

Yeast extract : A mixture of substances from yeast.

Yeld : Northern term for a ewe which is not carrying lambs when expected to be pregnant.

Yellow rust : A disease of cereals which is generally controlled when treatments for other diseases are made. Yellow pustules appear on the leaf and develop between the veins to give a striped effect.

Yellowfin tuna : These tuna reach about 300 pounds in weight. They feature a pale pink flesh that is relatively mild. Also called "ahi."

Yellowtail : A large game fish (up to 100 pounds) from the jack family with a flavor and texture resembling tuna. May be prepared in any manner suitable for tuna.

Yersinia pestis : Etiologic agent of plague

Yew : An evergreen hardwood tree noted for it's use in making longbows. Common in churchyards it has many myths attached to it.

Yield : Plant part harvested and the quantity of it. In agriculture, necessarily related to a specified crop or crops or to a group of animals or to an area, and to a period of time. For multipurpose trees, the amount of each specified part harvested.

Yield calibration : Procedures used to calibrate a yield monitor for specific harvest conditions such as grain type, grain flow, and grain moisture.

Yield checker : Monitors the loss of meat from deboning operations.

Yield maps : A representation of crop yields collected on-the-go by a harvester equipped with an instantaneous yield monitor. Each location/site (pixel) in a field is assigned a specific crop yield value.

Yield mapping : Is a yield monitor coupled with a GPS. Each yield reading is tagged with a latitude and longitude coordinates, which is then used to produce a yield map.

Yield monitor : A yield-measuring device installed on harvest machines. Yield monitors measure grain flow, grain moisture, and other parameters for real-time information relating to field productivity.

Yield per recruit : A model that estimates yield in terms of weight, but more often as a percentage of the maximum yield, for various combinations of natural mortality, fishing mortality and time exposed to the fishery.

Z

Zone : An area distinguished by a range of annual average minimum temperatures, used in describing plant hardiness.

Zone of elongation : The section of the young root or shoot just behind the apical meristem, in which the cells are enlarging and elongating rapidly.

Zoo blot : Hybridization of cloned DNA from one species to DNA from a range of other organisms to determine the extent to which the cloned DNA is evolutionarily conserved.

Zoo fish : Fluorescence in situ hybridization technique, probing metaphase chromosomes of one species with DNA from another species. The technique allows inferences to be made regarding the evolutionary relationships between species.

Zoom : To enlarge or decrease the scale of an image that is being displayed. One can "zoom out" of a yield monitor image and enlarge it in a progressive scaling of the entire image or one can "zoom in" decreasing the scale.

Zoonoses : A biologically heterogeneous group of infectious diseases.

Zoonosis : A disease that can be transmitted from animals to people.

Zoonotic disease : Infectious diseases naturally transmitted from vertebrate animals to humans. Some of these diseases can be harbored in a vertebrate animal but there might be a vector involved in transmission, so that is still a zoonotic disease because it is harbored in a vertebrate animal. Additionally the disease may be food or water borne, so you don't need to have direct contact with an animal to acquire a zoonotic disease.

Zoonotic infection : Refers to infectious microorganisms that have the potential to cause disease in humans. Public Health is the study of zoonotic infections.

Zygmorphic : Capable of being divided into two symmetrical halves only by a single longitudinal plane passing through the axis; all orchid flowers are normally zygomorphic

Zygonema : Stage of meiotic prophase during which chromosome synapsis occurs.

Zygospore : A thick-walled resistant spore developing from a zygote resulting from the fusion of gametes in the course of isogamy.

Zygote : Any spore formed by conjunction of two gametes (sex cells); loosely, a zygospore.